Fashion Fictions

Fashion Fictions

Imagining Sustainable Worlds

Amy Twigger Holroyd

BLOOMSBURY VISUAL ARTS
LONDON • NEW YORK • OXFORD • NEW DELHI • SYDNEY

BLOOMSBURY VISUAL ARTS
Bloomsbury Publishing Plc, 50 Bedford Square, London, WC1B 3DP, UK
Bloomsbury Publishing Inc, 1359 Broadway, New York, NY 10018, USA
Bloomsbury Publishing Ireland, 29 Earlsfort Terrace, Dublin 2, D02 AY28, Ireland

BLOOMSBURY, BLOOMSBURY VISUAL ARTS and the Diana logo are
trademarks of Bloomsbury Publishing Plc

First published in Great Britain 2026

For legal purposes the Acknowledgements on p. xiv constitute an
extension of this copyright page.

Cover design: Adriana Brioso
Cover illustration: *Dreaming of parallel worlds* © Helen Merrin

Bloomsbury Publishing Plc does not have any control over, or responsibility for, any
third-party websites referred to or in this book. All internet addresses given in this
book were correct at the time of going to press. The author and publisher regret
any inconvenience caused if addresses have changed or sites have ceased
to exist, but can accept no responsibility for any such changes.

A catalogue record for this book is available from the British Library.

Library of Congress Control Number: 2025937719

ISBN: HB: 978-1-3504-3562-9
         PB: 978-1-3504-3563-6
       ePDF: 978-1-3504-3565-0
      eBook: 978-1-3504-3564-3

Typeset by Integra Software Services Pvt. Ltd.
Printed and bound in India

For product safety related questions contact productsafety@bloomsbury.com

To find out more about our authors and books visit www.bloomsbury.com
and sign up for our newsletters.

For Asa

Contents

Illustrations

Acknowledgements

Writing an adequate acknowledgement for the support that has made this book possible is, honestly, impossible. The whole Fashion Fictions project hinges entirely on the input of others, on the endless creativity, enthusiasm and radical hope of an ever-shifting, ever-growing global community of contributors. Many of those contributors are named in the List of Illustrations and the endnotes of this book. Many are not, for there are dozens more wonderful contributions than I have managed to cram into these pages. And countless people have supported the project's development in ways other than contributing a fiction, prototype or enactment: by helping to facilitate or document workshops, by filming, photographing, piano-playing; by spreading the word, coordinating projects, sharing ideas. I cannot name you all, but I send sincere thanks for making my idea of radical and collective speculation for fashion into a reality.

Special thanks are due to Matilda Aspinall, who worked as Research Fellow on the Fashion Fictions project from 2021–22 and made a significant contribution to the generation and analysis of data for this book, and to Sally Cooke, who has brilliantly supported the development of impact activities for the project. I am grateful to Nottingham Trent University for its support and funding, and to the Arts & Humanities Research Council for the Research, Engagement and Development Fellowship (AH/V01286X/1) that made the intensive research for this book possible – and provided the funding that enabled its open-access publication. Many thanks to Kate Fletcher and Thomas Binder for their wisdom and guidance in the development of the project, to Helen Merrin for the fantastic illustrations that bring the worlds to life, to Georgia Kennedy and Rosie Best at Bloomsbury, to my colleagues at NTU and to the reviewers who helped me to make this work the best it can be. I am thankful for my Warrior Hearts and Assembly friends, and my Union of Concerned Researchers in Fashion comrades, who remind me to see the big picture and remember what all this is for.

Thank you to my sons, Caspian and Asa, for holding possibility wide open while I tap away at my laptop. 'In this game, lunchtime's not over.' 'In this game, I have gecko powers.' 'In this game, I'm slipping through a crack.' 'In this game, sand is orange.' 'In this game, when we get to the icecream van it's tomorrow.' Every one blows my mind.

And thanks to Simon for listening to me waffle on and still always making the tea.

Data Access Statement

The dataset of material generated in four Fashion Fictions prototyping workshops and four enactment activities – the analysis of which forms the basis of this book (see page 43) – is available from Zenodo at http://doi.org/10.5281/zenodo.13369853. Access to the data is restricted to bona fide researchers, to ensure legitimate use of the material.

The creative outputs discussed in the book – written fictions, visual and material prototypes, and reports of embodied enactments – are openly available at https://fashionfictions.org, while a spreadsheet presenting an interpretive content analysis of the first 120 worlds (see page 50) is openly available at http://doi.org/10.5281/zenodo.6991840.

World Index

44
6
45 19 36 78 165 19
100 17 42
ODOUR
SEW
COLOUR
ANAESTHESIA
TRIBAL
DIGREE
TEXTILE
TALENT
GARMENT
YOUR OWN
GROW
JELLYFISH
WEAR YOUR HEART
ON YOUR SLEEVE
MANTRA
BODY
ARMOUR
3
GIVE A STORY
PERFORMANCE
IRONING
YOUTH
WEAR
FOOTY KIT
GAME CHANGER
MENDING ISLAND
INHERIT IT
SPEAK EASY
FLAMBOYANCE
SPARE PARTS
ZERO WASTE PRIDE
GIVE A STORY
REPAIRIST
ROCKSTAR
NO MORE MORE
FASHION IS ECOCIDE
VIRGIN CLOTH
ENLIGHTENED ONLY
PATCH PATINA STAIN STYLE
HYPER
LOCAL
PEOPLE
PLANET
TEACH
SHARE
TEXTILE
BAPTISM
HEAD
CRESTS
TAIL
SKIRTS
STYLE
BIRTHRIGHT SILK
VOTE
LOCAL
MEND
HOLES
INSECT
POSSIBILITY
RESOURCE
SAME CLOTHES
EVERY DAY
POSTCODE
GARMENTS
DO NO HARM

1

The Place Between

How change looks

'How change looks.'

This bold – if somewhat cryptic – statement, printed in an understated typeface on the brown paper bag of a popular fashion chain, catches my eye as shoppers saunter past on a sunny day in Nottingham's historic Old Market Square.

Later, I search for further context on the brand's corporate website and find that the slogan has a neat double meaning. The high-street behemoth is laying claim to both *change* in the sense of fashion, and *change* in the sense of transition towards sustainability. While the carefully worded text is specific to that company, it can easily stand in as an encapsulation of deeply problematic attitudes to fashion, and to sustainability initiatives, that are commonly found across the industry.

The high-street shops of Nottingham, much like those in Detroit, Dubai and Durban, are part of a mainstream fashion system that stretches across the globe. As Alice Payne explains, this is not a single homogenous system. There are 'myriad versions, played out in different cultures and cities'.[1] But in all of these iterations, key characteristics dominate: industry-driven trends, an uncanny homogeneity of styles, and the prioritization of business concerns over ecology, culture and wellbeing. This fashion system reaches deeply into the societies in which it is established, framing all clothing decisions – even those of people who feel no conscious interest in fashion.[2]

It is often claimed that the explosion of ready-to-wear clothing since the mid-twentieth century, and particularly the development of the fast-fashion sector in recent decades, has 'democratized' fashion by making garments affordable for all. Yet this growth in accessibility has come at a cultural cost: it has crowded out other ways of participating in fashion. Making clothes at home, for example, was once widespread, enjoyed by many as an accessible way of people providing for themselves and having

Figure 1.1 *Dreaming of parallel worlds.*

agency over the ways in which they presented themselves to the world. But the growth of readymade clothing made that into a choice, then a niche, then an expensive niche.[3] While home sewing is regaining popularity today, supported by the connective power of the internet, it is still absent from the esteemed spaces of fashion culture: the catwalk, the flagship store, the glossy magazine. As the mainstream fashion system has spread across the world, it has also erased locally rooted, materially light and culturally meaningful systems of fashioning the body. Erica de Greef explains that 'these alternative, so-called non-western or "other" fashion systems have been relegated to the margins, often made redundant, and defined as traditional, non-fashion or even, anti-fashion'.[4]

Thus – to return to the bags swinging in the hands of the Old Market Square shoppers – clothes purchased from a high-street fashion store, designed and produced by a global supply chain to correspond with globalized trends, are indeed *how change* (in the sense of fashion) *looks* today. Yet this is not all that fashion could, or should, be. There are many, many other ways of living with our clothes.

The production, use and disposal of clothing in the mainstream fashion system causes countless environmental and social problems: carbon emissions, water pollution, illegal landfills and abuses of workers' rights, to highlight just a few. These problems are well documented and have risen in profile in recent years.[5] The impacts of the fashion industry are, of course, part of a much bigger story about contemporary lifestyles and ecological devastation. As Jason Hickel explains, 'the global economy … is now dramatically overshooting what scientists have defined as safe planetary boundaries, with devastating consequences for the living world'.[6] Many in the fashion industry promise that we can address environmental and social challenges via a better version of business as usual: renewable energy, transparency schemes, improved efficiency, new technologies for production and recycling. Yet the number of garments produced globally is reported to have doubled between 2000 and 2015,[7] and production continues to rise.[8] While the impacts of an individual garment may have been reduced, as long as the volumes being produced continue to grow, then there is little chance of any significant reduction in overall impacts. If the fashion system is to be brought into balance with the living world, we need to contend with volume.

The impacts of human activities on ecological systems are linked to the use of resources, from extraction and production to consumption and disposal. These resources provide both the stuff from which goods are made and the energy needed for their production and use. Global resource use has risen significantly over the past fifty years, to a total far beyond sustainable limits. A recent study, working on the basis that all citizens of the earth should have a fair share of the planet's resources, has shown that 'high-income countries, which represent only 16 per cent of the world population, are responsible for 74 per cent of resource use in excess of fair shares and are therefore the primary drivers of global environmental degradation'.[9] To address this imbalance, rich countries would have to reduce their resource use by an average of at least 70 per cent.

The picture is similar if we examine carbon emissions. High-income countries in the global North bear the greatest responsibility for emissions, and for the devastating environmental impacts that they cause. Again, dramatic reductions are needed: a 2021 study by the Hot or Cool Institute demonstrated that the emissions of high-income countries need to fall by 91–95 per cent by 2050 in order to stay within the carbon budget for 1.5 degrees of warming above pre-industrial levels.[10] If we look at the fashion sector specifically, we see the same sort of picture. Another report by Hot or Cool quantified the reduction in the carbon footprint of clothing consumed in G20 countries that will be needed – this time by 2030 – to remain on the pathway to the 1.5°C target. It found that footprints must be reduced by 60 per cent on average during this period, rising to 83 per cent for the richest fifth of wearers in the UK.[11] All three studies emphasize that technological improvements alone will not be enough to achieve these staggeringly ambitious targets: unprecedented shifts in consumption patterns will be required. If this scale of change appears unachievable, we must keep the alternative in mind. As a 2022 report from the Intergovernmental Panel on Climate Change (IPCC) starkly states, 'any further delay in concerted anticipatory global action … will miss a brief and rapidly closing window to secure a liveable and sustainable future for all'.[12]

* * * * * * * *

If we want to tackle the globalized fashion system's culture of overproduction, where do we start? For me, we must look at the capitalist logic by which the system operates. Capitalism is an economic system in which wealth – capital – is invested to generate more wealth. It divides those who own the resources needed for production from those who sell their labour in order to make a living, and is guided by the principle of the free market: open competition, with little or no regulation. Capitalism is driven by the search for profit, which can be found by finding new markets or by inventing or finding new things to sell. Indeed, the mission of the system is 'unlimited and incontestable economic growth'.[13] As Martin Parker and his co-authors explain, 'capitalism and its quest for accumulation rests on producing, selling and consuming ever more'[14] – hence those ever-growing mountains of clothes.

Many would argue that the capitalist system drives development and innovation and is the most efficient way of allocating resources, to the benefit of all. Yet evidence shows that capitalism has led to increased inequality, both globally and within national economies; inequality, in turn, leads to widespread negative impacts, from poor health and educational outcomes to increased violence.[15] Furthermore, the system causes ecological devastation – partly because neither producer nor consumer are required to bear the environmental costs of production. Overall, the incessant economic growth of capitalism is underpinned by a simple formula: taking more, from both ecological systems and human labour, than you give back.[16] This extraction wreaks ecological and social damage, usually in poorer parts of the world that are far from the places in which the majority of the goods or services are consumed. As Hickel explains, 'The ecological crisis is an inevitable consequence of this system.'[17]

Capitalism's extractivist mentality is deeply bound up with the paradigm of modernity, which arose during the Renaissance and, as Arturo Escobar describes, 'crystallized toward the end of the 18th century into a configuration of knowledge … in which the figure of Man was the foundation of all possible knowledge'.[18] Richard Norgaard explains that modernity 'promised control over nature through science, material abundance through superior technology, and effective government through rational social organization', accelerating human progress.[19] Astonishing advances have certainly been delivered, for example in terms of global life expectancy and health outcomes.[20] Yet, Norgaard argues, progress has been betrayed; its pursuit has caused global environmental degradation and deep social injustices.

Figure 1.2 *Overproduction, overconsumption and the myth of endless growth.*

One of the ways of thinking embedded in modernity is dualism: the separation of mind from body and humans from nature. From this perspective, the natural world is merely a resource for humans to exploit. Historical colonization was driven by a related, and also deeply problematic, dualism, which framed Europeans as superior to people in other regions – and led to further devastating exploitation. As Escobar explains, 'This dualist ontology was fundamental for the development of patriarchal capitalism, colonialism, conquest, and slavery and it remains at the heart of globalization.'[21] Decolonial scholars such as Vanessa Machado de Oliveira thus use the hybrid term modernity/coloniality 'as a reminder that the benefits we associate with modernity are created and maintained by historical, systemic, and ongoing processes that are inherently violent and unsustainable.'[22]

The need to challenge the model of endless growth and the systems of extraction that underpin it is now surely apparent. A number of 'post-growth' movements have arisen in response to this need; all recognize environmental limits and aim to benefit human wellbeing without economic growth. One such movement, degrowth, was launched in France in 2001 and is now a vibrant and complex field of academic inquiry and activism.[23] While nuanced understandings vary, degrowth can be defined as 'an equitable downscaling of production and consumption that increases human well-being and enhances ecological conditions at the local and global level, in the short and long term.'[24] The authors of a recent book, *The Future is Degrowth*, explain that the movement explicitly criticizes the dominance of growth and proposes possibilities for the radical reorganization of economy and society.[25] Degrowth is therefore quite different to 'green growth', which attempts to make capitalism sustainable without disrupting its underlying principles.[26] Green growth proposes to protect ecological systems by 'decoupling' economic growth from the use of the earth's resources, via improved efficiency and emerging technologies. The sustainability initiatives put forward by the fashion industry overwhelmingly fall within this domain. Yet rigorous scientific studies have shown that decoupling is physically impossible: economic growth 'cannot plausibly be decoupled from growth in material and energy use.'[27]

The two concepts represent two very different approaches to sustainability. Green growth aims to do more with less, whereas degrowth aims to reinvent the notion of prosperity to focus on the wellbeing of humans, other species and the planet as a whole.[28] An economy shaped by degrowth would thus be organized to meet the fundamental human needs of the global population, rather than pursuing growth for its own sake. Crucially, degrowth is based on global equity, guided by the prospect of 'a good life and social justice for all'.[29] It recognizes that most countries in the global South could increase their use of resources to meet the human needs of their citizens while remaining within planetary boundaries.[30] Reductions in activity, therefore, are reserved for those countries that have already had far more than their fair share of resources.

A theory of learning and change proposed by Stephen Sterling provides another way of distinguishing between green growth and degrowth. As Sterling explains, first-order change – such as green growth – 'refers to doing "more of the same", that is, change within particular boundaries and without examining or changing the assumptions or values that inform what you are doing or thinking.' Second-order change – such as degrowth – 'refers to a significant change in thinking or in what you are doing as a result of examining assumptions and values'.[31] For me, the most powerful work deals not only with growth and degrowth, but also with modernity and the prospect of a paradigm beyond modernity. This represents third-order change: a transformative shift of consciousness based on 'the experience of *seeing* our worldview rather than *seeing with* our worldview so that we can be more open to and draw upon other views and possibilities'.[32] Machado de Oliveira, for example, discusses the notion of 'hospicing modernity': letting go of ways of thinking and being associated with modernity/coloniality, acknowledging the deep complexities of this process and creating 'new, fertile soil for other possibilities of existence to emerge'.[33]

As Hickel explains, a reorganization of the economy would require decisions about which areas of production and consumption in industrialized countries should be radically scaled back – such as those 'designed purely to maximize profits rather than to meet human needs … or advertising strategies intended to manipulate our emotions and make us feel that what we have is inadequate'.[34] It seems inevitable that the globalized mainstream fashion system, with its rampant overproduction, would be high on the list. In fact, fashion presents a particularly fertile ground for exploring degrowth ideas: it is a complex tangle of consumerism and human connection, material products and intangible experiences, showing off and looking within. It has an influence that extends far beyond clothing and thus has the potential to act as a powerful lever for change.

What kind of fashion systems would we build in place of those that exist today? *Earth Logic Fashion Action Research Plan,* a 2019 publication by Kate Fletcher and Mathilda Tham, provides a comprehensive and inspiring framework for exploring fashion in a post-growth, or 'earth logic', context.[35] The plan provides six 'landscapes' that 'set out progressive areas for transformation of the fashion sectors' for use by researchers, practitioners and decision makers.[36] Three landscapes – less, local and plural – focus on fashion activities. Another three – learning, language and governance – focus on processes needed to create the conditions for a new paradigm. While the invitation of *Earth Logic* is open-ended, it is certain that a new paradigm will involve fundamentally different ways of understanding fashion. For initial inspiration we could look to M. Angela Jansen, who proposes the use of fashion as a verb to describe a plural 'multitude of possibilities' for fashioning the body.[37]

Returning once again to the feel-good slogan of the high-street chain, we can see that incremental 'eco' strategies commonly used by the fashion industry – described by Lucy Siegle as 'ad-hoc, ineffective and wilfully conservative'[38] – are indeed *how change* (in the sense of transition towards sustainability) *looks* in the global North today. These initiatives represent business as usual, hidden by a superficial facade of first-order change. They stand in stark contrast to John Ehrenfeld's powerful definition of sustainability, which I use as a guiding vision throughout this book: 'the possibility that humans and other life will flourish on the Earth forever'.[39] As long as the fashion industry's initiatives are rooted in a paradigm of growth, they cannot nurture this flourishing. They cannot deliver the absolute reduction in resource use that is urgently needed, nor address the violence of coloniality. Stepping back, it is clear that the mainstream fashion system has not only dominated our thinking about what fashion is, and in the process closed out other ways of doing fashion. Its emergent sustainability arm has also dominated our thinking about what change is, and in the process closed out other, far more meaningful, ways of transforming the mainstream fashion system.

Imagining otherwise

Ideas that challenge the status quo such as degrowth, whether in the field of fashion or in society more broadly, are dismissed by many as naive or impossible. The idea of redesigning the economy seems too big to be achieved by any individual, any organization or even any nation. While the merits of degrowth versus green growth can be debated, the deep-rooted sense that green growth is the *only* option available presents a much more stubborn challenge. In contemporary society, many of us cannot imagine radical change; minor tweaks to the status quo represent the only possible path.[40] Our view of the future, it seems, is based on 'the present –"our way of life"– simply stretching all the way to infinity, give or take a few new electronic gadgets'.[41]

This sense that the world feels fixed, the future foreclosed, is reflected in what Mark Fisher famously described as 'capitalist realism': 'the widespread sense that not only is capitalism the only viable political and economic system, but also that it is now impossible even to imagine a coherent alternative to it'.[42] Indeed, as Arturo Escobar notes, 'one of the most pernicious effects of today's dominant political, economic, and belief systems has been to narrow down, if not colonize, the notion of reality and, hence, to drastically restrict possibility and foreclose the imagination of radically different futures'.[43] This constrained perspective has far-reaching consequences, for the images of the future that we carry – whether consciously or unconsciously – indirectly shape the future. In fact, as sociologist Erik Olin Wright argues, 'the actual limits of what is achievable depend in part on the beliefs people hold about what sorts of alternatives are viable'.[44] If we feel that the world is fixed, we do not bother to explore ideas that we consider to be impossible, and therefore do not have the chance to bring them into the light. In a self-fulfilling prophecy, they remain impossible and we find ourselves locked into an unsustainable and unsatisfying system. To break the deadlock, we need imagination.

Tania Zittoun, Hana Hawlina and Alex Gillespie define imagination as 'the process by which we temporarily leave the here-and-now of current experiences, to explore and play with the past, the future, and alternative spheres of experience'.[45] Unlike thinkers in psychology and philosophy who frame imagination as solely a personal faculty, Zittoun, Hawlina and Gillespie take a sociocultural

Figure 1.3 *In Fashion Fictions we use embodied enactment to explore imagined scenarios – such as the ritual garment exchanges of the fictional World 27.*

perspective, understanding that imagination 'arises at the intersection of immediate experience, personal history, culturally shared meaning complexes, and symbolic or cultural resources (such as books, films, narratives)'.[46] They highlight several dimensions of imagination, including temporality (imagining the past, future or alternative presents) and generalization (imagining at an abstract or specific level). Through imagination we can think beyond our present reality to engage with the possible, or what we believe *could be*. Moreover, we can push into the impossible, exploring propositions that we consider to have no prospect of actualization. But impossible propositions can become possible or even actual: the boundaries between the categories can shift. The idea of putting people on the moon, for example, was initially deemed impossible, but eventually happened; the same shift can be observed in the development of various social movements and political ideas. Thus, as Zittoun, Hawlina and Gillespie state, 'imagination acts precisely as the process that sustains, nourishes, and transforms the possible'.[47] In terms of sustainable transitions, we can drive change by giving ourselves permission to imagine and develop ideas that we think could not come to pass, ideas that fall far beyond the realms of possibility.

The process of imagining a better future society can be described as the social imagination – or, alternatively, utopianism. Lisa Garforth explains that although the latter term may bring to mind 'rigid blueprints of perfection, totalitarian master plans or fantastical idealism',[48] today it is used to discuss tentative, partial and contingent visions that seek to 'stimulate critical and creative reflection on alternatives to the way things are'.[49] Geoff Mulgan argues that in recent decades our collective capacity for social imagination has diminished. In a report entitled *The Imaginary Crisis,* he observes that mainstream culture supports us to readily imagine apocalypses, but not better worlds.[50] Mulgan identifies a range of drivers for this shift, including a culture of individualism, the pull of logic and rationality and a reduced sense of personal agency.[51] Garforth likewise discusses a decline in utopianism, driven by the incessant change, global networks and growth-focused economics of the era defined by Zygmunt Bauman as 'liquid modernity'.[52] As Garforth argues, in this context 'utopianism is colonized by capitalist logistics; desire is attached to commodities; future dreams become individualised lifestyle aspirations'.[53] Thus, John Wood notes, 'while, as voters and consumers, we have become experts at choosing and complaining, we have forgotten how to envisage what we really want'.[54]

Mulgan proposes that the decline in imaginative capacity matters because we are facing global challenges of a staggering scale, from the climate crisis to ageing and deep inequality. As he observes, 'Each of these alone would put huge strains on our social institutions. Add them together and it's clear that we need a very major and rapid boost in our capacity to imagine and design better social arrangements.'[55] Rob Hopkins agrees: 'I worry that we have created a culture, a kind of perfect storm of factors, that are profoundly ruinous to the human imagination at the worst possible time in history for that to be the case.'[56]

Mulgan and Hopkins are two voices among many who highlight imagination as a societal necessity and are working to rebuild this vital collective capacity – often with a particular orientation. The Institute for Radical Imagination, for example, is an international organization that aims to 'bring together art, activism and pedagogy in order to transition towards a post-capitalist society'.[57] Social justice activists also speak powerfully of the power of imagination. Talila A. Lewis, an abolitionist community lawyer, educator and organizer, proposes:

When we create space for ourselves and others to dream, we embody recurring hope, active love, critical resistance, and radical change. We are reminded that those who came before us dreamed of that which no one thought could exist … their dreams are the reasons we now are living the 'impossible.'[58]

If we are to regain our capacity for utopianism and social imagination, it may be helpful to consider the various manifestations of these impulses in the past. Garforth explains that utopianism can be thought of as an inherent human instinct; she highlights various longstanding folk and religious narratives that envision better worlds.[59] Mulgan identifies a variety of methods for imagining better futures, including fiction and poetry; experimental communities and settlements; political and social movements; speculative social science; entrepreneurship; events such as London's Great Exhibition of 1851; and, more recently, films and video games.[60]

* * * * * * * * *

Fiction has long been a vibrant arena for utopian thought. Thomas More's *Utopia,* the book that first coined the term, was written over 500 years ago, while *The Blazing World,* a 1666 book by Margaret Cavendish, depicted the empress of a utopian kingdom.[61] Jumping forward to the nineteenth and early twentieth centuries, William Morris's *News from Nowhere* and Charlotte Perkins Gilman's *Herland* demonstrated the capacities of the novel for exploring socialist and feminist utopias.[62] The societal shifts of the 1960s and 1970s saw a new era of utopian writing, often with a focus on environmental concerns, including Ernest Callenbach's *Ecotopia* and Ursula K. Le Guin's *The Dispossessed.*[63] Recent additions that respond to contemporary issues include inventive formats such as *Everything for Everyone: An Oral History of the New York Commune, 2052–2072* and *Octavia's Brood,* a collection of stories from social justice movements. These fictional works are influential in giving people a sense of just how different the social order could be. Le Guin described her work as 'offering an imagined but persuasive alternative reality, to dislodge my mind, and so the reader's mind, from the lazy, timorous habit of thinking that the way we live now is the only way people can live.'[64]

A much more recent development in social imagination is design fiction, a term coined by science fiction writer Bruce Sterling in 2005.[65] Another term for the same type of work is speculative design; its origins are commonly traced to Anthony Dunne and Fiona Raby's 2013 book *Speculative Everything: Design, Fiction, and Social Dreaming.*[66] Both terms now have multiple clashing interpretations and diverse applications, from commercial consultancy[67] to the thoughtful interrogation of assumptions in the development of meaningful design briefs[68] and research investigating social change.[69] Across these varied contexts, design fiction is generally used to generate and materialize a speculative proposition, typically through models, prototypes or films.[70] As Thomas Markussen, Eva Knutz and Tau Lenskjold note, 'Like a fictional text, a design fiction artefact projects a new actual world of its own that we can experientially engage in and where some fictional facts must be taken for granted.'[71] The artefact thus prompts us to contemplate alternative possibilities and reflect on present-day situations.[72]

Much existing practice in this field is based on dystopian visions of technological change and neoliberal capitalist systems – that is, those that promote unfettered free trade. *Manufacturing Monroe,* a video by Emily Hayes, illustrates this tendency: it portrays a fictional tissue engineering factory that manufactures small sections of dead celebrities' bodies.[73] *88.7: Stories from the First Transnational Traders,* a work of speculative design by Tobias Revell, presents a scenario in which neoliberal

Figure 1.4 *Otto von Busch's speculative project* Fashion suX *explores a fictional sustainable fashion movement that fuses straight-edge punk subculture with sewing practice and related iconography. Among the artefacts created for* Fashion suX *are garments, patches, accessories, zines and posters.*

expansion has led nation-states to the brink of collapse.[74] Various intentionally mundane documents crafted by Revell, including charts, letters, designs and legal statements, bring this fiction to life.

Speculative design can equally explore more enticing visions. *Fashion suX* by Otto von Busch, for example, imagines a sustainable fashion movement that is very different to real-world manifestations (Figure 1.4). To create his vision, von Busch built on the real-world phenomenon of straight edge, a punk subculture based on abstinence from recreational drugs and the promotion of veganism and animal rights.[75] His speculative interpretation of straight edge has a distinctive fashion-focused culture:

The project specifically examines the underground fashion and craft movement that called themselves suXers (sometimes referred to as 'sustainable fashion Straight Edge'). Radically opposing the 'do-good' ethics of consumerist sustainability, the suXers embody an ethic that imbues not only clothes and lifestyle but also an infuriated rejection of the fashion system's sartorial betrayal.[76]

Figure 1.5 *In her speculative design project* Mending with Mycelium, *Emma Fukuwatari Huffman explored the possibilities for collaborating with mycelium to mend the worn-out soles of sneakers and imagined an alternative reality in which this practice would be normal.*[77]

As the design fiction field has matured, commentators have highlighted problematic aspects of some projects. Tony Fry, for example, notes that, despite the potential of speculative design to address substantial predicaments, 'it so often spirals down to "solutions" delivered by new products and services, and "speculative techno-visions" aiming to go beyond the perception and limits of existing technology'.[78] A pan-European education project, SpeculativeEdu, recognized this issue and has sought to redirect speculative design practice away from dystopian and technocentric visions.[79] Pedro Oliveira and Luiza Prado, meanwhile, criticize the power dynamics embedded in the gallery presentation of design fiction artefacts: 'the designer, as the enlightened subject, speaks and exhibits; the silent spectators in the audience merely listen and observe'.[80] An alternative to this one-way engagement can be found in participatory speculation activities, sometimes known as collective imagination activities. These activities involve diverse stakeholders in the process of speculation and arise in a variety of contexts, including design anthropology, futures studies, interdisciplinary research and civic initiatives (see Box 1.1 for further reading).

Some activities ask participants to devise fictional worlds or create speculative prototypes via guided activities and creative workshops. *The Thing From the Future* by Stuart Candy and Jeff Watson, for example, prompts people to envision alternative futures via a user-friendly deck of cards,[81] while Ann Light's *On Some Other World* workshop invites participants to develop and represent imagined counterfactual worlds through talking, writing and making.[82] A large-scale civic project in Munich used a lo-fi yet highly engaging making workshop to explore visions of the city in 2036;[83] the Alpine Community Economies Laboratory also focused on futures in a specific region and produced a workshop toolkit for use in other contexts.[84] Another type of work takes the form of temporary immersive installations and encounters, making a future vision accessible in the present 'as a landscape to venture into'.[85] *Borrowed Scenery*, a project by transdisciplinary network FoAM, brought to life an alternate reality in which plant and human life are deeply intertwined via 'a speculative "patabotanical lab"'; members of the public were recruited by fictional 'research assistants' to support various participatory activities.[86] Some projects invite participants to experience speculative propositions in their everyday lives over a longer period, such as the initiative led by Kakee Scott, Conny Bakker and Jaco Quist that invited participants to devise and then explore speculative bathing practices in their own homes for two weeks, and to document their experiences.[87]

Mulgan highlights the importance of opening up social imagination processes to diverse participants:

> if you care at all about emancipation it must matter that seriously organised social imagination is being so monopolised by the already rich and powerful (such as think-tanks in California funded by, and reflecting the narrow worldview of, male billionaires), and so little is being done to shape a world in line with the interests and values of the great majority.[88]

The visions generated by the rich and powerful tend to focus, unsurprisingly, on furthering their own interests. As Ruha Benjamin asks, 'is it any wonder … that those in power work tirelessly to squash us from having radical imaginations that dare to envision a world in which everyone can thrive?'[89]

Even if convinced of the political importance of involving diverse groups in social imagination activities, some might worry that people without specialist training lack the expertise to generate visions of alternative worlds. Garforth, drawing on the work of German philosopher Ernst Bloch, argues that this is not the case. Bloch identified utopian impulses in many aspects of everyday life, from religion to daydreams and even advertising, and argued that the ability to anticipate the future is part of the human psyche. Utopia does not, therefore, require a special way of knowing: it is a capacity shared by us all.[90]

Box 1.1 Further reading

Two recent articles provide valuable overviews of the diverse and fascinating academic work in participatory speculation. 'Forms of Participatory Futuring for Urban Sustainability: A Systematic Review' by Rike Neuhoff, Luca Simeone and Lea Holst Laursen (*Futures* 154, 2023) reviews more than 100 research papers to identify three approaches used in this field; 'public futuring for social learning' is most relevant to Fashion Fictions.[91] 'Social Dreaming Together: A Critical Exploration of Participatory Speculative Design' by Pedro Gil Farias, Roy Bendor and Bregje van Eekelen (*Participatory Design Conference 2022*, 2022) presents another systematic review of published projects and proposes eight levels of participation in speculative design, from spectatorship to ownership.[92]

Earlier work that has informed and inspired the Fashion Fictions approach includes 'Collective Scenarios: Speculative Improvisations for the Anthropocene' by Renata Tyszczuk (*Futures* 134, 2021), which presents thought-provoking insights from a series of speculative research, arts and public engagement projects[93] and 'Near Future School: World Building Beyond a Neoliberal Present with Participatory Design Fictions' by James Duggan, Joseph Lindley and Sarah McNicol (*Futures* 94, 2017), which reports on the use of participatory design fiction practices with young people to open up alternative and plural futures.[94]

A distinctive strand of participatory speculation has developed in the disciplines of anthropology and design anthropology; the collections *Anthropologies and Futures*, edited by Juan Francisco Salazar et al. (Bloomsbury, 2017) and *Design Anthropological Futures*, edited by Rachel Charlotte Smith et al. (Bloomsbury, 2016) present a variety of fascinating work. The interdisciplinary *Anticipation* conference brings together the latest research that explores 'how ideas of the future inform action in the present'.

Participatory speculation is perhaps less prevalent in fashion than in other fields. Clarice Carvalho Garcia's doctoral research is an important contribution that takes a critical view of traditional fashion forecasting practices and tests an innovative methodology that prompts participants to create and explore distinctive and varied imaginative scenarios.[95] This work is presented in a recent article, 'Fashion Futuring: Intertwining Speculative Design, Foresight and Material Culture Towards Sustainable Futures' (*Futures* 153, 2023).[96] *Fashion Futures 2040*, a project led by Cosette Joyner Martinez and Katia Dayan Vladimirova, invited an international group of researchers to speculate on futures of sustainable fashion consumption, generating four scenarios that are profiled in a downloadable report.[97] *Radical Fashion Exercises: A Workbook of Modes and Methods,* edited by Laura Gardner and Daphne Mohajer va Pesaran (Valiz, 2023), is a practical handbook that presents more than 100 activities, prompts and workshops that challenge the norms of fashion; one section of the book focuses on 'imagining and dreaming'.

A great deal of pioneering activity in this field takes place outside academia. *Our Futures: By the People, for the People,* published by NESTA in 2019, provides a valuable overview of participatory futures techniques for civic society,[98] while *From What Is to What If: Unleashing the Power of Imagination to Create the Future We Want* by Rob Hopkins (Chelsea Green, 2019) is an accessible and inspiring read. The Joseph Rowntree Foundation collaborates with like-minded organizations to support collective imagination practices in diverse settings. One valuable output is the freely accessible Collective Imagination Practices Toolkit.[99]

* * * * * * * *

This book explores the new discoveries that can emerge when we use participatory speculative activities to open up positive visions of alternative fashion systems. It draws on Fashion Fictions, an international project that I founded in 2020 in order to bring people together to generate, experience and reflect on engaging fictional fashion worlds. The project has an ethos of openness, with anyone, anywhere invited to participate as an individual or to organize their own activities. These activities are supported by a host of guidance resources available on the website, aimed at adults and children.[100] More than 6,000 people have been involved at the time of writing; while some of those taking part bring specialist fashion expertise, every participant brings expertise that is just as valuable: that gained from the wearing of clothes, day in and day out.

Participants are spread across six continents, with contributions catalyzed by online workshops and localized activities. This diversity is crucial as it enables the project to benefit from ideas emanating from different cultural contexts, which respond to different contemporary realities and offer different visions of preferable fashion systems. The entire project is based on Creative Commons Attribution-ShareAlike 4.0 International licences, supporting the aim of collective creativity. The licences allow contributors to pick up, develop, remix and respond to material created by others (providing that we credit the original author and share any adapted material using the same licence). As adrienne maree brown comments, 'if we want worlds that work for more of us, we have to have more of us involved in the visioning process. One of the ways we perpetuate individualism is by ideating alone, literally coming up with ideas in solitude and then competing to bring them to life.'[101]

The project creates a safe space to investigate what alternative fashion systems might look like and to think things through critically and creatively. Along the way, it aims to generate an expanded sense of possibility: a feeling that radical change can happen – and might involve ideas that currently feel impossible. The project allows us to pause and ask ourselves: *what do we wish for?* To do this, we explore 'what if' questions to imagine contemporary realities in parallel worlds: worlds that have split off from our own at some point in history, and taken a different path. We imagine positive and enticing worlds, in terms of individual satisfaction, social justice and sustainability. We imagine worlds that are physically possible, but push beyond what feels plausible today – understanding plausibility as a socially constructed sense of what is possible.[102]

While the notion of post-growth fashion systems guides the project as a whole, the invitation to contribute is more open: I simply encourage people to question the fashion system's established norms in their speculations and participants are welcome to interpret this prompt in whatever way they wish. This invitation generates a diverse range of responses – from minor amendments of the existing mainstream fashion system to radical reimaginings of life on earth – and all contributions submitted to the project are displayed on the website repository.[103]

Fashion Fictions has a three-stage structure that loosely maps on to three areas of social imagination already discussed: written fiction, speculative design and participatory enactment. At Stage 1, we create 100-word outlines of fictional fashion cultures and systems, known as 'worlds'; at Stage 2 we build on these outlines, generating visual and material prototypes known as 'explorations'; at Stage 3 we find ways to enact and experience the prototyped worlds, in activities known as 'enactments'. At each stage, and in the project as a whole, I have sought to design a structure that catalyzes activity while allowing participants a significant level of ownership over the form and focus of their contribution.[104] In Chapter 2, I will provide further detail on each of these stages (which can, if desired, easily be adapted to speculate on aspects of everyday life other than fashion; see parallelpresents.org). Through these diverse activities, the project seeks to open up the conversation about sustainability in fashion. In her book *Bad Environmentalism: Irony and Irreverence in the Ecological Age,* Nicole Seymour outlines the sensibilities typically associated with environmentalism, including guilt, shame, prescriptiveness, sentimentality, sincerity and self-righteousness. Similar observations could be made about sustainable fashion: its overriding tone is wholesome, privileged and moralistic – and largely focuses on consumer choices, rather than a more expansive view of the fashion experience. Seymour argues that a broader repertoire of affective modes such as irreverence, frivolity, irony, perversity and playfulness might 'enable us to create new modes of resistance, new forms of community, and new opportunities for inquiry into environmental crisis'.[105] The thinking underpinning Fashion Fictions runs along similar lines. I have a hunch that tapping into a broader spectrum of sensibilities, aesthetics and spheres of knowledge will allow us to bring much more of ourselves to the collective process of transforming our fashion systems. It could also inspire us to act: Michele-Lee Moore and Manjana Milkoreit argue that 'the inputs for action in the present are generated, in part, through emotions activated in response to imaginations of the future'.[106]

Overall, the project aims to support transitions towards sustainable, post-growth fashion systems by reshaping public, professional and academic understandings of the possibilities for sustainable fashion: by expanding our collective sense of *how change* (in the sense of transition towards sustainability) *looks*. It acknowledges the huge reduction in resource use that will be needed if we are to develop fashion systems that work within ecological limits. Such systems will involve different social and cultural norms, different economies, different ways of living with our clothes. After all, as sociologist John Urry states, 'to slow down, let alone reverse, increasing carbon emissions and temperatures requires the reorganization of social life, nothing more and nothing less'.[107] We need to move from incremental changes to the design and manufacture of clothes to radically different ways of fashioning our identities. We need to completely reimagine *how change* (in the sense of fashion) *looks*.

Figure 1.6 *Fashion Fictions workshops offer the opportunity to think playfully about alternative fashion systems, asking ourselves:* what do we wish for?

Embracing the impossible

Many of the books and speculative design projects discussed earlier in the chapter fall within the realms of science fiction. Science fiction can be defined as 'a genre (of fiction, film, etc.) in which the plot or setting features speculative scientific or technological advances or differences'.[108] As theorist Brian Attebery explains, this focus plays out through a science-based vocabulary, through recurring icons such as the robot, the monster, the spaceship and the city, and through recurring situations such as first contact with species from other worlds.[109] While novels that we would now categorize as science fiction appeared throughout the nineteenth and early twentieth centuries, it was in the 1940s and 1950s that science fiction coalesced into a genre through pulp fiction publications.[110]

In some respects, the approach to speculation used in Fashion Fictions corresponds with the science fiction genre. In particular, we are trying – to varying degrees – to imagine ways of living with our clothes that might involve different ways of organizing our activities and different economic systems. But in other ways, science fiction is a mismatch for the values of Fashion Fictions. In contrast to the genre's focus on science and technology (which, as discussed earlier, is also present in much design fiction), this project seeks to place at centre stage a quotidian aspect of human life: the ways in which we dress our bodies. We speculate on this personal, embodied, intimate, material and social act in terms of human-material relationships and socio-material systems, rather than emerging technologies; we are interested in social innovation, rather than technological fixes.[111] While some people, entranced by the potential of the metaverse, may envision a future of digital dress, I cannot help but observe that we have dressed in material textiles for millennia and sense that this fact is not going away. The project is therefore driven by the notion that change is needed in the ways we use and live with these textiles, not in innovation that seeks to replace them.

There are other ways in which the values of Fashion Fictions clash with those of science fiction. Underlying the vocabulary, icons and settings of science fiction is the 'megatext of science': that is, the collective set of attributes, images and conventions, all rooted in science, that are shared across the genre.[112] The science fiction megatext includes the incessant march of technological progress, whether presented in the form of prediction, cautionary tale or critical commentary. While particular stories might question how technology will develop, the path it might take or the implications it might have – and often highlight the downsides of this progress – the onward march is nonetheless present. As Farah Mendelsohn puts it, 'science fiction is the literature that wants the universe to be rational'.[113] The notion of technological progress, along with companion notions such as rationality, lies at the heart of modernity. Thus, the megatext of science fiction is deeply rooted in the values of modernity/coloniality that, I would argue, have led to the planetary crisis we face today. The movements with which the project is aligned, such as degrowth, earth logic and hospicing modernity, seek to challenge and deconstruct these values, rather than reinforce them.

Contributions to the Fashion Fictions project suggest that others feel a similar pull. Certainly, there are fictions that mirror common science fiction themes: in **World 70**, for example, space exploration has led to bio-monitoring spacesuits, cleaned by electricity, being worn by all.[114] Yet a far greater proportion of the contributions at all stages of the project suggest a desire for ideas that tap into deep-rooted cultural patterns, a sense of myth and even a taste for poetically oriented magical thinking, rather than science fiction-inflected stories of technological progress.

With the benefit of hindsight, it feels clear that the conceptual foundation of Fashion Fictions should be found outside the sphere of science fiction, and indeed it is the genre of fantasy – a neighbour of science fiction in the 'supergenre of the fantastic'[115] – that first informed and inspired this work. The initial use of fantasy as inspiration was entirely instinctive, guided by an understanding of the world – or worlds – gained from books I devoured in childhood. The books are the Chrestomanci series by Diana Wynne Jones, a critically acclaimed fantasy author, and particularly one book from the series, *The Lives of Christopher Chant*, published in 1988. The eponymous character is a seemingly ordinary boy who is able to travel to other worlds in his dreams, and – through a series of hair-raising adventures – turns out to be a powerful nine-lifed enchanter.

Figure 1.7 *World 152 reflects a common appetite for myth and ritual in Fashion Fictions. The original Stage 1 fiction states that 'clothes are perceived as mediums of spirituality';[116] in this Stage 2 interpretation, designers are seen as religious leaders who are influenced by folklore and ancient customs.*

Having borrowed the book from my local library, I guess that I cannot have read it more than two or three times as a child. Yet Jones's evocative portrayal of the multitude of parallel worlds that Christopher explores made a deep and lasting impression on me, to the extent that it has become ingrained to my understanding of imagination and possibility. Where others might use a mental map for speculation based on quantum physics or the fiction of H. G. Wells, I think of Christopher stepping past the fireplace in his bedroom to stand in The Place Between, a valley of shapeless rocks, contemplating dozens of paths leading down into similar-yet-different worlds.[117] Charlie Butler has written about Jones's interest in the notion of the multiverse, rather than a single 'other world' as found in many fantasy and science fiction works: "'The world is not enough," Diana once said, and for her this was true. Her imagination shuffled universes like cards, or bent them into origami shapes.'[118]

The multiverse of the Chrestomanci series takes the form of parallel worlds that split off from one another at decisive moments in history. As Christopher's teacher Flavian explains:

All the worlds were probably one world to begin with – and then something happened back in prehistory which could have ended in two contradictory ways. Let's say a continent blew up. Or it didn't blow up. The two things couldn't both be true at once in the same world, so that world became two worlds, side by side but quite separate, one with that continent and one without. And so on …[119]

This notion has directly influenced Fashion Fictions: the project's speculations take place in present-day alternative worlds – parallel presents – that have split off from our own at some point in history. Many writers have explored this counterfactual history device. In *The Yiddish Policemen's Union* by Michael Chabon, for example, the USA implements a 1940 proposal to resettle European Jews in Sitka, Alaska, creating a Yiddish-speaking metropolis. *The Years of Rice and Salt* by Kim Stanley Robinson covers a much longer timespan, imagining a world in which the Black Death almost entirely wiped out the population of Europe. The approach can also be used in speculative design; Sascha Pohflepp's project *The Golden Institute* visualizes a world in which Jimmy Carter won the 1980 US election, enabling the development of renewable energy initiatives.[120] These counterfactual fictions reframe the present day, questioning cultural, political and technological norms.[121]

In Fashion Fictions, we speculate sideways into endless parallel presents, rather than forward into the future. While futures are implicitly present in any work of imagination that is 'mindful of all the other ways the world could be',[122] in Fashion Fictions this interest is channelled through the 'surrogate' of parallel worlds.[123] This indirect approach feels like the right fit for a project seeking to disrupt assumptions of technological progress. When we look forward in time, the idea that technology will become increasingly embedded in every aspect of life is hard to avoid, particularly when extrapolating from trends in today's society. Sidestepping the future also helps to mitigate fashion's complicated relationship with time. On one hand, the fashion industry dwells in the near future, with trend forecasters anticipating our wants and needs in the months and years to come. At the same time the fashion system constantly delves into history through the revival of past styles, 'play[ing] promiscuously with the past'.[124]

Beyond these considerations, the most important reason for speculating sideways is that projecting into the future has the potential to close down, rather than open up, the expanded sense of possibility that the Fashion Fictions project seeks to nurture. Placing a vision in the future implicitly raises the question of how such a vision could be achieved: what the path from here to there could be. Radical scenarios can therefore be dismissed as hopelessly naive, limiting the scope of our collective imaginings just at the time when we need to be exploring with wild abandon.

* * * * * * * *

Fantasy may seem like a surprising choice as the conceptual foundation for Fashion Fictions. The project is not concerned with magic or witchcraft; the swords-and-sorcery vision that the word tends to evoke is just as ill-fitting as that of spaceships and robots. While I seek to guide the speculation away from emerging technologies and the conquering of space, I do not wish to wander into the territory of lazy nostalgia and bucolic idealism. Yet the fantasy genre is much broader than this cliched image, and the underpinning characteristics of fantasy have much to offer the speculation that I seek to cultivate.

Brian Attebery identifies a central characteristic of fantasy as the impossible: 'some violation of what the author clearly believes to be natural law'.[125] As he explains, 'fantasy treats these impossibilities without hesitation, without doubt, without any attempt to reconcile them with our intellectual understanding of the workings of the world or to make us believe that such things could under any circumstances come true'.[126] Earlier in the chapter, I discussed the impossible as an element of imagination and highlighted its importance for sustainable transitions. The most obvious impossible aspect of Fashion Fictions is the parallel-worlds premise: the existence of countless parallel worlds that are similar to our own, save for certain aspects of the fashion system and surrounding economic and cultural norms, is an impossible notion.

But what about impossibility in the fictions themselves? From one perspective, the visions created in the project do not extend into the impossible. One of the parameters that has guided contributions to the project from the start is the need for the fictional fashion cultures and systems to be physically possible – not relying on magic wands, time travel or alien technologies, for example. The structure of the project, therefore, explicitly directs contributors not to break laws of biology and physics. Yet possibility should not relate only to physical factors; it should also take into account our *sense* of what can and cannot happen, in social terms. (Strictly speaking, this is plausibility, rather than possibility; given the project's focus on social and cultural systems, the two categories are closely connected.) Attebery acknowledges that our framing of the impossible is affected by our collective sense of the possible,[127] while Kathryn Hume refers to fantasy as 'departure from consensus reality'.[128]

As I noted earlier in the chapter, a viable alternative to capitalism feels, for many, impossible. In fact, Arturo Escobar notes, *any* world 'beyond the dominant notions of life and the human that have come to prevail in the West and beyond it' could be placed in the realm of the impossible. Thus, fictions exploring post-growth worlds and visions beyond modernity/coloniality sit beyond plausibility. Indeed, it was this consensus that initially prompted Fashion Fictions. I came up with the project's underlying principles in response to the frustration I felt when ideas for alternative fashion systems were quickly shut down by statements along these lines: *that's just not going to happen. It's not realistic.* (The irony, of course, is that business as usual – a growth-based economy on a finite planet – is a far more unrealistic long-term proposition.)

The project explicitly suggests that everything is on the table and up for discussion: economic systems, cultural norms, long-established clothing practices. It celebrates the value of imagining wildly; as Tania Zittoun, Hana Hawlina and Alex Gillespie argue, 'reversing or completely suspending reality from time to time can foster a playful and open-ended engagement with the world, loosening the fixation of how things are and questioning the existing state of affairs'.[129] Contributors are invited to suspend the critical voice that tells them a fictional system is impossible, and instead take the time to explore it. They are aided on this front by the parallel-presents structure, which is intended to disrupt lines of thought that search for a path between the present day and a desired future. Attebury points out that 'fantasy, by its structure, emphasizes the difference between fiction and life'.[130] To the contributors, we say: this is a fiction, it is not real and will not come true. But let us see what happens if we pretend for a while that it is real. *You're inventing a world. It doesn't exist. What is it like?*

The question of what the fictional world is like will never be fully answered within the space of the project: we place one or two aspects of fashion culture in the foreground and, inevitably, many other aspects remain vague and unresolved. Given the 100-word limit, the Stage 1 written outlines should be seen as playful thought experiments rather than comprehensive visions. Even when fleshed out as prototypes at Stage 2 and enactments at Stage 3, the worlds remain fragmented and incomplete, riddled with semi-apparent contradictions and confusions. This partiality does not diminish the fictions' utopian potential; as Lisa Garforth explains, 'the desire for a different and better way of being does not require the full-blown projection of an alternative'.[131] Another characteristic of the worlds is humour. I actively encourage Stage 1 contributors to make the stories of how their worlds split off from our own somewhat fanciful, and – if they wish – funny. (When weighing up options for my own Stage 1 worlds, I am generally guided by the version that amuses me the most.)

Due to these qualities, the fictions created by the Fashion Fictions community sit more in the sphere of 'tall tales' than serious visions. As Attebery explains, tall tales, like jokes and fantasy stories, have 'a certain contrived or constructed quality'.[132] They occupy what Richard Sandford calls 'subjunctive space': 'the kind of imagined settings that are contingent, conditional, offered not as futures seriously entertained as futures, but as alternatives posited for the sake of an argument or to illustrate a principle, a world that is not-yet but that is not hypothesised in a way intended to suggest it might ever be'.[133]

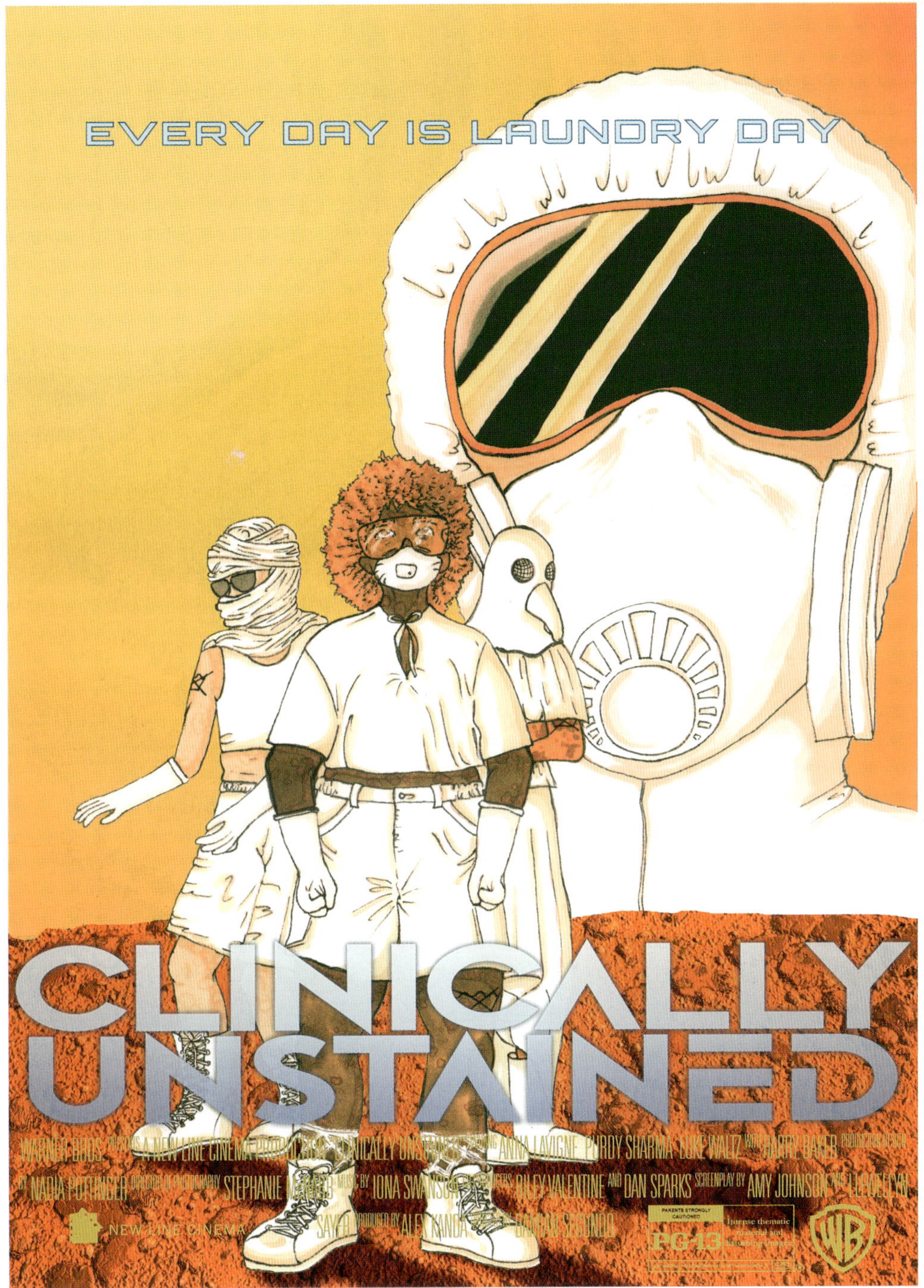

Figure 1.8 *The original World 97 fiction describes a world in which wearing stained and soiled clothing signi-fies style and prosperity.*[134] *This cleverly conceived poster, created as a Stage 2 prototype, advertises a film from World 97 about a hygiene–obsessed dystopia.*

This constructed quality may make the fictions seem unduly frivolous, or the exercise of generating them a waste of effort. Certainly, such criticisms have been levelled at Fashion Fictions. One Stage 1 contributor appended their fiction with the comment, 'I can not be too playful … Simply because we do not have enough time for that.' Yet play can have great value. Nicole Seymour argues that cultural works that draw on playfulness, irreverence and irony rather than sincerity are well suited to addressing horrors such as climate change[135] – and, I would add, the horrors of the mainstream fashion system. Diana Wynne Jones likewise highlights the importance of play: 'I venture to say that more important things can be conveyed like this, playfully, while people laugh, than by any other means.'[136] Indeed, as Richard Schechner notes, 'playing is double-edged, ambiguous, moving in several directions simultaneously. People often mix bits of play – a wisecrack, a joke, a flirtatious smile – with serious activities in order to lighten, subvert, or even deny what is apparently being communicated.'[137]

* * * * * * * * *

Diana Wynne Jones put her inclination for writing fantasy down to an unconventional upbringing and the outbreak of the Second World War when she was five. As she explained: 'I have never really lost this sense that the world is basically thoroughly unstable. I think this is why I tend to write about multiple parallel worlds – anything can happen and probably is doing somewhere.'[138] This sense of instability and openness perhaps explains why I find Jones's work to be such a vibrant source of inspiration for exploring alternative fashion systems. By imagining endless parallel worlds in Fashion Fictions – by finding our own Place Between – we are freed from the assumptions of technological progress that limit much speculative work and prompted to tap into modes of being that do not usually have a place in sustainable fashion discourse.

Accepting the impossibility of this task also liberates us from the stifling concern for how change will happen and allows us to speculate freely. One of the Stage 2 workshop participants, Alison, described her experience of building another world, and the freedom that she felt to imagine otherwise:

> We had to go there and start from there, rather than trying to take [our world] with us. And it gave it a slightly different perspective than if we'd just been asked to change something here – when you've got all of here already around us … even in your head, it feels quite a safe way of doing that, that exploring. And you can be quite radical with it all.

This process may appear escapist to some, but in fact the falseness of speculation is deeply connected with the real; it provides a powerful means of 'unsettl[ing] the present.'[139] As Farah Mendelsohn comments in her writing on Jones's work: 'creativity is a process of mixing one's internal self with external stimuli. There is no such thing as imagination, in and of itself. Imagination is dialectic: it is not about copying the world but about arguing with it.'[140] In Chapter 2, we will explore the many forms that these arguments can take.

127
76
81
258
44

2

Speculating sideways

Envisioning parallel worlds

Stage 1 of Fashion Fictions invites contributors to invent a parallel world in which people live differently with their clothes and to capture this world in a 'flash fiction' of just 100 words. After writing an initial five worlds to get things started in early 2020, I published a call for contributions. Catalyzed by a series of online workshops and affiliated projects at various higher education institutions, the worlds started to roll in. As I gained experience of supporting others to devise their worlds, I developed a flexible step-by-step guide for writing a fiction. Integrated into this process is an interactive generator that can be used either to illustrate useful elements of a fiction or to kickstart ideas (Figure 2.2). I published the guide on the project website, along with advice for anyone wishing to run their own world-writing workshop, and refined it further as time went on.[1]

In Fashion Fictions we aim to explore positive and enticing worlds: places we might want to live, or at least find out more about. When first presented with this challenge, many people find it hard to generate ideas – unsurprisingly, given the seeming intractability of the status quo. The fiction-writing guide encourages contributors to overcome this difficulty by first identifying an issue that they find particularly frustrating within the real-world fashion system. A small selection of frustrations, as recorded on the fiction submission form, provides an insight into the varied nature of these starting points: 'the cult of newness'; 'overloaded closets'; 'lack of inclusivity in the fashion industry'. The frustration can then be flipped to create a positive 'what if' idea. A frustration with the huge volumes of unworn clothes hanging in many wardrobes might, for example, inspire an idea based on wardrobes of limited size or the rationing of clothes, while a frustration with the dominance of Paris, New York, Milan and London might inspire a fiction in which the epicentres of fashion influence are found in the global South.

Figure 2.1 *Generating an abundance of fictional propositions, together.*

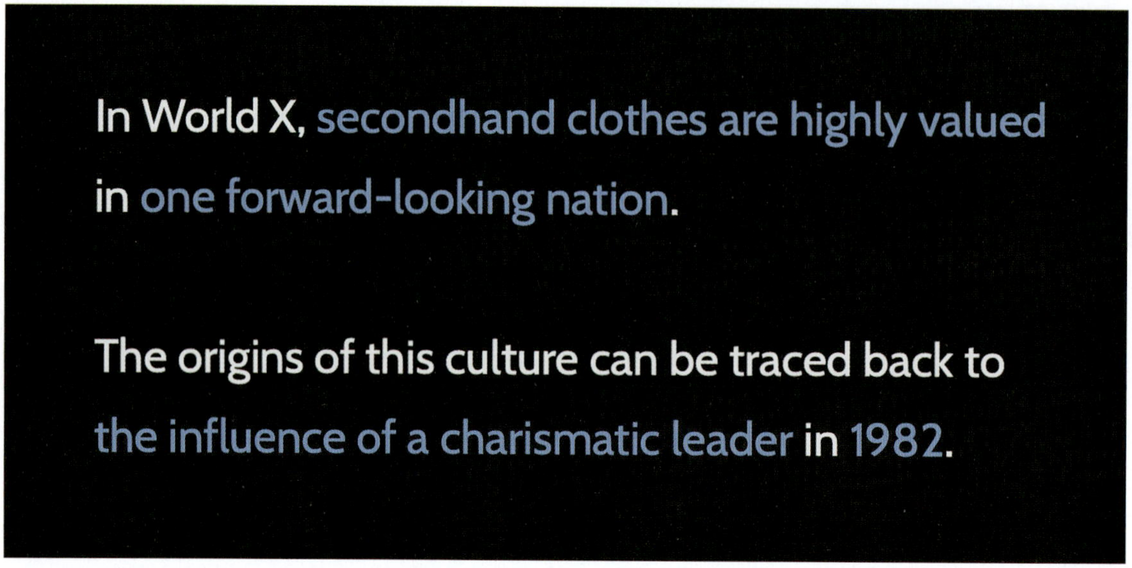

In World X, secondhand clothes are highly valued in one forward-looking nation.

The origins of this culture can be traced back to the influence of a charismatic leader in 1982.

Figure 2.2 *The interactive generator can be used to create brief outlines of parallel fashion worlds.[2] Each area of blue text rotates through multiple options, creating thousands of possible combinations.*

A criticism sometimes levelled at speculative design is the tendency for privileged designers to invent fictional scenarios – typically, dystopian visions such as widespread hunger – that are daily experiences for many communities.[3] When devising the Fashion Fictions structure I took this on board but realized that each contributor could only speculate on the basis of their own lived experience, and that this experience, underpinned by their cultural knowledge, will inform their sense of what is actual, possible, impossible and desirable.[4] For me, this is a feature rather than a bug: diverse perspectives enrich the project. I value the contributions from the global South, and particularly from settings in which the globalized mainstream fashion system has not (yet) come to dominate; I *also* value the dreams of those who are living in the thick of that system. Regardless of positionality or starting point, I encourage people to amplify their ideas and push beyond their own limits of plausibility, inspired by Donella Meadows' call for people envisioning better worlds to articulate 'what you really want, not what you think you can get'.[5]

In the next part of the process, contributors are guided to consider the context for the fiction, for example specifying whether the fashion culture being described is mainstream or underground, and whether it spans the world or is located in a particular region. Another important element is the backstory of the fiction: the narrative of how the parallel world came to develop differently to our own. As part of this backstory, I encourage world-writers to identify the juncture at which the paths of history diverged – described in science fiction circles as the 'Jonbar hinge'.[6] Some approaches to speculating in parallel presents start with an alternative outcome of a real-life historical event and work forward to the present day. For Fashion Fictions I encourage a different approach: first coming up with the present-day parallel and then generating the historical backstory.[7] Furthermore, I encourage people to create amusing and only semi-plausible backstories, incorporating invented rather than genuine junctures if they wish, as a strategy for creating diverse and engaging fictions. By drawing together the 'what if', the context and the backstory, and by giving consideration to the everyday fashion experience in the fictional world, a coherent vision can be presented – though the rigour of the 100-word limit generally forces the writer to make a savage edit that retains only the elements that they deem most important.

At the time of writing, more than 250 Stage 1 worlds have been submitted for inclusion on the project website, most by individuals and some by pairs or groups working collaboratively. Despite the brevity of each contribution, as a collection the fictions cover a broad variety of topics that extend far beyond the typical fashion and sustainability discourse. In addition to mentions of the clothing worn and the ways in which fashion production and consumption are configured in the fictional society, the worlds explore high-level issues such as economics and geopolitics. This kaleidoscope of visions chimes with Lisa Garforth's observation that 'there cannot be a single utopia of sustainability but rather a range of ideas, expressed in diverse forms, about how we can live better with the natures we have and have made'.[8] It is also reminiscent of the pluriverse, a concept that challenges 'the modern idea that we all live within a single reality or World'.[9] As Arturo Escobar explains, there are now, and have been in the past, many realities. He argues that acknowledging these many worlds – working with the idea of 'a world in which many worlds fit'[10] – is a powerful antidote to the singular worldview of modernity/coloniality. The pluriverse's disruption of a single truth, destiny or narrative is vital for post-growth possibilities.

* * * * * * * * *

Activity 2.1: Stage 1 – writing a world

This activity invites you to imagine a parallel world in which people live differently with their clothes, and to describe the world's fictional fashion system. It usually works best as an individual task. Before you start, note the rules of Fashion Fictions. All descriptions should:

- describe a contemporary reality in a parallel world, not the future in our world

- explore a positive and enticing culture, in terms of individual satisfaction, social justice and sustainability

- be physically possible but push beyond what feels plausible (to you) in the real world.

1. Identify one specific issue relating to our real-world fashion system that frustrates you. Consider how this issue could be reversed to create a positive vision. Alternatively, work directly with a focused idea for a positive fictional fashion system.

2. Develop your core idea – the distinctive essence of your parallel world – by thinking in detail about a 'what if' question driving your fiction. Be playful as you imagine your world. Include quirky elements to make it memorable.

3. Generate a 'backstory' for the world: an explanation for why its fashion system developed differently to the system in our own world. Identify an event in history – genuine or invented – that caused the fictional world to split from our world. This could be months, years or centuries ago.

4. Flesh out the idea and capture it in a 100-word fiction. Use the first fifty words to describe the core idea and the backstory. Use the second fifty words to describe the everyday fashion practices in your world and key aspects of its fashion culture.

For more detailed guidance on this activity, to access the interactive fiction generator and to share your world, visit fashionfictions.org/contribute-a-world.

Note that all Fashion Fictions processes can be easily adapted for non-fashion contexts by substituting the word 'fashion' for your area of interest: food, housing, transport and so on. See parallelpresents.org for further guidance.

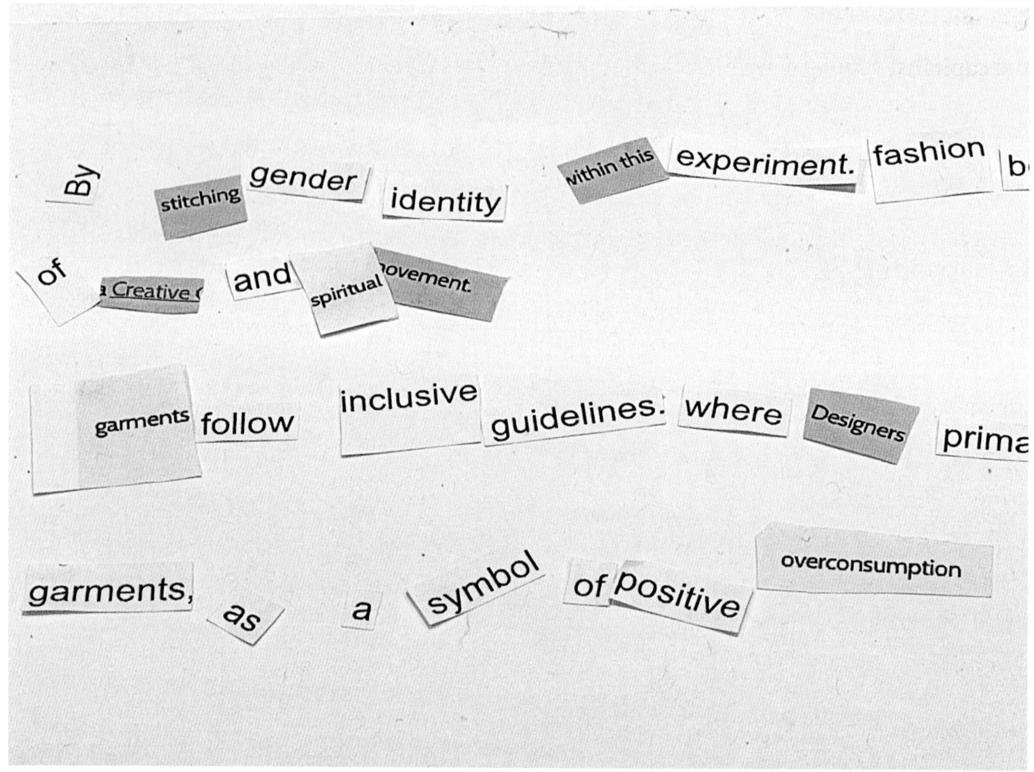

Figure 2.3 *An alternative way of creating a 100-word fiction is to adapt, rework or physically remix one or more existing worlds. The Creative Commons licence applied to each contribution allows for such adaptation, as long as the original creator is credited and the same licence is applied to the remixed version.*

The Stage 2 prototyping activity is highly flexible: it can be experienced in half an hour or can expand into an undertaking lasting several months, as for the students at various institutions who have created prototypes as major projects during their studies. In order to gain an insight into the experiences of people taking part in the prototyping process, I ran four two-day Stage 2 workshops in Nottingham between November 2021 and March 2022, building on an earlier pilot that had taken place in early 2020. To recruit participants I issued a number of open and targeted calls and received over a hundred responses. I then invited a selection of these people to join a workshop, with the aim of bringing together people with diverse positionalities – although a significant gender imbalance in those expressing interest meant that relatively few men took part. Between seven and twelve people attended each workshop, including: academics with expertise in fashion and sustainability, fashion theory and fashion history; fashion/textile industry professionals; and, importantly, people whose experience of the fashion system was solely personal rather than also professional or academic.

Stage 1 fictions were selected for exploration at my Stage 2 workshops via a two-stage process. First, I carried out an initial sift of the 125 worlds available at that time, prioritizing fictions that challenged, whether overtly or implicitly, the structures and norms of the mainstream fashion system and the capitalist economy within which it operates. This produced a long list of thirty-seven worlds; an international panel of six advisors, who brought diverse perspectives on fashion, sustainability and speculation, then voted for their preferred fictions, and the twenty worlds with the highest scores were selected. Five worlds were offered for exploration at each workshop and on each occasion four were selected by participants, with group sizes ranging from two to four people working collaboratively and, on a couple of occasions, one person working solo.

The first part of Stage 2 involves 'fleshing out' the fiction: developing an understanding of the world and thinking about its society and culture in more depth. While the Stage 1 fiction forms the foundation for exploration, I encourage participants to extend, adapt and even reinvent this text to suit their interests and understandings: to treat it as a 'seed' that 'allow[s] thoughts to go in all directions', rather than a fixed scenario.[11] Notes from the small-group discussions in the first part of the workshops record frequent questioning: *is the world like this, or like that?* Prompts to support the process encourage participants to consider what is celebrated and stigmatized, abundant and scarce in the world. By exploring these questions, the participants develop a shared, though often unresolved, understanding of the fashion system in their fictional world. Once this understanding is in place, they create a visual or material diegetic prototype – something that belongs *in* the fictional world – to represent its fashion system. I invite them to imagine that they have travelled to the parallel world and either taken a photograph or picked something up and brought it back to show us what life is like there.

As I explained in Chapter 1, Fashion Fictions was conceived as an escape from the pervasive 'realist' attitude: *that's just not going to happen.* Happily, my hopes were fulfilled at the Stage 2 workshops. Participants willingly suspended their disbelief and we managed, as Brian Attebery puts it, to 'evade the rational censor'.[12] This embrace of the impossible is a different mindset to that of much speculative

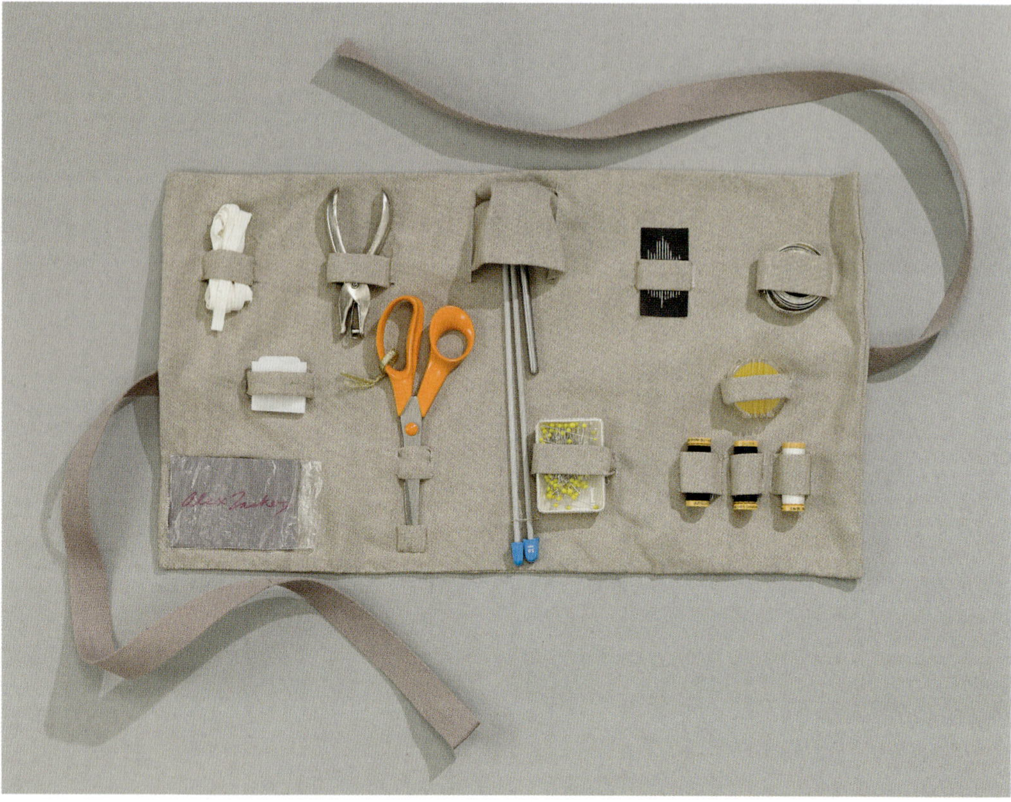

Figure 2.4 *This diegetic prototype was created at a Stage 2 workshop as a representation of life in World 9, in which learning to sew is a teenage rite of passage. This standard-issue sewing kit is presented to every young person on their sixteenth birthday by the Ministry for Artisans and Makers.*

design, which seems to adopt a rational approach more akin to science fiction: *this could really happen. Is that what you want?* I feel it is important to step away from rationality, not only because of its inherent connection to the paradigm of modernity/coloniality, but for a deeply pragmatic reason: after being involved in discussions about fashion and sustainability for twenty years, I do not believe that we are going to reason our way to a sustainable fashion system. Fashion performs such deeply personal, emotional and social functions that something beyond facts and logic is needed. We need stories, inspiration, qualitative insights into alternative modes of being. Gary K. Wolfe describes science fiction as 'the geography of reason' and fantasy as 'the geography of desire'.[13] Fashion Fictions occupies the latter of these territories: not anticipating what we think will happen, but rather exploring our collective desires for how life with clothes might be different. This sense of desire is crucial. As Rob Hopkins notes, 'we all need to get an awful lot better at the cultivation of longing … I've always felt that unless we are able to cultivate a deep and visceral longing for a low carbon future, we have no chance of ever creating it.'[14] In Fashion Fictions, we indulge ourselves in fantasy, in longing, to forge new pathways to change.

Activity 2.2: Stage 2 – making a prototype

This activity asks you to create a visual or material prototype to represent everyday life in a fictional fashion system. It works well as a collaborative activity, because a range of perspectives feed the development and discussion of ideas, but can also be carried out individually.

1. Choose a Stage 1 fiction from the website (fashionfictions.org/the-worlds) or use your own Stage 1 fiction (see Activity 2.1).

2. Flesh out your understanding of your chosen world. Use the information provided in the original text but also bring in your own ideas, aiming for an engaging and positive vision that stretches the imagination in unexpected directions.

3. Generate ideas for an object or image that you could create to represent everyday life in the fictional world. Imagine that you have travelled to the world and brought something back, or taken a photograph, to show people what life is like there.

4. Select the idea that communicates the distinctiveness of the fictional fashion system most effectively and create your prototype.

5. Write a short text to explain your prototype. Remain within the fiction: write from the perspective of a traveller who has just returned from the parallel world.

For more detailed guidance on this activity and to share your prototype, visit fashionfictions.org/contribute-exploration.

Figure 2.5 *Working with pre-existing imagery, such as magazine pages, can be a productive and thought-provoking way of creating a Stage 2 prototype.*

Bringing the worlds to life

While fantasy depends on conjuring visions of impossible places and plots, it is not devoid of real-world references. After all, as Brian Attebery explains, all stories involve elements of mimesis and fantasy. He describes mimesis as the faithful imitation of everyday life and fantasy as the notion that anything can happen – or, more memorably, 'mimesis tells what is and fantasy tells what isn't'.[15] Despite the contrasts between these modes, a mix of both is needed in any work of fiction:

> Mimesis without fantasy would be nothing but reporting one's perceptions of actual events. Fantasy without mimesis would be a purely artificial invention, without recognisable objects or actions … Fantasy depends on mimesis for its effectiveness. We must have some solid ground to stand on, some point of contact, if only with the language in which the story is communicated.[16]

Fantasy, then, always makes some references to the familiar, whether at a general level – trees, humans, gravity – or a more culturally specific level – David and Victoria Beckham, barkcloth, tic-tac-toe. The same is true of imagination more generally: as a social and cultural process, it draws on shared meanings, experiences and resources from the real world. Indeed, as Tania Zittoun, Hana Hawlina and Alex Gillespie explain, 'the actual and the possible' – and, I would add, the impossible – 'are not opposites, but deeply interconnected'.[17]

Much of the fiction by Diana Wynne Jones that has inspired Fashion Fictions is categorized as 'low' or 'real-world' fantasy: stories that consciously draw in elements recognizable from everyday life. Unlike the enclosed worlds of many fantasy authors, works of low fantasy 'describe settings that seem to be real, familiar, present-day places, except that they contain the magic characters and impossible events of fantasy'.[18] The magic realists of Latin America such as Gabriel Garcia Marquez likewise blend the familiar and the fantastical, creating worlds that are, in Attebery's words, 'at once solid and slippery'.[19] As he comments with reference to horror writers who also use everyday real-world settings, the stories 'derive their effectiveness from the apparent ordinariness and security that they breach'.[20]

We take a similar approach with the Fashion Fictions fantasies. The premise is that these worlds are much like our own, save for the particular aspects that we select for manipulation. For example, we might imagine a world in which every village has a shared wardrobe. Every aspect of the world would potentially be up for discussion: societal notions of ownership, what the clothes are like, how this arrangement affects interpersonal relations. But in general, the default would be a blurry version of the status quo: the real-world norm is assumed to be the case, unless we actively choose to disrupt it. Every world is thus a blend of the familiar and the unfamiliar.

The Stage 1 fictions vary widely in how far they depart from the real world. Some are close enough to feel somewhat possible (save for the parallel-world conceit), while others reimagine the whole of human civilization, with millennia-long invented histories that have implications for every aspect of society and culture. Most sit somewhere in between, challenging selected aspects of everyday life, with a focus on fashion. Stage 2 presents another opportunity for participants to consider how close to real life they wish their fiction to sit and which aspects of society and culture they wish to challenge. At both Stage 1 and Stage 2, specific real-world references are often incorporated as a way of making the fiction feel real and three-dimensional.

Another bridge between the fictional parallel worlds of Fashion Fictions and the real world is offered by the resources used in the workshops and enactments. At my Stage 2 workshops, I provided a selection of basic materials and equipment including assorted papers, stationery, art supplies, haberdashery and textile tools. Two iPads were available and many participants used their own digital devices, while a photographer was on hand to support groups to create still and moving imagery. Each group was given a small budget to spend on additional supplies; some groups bought

Figure 2.6 *Stage 2 prototypes can be made using physical or digital processes, or a combination of the two. In this workshop, a photograph of a closed-down department store in Nottingham city centre is being considered for use as part of the prototype.*

nothing, while others purchased secondhand clothes and other objects, magazines and sundry small items. Some participants also brought items from home, typically craft supplies and textile samples. By using these assorted resources to create their prototypes, the participants made many decisions – both consciously and unconsciously – about the fictional worlds and the nature of the items that would be found there.

Reflections from the Stage 2 workshops indicate that these engagements with the concrete – in terms of both references and resources – helped to make the world feel closer by providing a 'perceptual bridge' between fiction and reality.[21] Workshop participant Annebella, a fashion historian, noted that the fictions 'might seem sort of off the scale initially, like these mad fantasies. But once you start breaking them down into the detail, they're only one step away from wherever you already are.' Drawing on her knowledge of historical utopian impulses, she continued, 'Our fantasies are really conditioned by our present realities … our utopias are very much rooted with one foot in the present.' Lisa Garforth agrees:

> Utopias are doubly social. They are a product of, expressive of, particular social conditions, and they are about the possibility of a transformed society. The content of any utopian expression is irreducibly shaped by its social context. Utopias appear to be about an elsewhere or an alternative future – but the very act of imagining otherwise points to problems, lacks and issues in the present. Utopias reveal what is wrong with the societies we have.[22]

The interplay between the fictional world and the real world is at its most apparent at Stage 3, when we invite participants to enact speculative propositions. Such experiments are based on 'a playful mode of trying out how everyday life might play out differently'[23] and seek to examine the embodied experiences of participants as they encounter the fictional worlds made (somewhat) real. I ran a pilot Stage 3 enactment in early 2020 and built on this experience to organize four Stage 3 enactments as research activities between February and August 2022, involving participants from the earlier Stage 2 workshops and some new recruits. The development of these Stage 3 activities was itself a creative act: for each one I picked up an element from a world explored at a preceding prototyping workshop – often an idea from the group's discussion, rather than the prototype itself – and created a structured activity focusing on aspects of the fiction that felt particularly exciting and unfamiliar.

Two enactments – the pilot and the first of the later activities – involved geographically dispersed participants enacting a practice from a fictional world one day a week for six weeks, sharing updates and reflections via comments, images and other media posted to a WhatsApp group.[24] For another 'remote' enactment, small groups posted garments to one another in a round-robin format and created collaborative texts to describe each item.[25] The other two enactments were in-person events, where participants came together to interact in person and experience particular places, materials and practices.[26] Following the conclusion of the four research enactments I experimented with open Stage

Figure 2.7 *The enactment of World 54, in which production of new textiles is severely limited, took place in a large music rehearsal room. Participants stepped into the fictional world together, experiencing a resourceful yet opulent fashion culture based on the use of sheets, curtains and versatile straps.*

3 opportunities, in the format of 'wardrobe challenges' coordinated via digital platforms.[27] While these participatory enactments and challenges took a variety of forms, they all depended on the merging of real and fictional worlds. Through their activities, each participant was able to act in and experience both real world and fictional world, with their focus shifting dynamically between the two. Along the way, they built the world further, constructing new understandings – some personal, some shared – about life in the fictional culture.

Activity 2.3: Stage 3 – creating an enactment

The final stage of Fashion Fictions invites you to enact a fashion-related practice or event from a fictional fashion world as a way of experiencing an alternative fashion culture in an embodied way. An enactment could be individual but is particularly effective as a group activity, whether involving direct collaboration or the sharing of individual experiences.

1. Choose a Stage 1 fiction from the website (fashionfictions.org/the-worlds) or use your own Stage 1 fiction (see Activity 2.1). Alternatively, use a Stage 2 prototype (see Activity 2.2) as your starting point.

2. Consider life in the fictional world and identify everyday fashion practices and/or events that take place there. The practices/events may be present in the fiction selected in Step 1 or may emerge from your thinking as you interpret and discuss the fictional world. Feel free to take the fiction in an unexpected direction to create an engaging vision.

3. Generate ideas for possible ways that you could enact the practices/events in the real world. Enactments could take many forms, such as a one-day live event or a commitment to perform the world's practices one day per week for a period of time.

4. Select the idea that will offer the most immersive and compelling experience of an alternative fashion culture or system and plan your enactment. Brief participants fully on the fictional fashion culture/system they will be performing.

5. Conduct your enactment, aiming for a playful and informal ethos.

For more detailed guidance on this activity and to share your enactment, visit fashionfictions.org/contribute-enactment.

Figure 2.8 *Moorlands Primary School in Huddersfield, a town in northern England, organized a large-scale enactment of World 127, in which climate change drives an inventive umbrella recycling culture.*[28] *In this interpretation of the fictional world, umbrellas are not only recycled but also used to send messages and to celebrate significant events. The project culminated in a carnival parade to mark the real-world royal coronation.*[29]

* * * * * * * *

In Fashion Fictions workshops I have observed that by the time the speculation or enactment activity is drawing to a close, the fictional world has become quite real to the participants and the real world can feel somewhat alien. Mette Gislev Kjærsgaard and Laurens Boer, writing about the speculative design process, describe this sense of distance as defamiliarization and highlight the centrality of the concept in traditional anthropological practices.[30] Another term for defamiliarization, used in some of the fields discussed in Chapter 1, is estrangement; Garforth discusses 'estrangement from taken-for-granted social arrangements' as part of the process of utopianism,[31] while Attebery highlights the importance of estrangement in works of science fiction and fantasy. Discussing the work of Ursula K. Le Guin, he explains that the author 'effectively "estranges" us from conventional gender roles: we turn from her world … to the world surrounding us and both look strange, unlikely, awkward, and fascinating'.[32]

Another way of framing estrangement is the rather more enticing notion of wonder. Wonder is a versatile concept: both verb and noun, with varying popular and academic interpretations dating back to ancient Greek philosophy.[33] Some of these interpretations relate to a process of questioning and a new perception of the familiar world, as if seeing through different eyes. Vlad Glăveanu defines wonder as 'a particular type of experience whereby the person becomes (more or less suddenly) aware of an expanded field of possibility for thought and/or action and engages (more or less actively) in exploring this field'.[34] In his conceptualization, this powerful yet everyday process shares characteristics with awe, contemplation, pondering and curiosity – and involves both immersion and detachment, passive observation and active exploration.[35] In the context of Fashion Fictions, wonder generates a fresh perspective on our real-world experiences of fashion and new insights about aspects of contemporary life that usually feel so familiar as to be utterly unquestioned. It causes us to challenge that which we thought was fixed and to revisit our own taken-for-granted assumptions about how things are. Furthermore, it prompts us to see possibilities where we previously did not – and, as we will see in Chapter 7, to start to explore these possibilities.

In order to help the wonder generated by the workshops to be sustained, I wanted to find ways of crystallizing participants' thinking to create an accessible resource of inspiration and courage; both will surely be needed if we are to transform the status quo. With this in mind, I started to invite those completing a Fashion Fictions activity to capture a thought via one of three paths: *questions, ideas for action* and *precedents*. Such thoughts might connect directly to the fictional world that the participant explored, but could equally be seemingly unrelated thoughts that arose through the process of speculation and reflection.

The first path, *questions*, involves questions about the status quo that arise when looking with fresh eyes, typically relating to *how* or *why* things are the way they are. The second, *ideas for action*, identifies things that the contributor would like to see happen in the real world, guided by longing and desire rather than practicality or rational thought. For these ideas – as for the other two paths – contributors can think personally or collectively. For example, an idea for action may be a personal act that the participant intends to undertake as a result of the workshop, but could equally be a high-level policy proposal that would not look out of place in a bold manifesto for transformative change. Thus, while in the speculative stages a participant acts as a creator (Stages 1/2) or a fictional citizen (Stage 3), for the purposes of wonder they can act in the mode of citizen and policymaker.

The third and final path, *precedents*, concerns contemporary or historical examples of better ways of living with our clothes. These are practices or arrangements that currently happen, or happened in the past, in the real world, which could offer vital inspiration to others. I have found that various precedents – whether personal or collective – are often mentioned during the process of speculation, and have woven some into the pages of this book. Making connections between a speculative vision and lived experience is an instinctive and natural process. As Attebery notes, 'As soon as it is announced that the world we are reading about bears no relation to our world, we begin to make connections.'[36] (You might experience this phenomenon as you encounter the worlds for yourself.) Fashion Fictions thus acts as a hook, pulling forgotten or underappreciated examples into the light.

Bearing in mind that the consumption-intensive globalized mainstream fashion system is a relatively recent development, there is a huge historical scope to work with when contemplating possible precedents. As Thomas Princen notes, 'In the vast bulk of history … humans have been figuring out how to live *with* earth's bounties and *within* its boundaries.'[37] Furthermore, although today's globalized fashion system can seem all-consuming, it is riddled with alternative practices such as mending, sharing, swapping and bartering. In fact, the same is true of capitalism more generally; this seemingly dominant system is actually 'partial, fragmented, and has always existed alongside, or even dependent upon, non-capitalist alternatives.'[38] Cameron Tonkinwise argues that transitions towards sustainability will therefore mean

> finding and amplifying all the ways of being in the world that are persistently non-capitalist, that defy technological ratcheting of expectations around efficiency and comfort and instead entail everyday practices of sustainment … localist systems of resourcing, commons and shared resource use, ways of consuming time that are regenerative of ecosystem health and diversity.[39]

Overall, then, we can see that Fashion Fictions uses structured speculation as a route to open-ended wonder: speculation takes us away from the real world while wonder brings us back, with fresh eyes and a more open mind. The playful speculative task leads to the unmaking of social norms and simultaneous contemplation of how the real world might be configured otherwise. In fact, it can cause a collective shift, from resignation to an energetic appetite for change. In a delicious paradox, it is by imagining the consciously impossible that new and different real-world paths forward come into view.

Others have made the link between these companion processes: Cally Gatehouse, for example, discusses how her participatory speculative design workshops generate a sense of wonder. She observes that speculation 'requires a faith that asks us to leap blindly', whereas wonder 'allows us to feel our way along boundaries and ask how they might be redrawn'.[40] The questioning of wonder has an open-ended quality; as Glăveanu explains, it 'opens us up to multiple answers and, above all, the possibility that none of them are correct, that there is much more that we still do not understand and we should continue to think about'.[41] I would add that in the case of Fashion Fictions, the sensibility of speculation is humorous and playful, while that of wonder is earnest and courageous: the tone is that of people who, through a satisfying session of play, develop a new-found determination that change will – must – be possible.

Activity 2.4: Capturing wonder

This reflective activity invites each participant to capture their thoughts in the final stage of a Fashion Fictions workshop or project (as described in the activities in Chapters 2–5), when the sense of wonder – a new perspective on their real-world experiences of fashion – is fresh. It is intended for people working in a group, but can be adapted for individual use. Resources are available to support this activity, whether in person or online.[42]

Wonder is channelled along three paths, each of which is associated with a different motif:

- Questions about the real world (feathers): a question about how or why things are how they are.

- Precedents – real-world examples (shells): a contemporary or historical example of a better way of living with our clothes.

- Ideas for action in the real world (leaves): something you want to see happen; be guided by desire, not practicality.

For all three themes, participants can think personally or collectively; contributions might connect to a particular fictional world or a different strand of thought that arose through discussion or reflection.

1. Familiarize yourself with the three wonder paths.
2. Spend a few minutes in silence thinking about your ideas and working out the wording for one question, precedent or idea for action. Capture it concisely – think of it as a headline or slogan.
3. Write your statement or question on the relevant motif.

4. Gather together, in a circle if you are working in person. One by one, say your name to locate yourself and then share your question, precedent or idea for action with the group.

5. Pin each question, precedent or idea for action on a pinboard or washing line (real or digital) for others to read.

6. After the workshop, carry this sense of wonder and possibility into the wilds of the real-world fashion system.

Figure 2.9 *At the wonder-capture activity that concludes some Fashion Fictions workshops, participants note their thoughts about the real world in the form of questions, precedents (contemporary or historical examples of better ways of living with our clothes) or ideas for action.*

Exploring the book

The next four chapters explore overarching themes that I have identified through my research examining the Fashion Fictions project. I explored ideas for these themes by analysing the wealth of data – extending to more than 1,200 pages of material – generated in the Stage 2 workshops and Stage 3 enactments outlined in this chapter.[43] This data enabled me to access not only the participants' creative outputs, but also the many fascinating conversations and practical explorations that took place during the process of developing, resolving and reflecting on these outputs. Through an extensive thematic analysis process, which involved months spent coding the Stage 2 workshop data – comprising transcripts, photographs and many different types of notes – and generating, reviewing and defining themes from the codes, I was able to identify the themes that I highlight in this book.[44] I then used these themes to investigate related insights within the Stage 3 enactment data, which took different forms depending on the activity: written comments and reflections, photographs, short videos and audio recordings. The entire collection of worlds, prototypes and enactments that had been submitted for the website at the time of writing provided valuable material that further fleshed out each theme.

From many potential areas of focus, I selected those that feel ripe with radical possibility, that are bursting to expand the field of fashion and sustainability into underexplored territories of thought and action. All of the themes arose in discussions about highly diverse worlds and prototypes, suggesting that they resonate across contexts as people gesture towards alternative systems. In each chapter, I use the fictions – and, importantly, those discussions that took place as they were prototyped and enacted – to lead me to theoretical concepts and real-world insights that shed light on the ideas being discussed, with the aim of creating a patchwork of the speculative and the real, the practical and the theoretical.

Chapter 3 explores the role of stories and language in both real-world contexts and the fictions created for the project. The process of enacting worlds is one area of focus, highlighting the value of embodying and performing stories and thus blending reality and fiction. The enactments of World 27, in which garments are valued for the stories they carry, and World 62, in which garments must be described in words rather than communicated in images, provide case studies.

Chapter 4 turns to the interconnected themes of nature and spirituality, considering topics such as the complex relationship between fashion and nature; the emergence of hybrid human/nonhuman communities; and decomposition and humbleness. Nature-centric World 91, in which mushrooms are hailed as spiritual guides, is considered in detail.

In Chapter 5 I expand the notion of community into a consideration of place and togetherness. The chapter explores the locations, places, celebrations, rituals and dynamics of fashion, taking in ideas such as local distinctiveness, connection and solidarity. Various fictions and prototyped worlds are discussed, with a particular focus on Stage 3 enactments: we return to the story-focused World 27, first discussed in Chapter 3, and explore World 54, in which trends manifest through styling rather than consumption.

Chapter 6 discusses the organization of fashion systems at various scales, from specific initiatives to the role of the state in shaping behaviour through policy and legal interventions. I consider the tension between restriction and self-expression and explore the need for limits and adaptation in an uncertain world. A return to the World 54 enactment, discussed in the previous chapter, provides an opportunity to focus on the resourcefulness that often arises in response to restriction.

To conclude each of the four thematic chapters I summarize a set of ideas that feel worthy of being carried forward in practice and research. The ideas are phrased as questions, intended to provoke new creative and activist lines of enquiry.[45] I also highlight potential pitfalls: common challenges that can present themselves when exploring the territory under discussion.

In Chapter 7 I draw the threads of the preceding chapters together in a discussion that focuses on real-world change. I discuss three ways in which Fashion Fictions contributes to change: by creating an expanded sense of possibility; by contributing new stories to the discourse around fashion and sustainability; and through hands-on action. I propose an alternative way of using the Fashion Fictions structure – playing in *prefigurative,* rather than *speculative* mode – that can generate visions for alternative organizations and practices, and bring them to life through repeated, extended or open-ended enactments.

Despite its basis in the speculations generated by participants in the first years of the Fashion Fictions project, this is not a purely retrospective book: there are various invitations to get involved. Activities 2.1–2.4 include instructions for the three stages of Fashion Fictions and the reflective wonder-capture activity. In Activities 3.1, 4.1, 5.1 and 5.2 you will find four 'recipes' for Fashion Fictions enactments: invitations to step into a speculative world for yourself. Activity 7.2 provides instructions for working with the Fashion Fictions structure in prefigurative mode. More detailed guidance for the various activities can be found by exploring the Fashion Fictions website.[46]

A note of caution: with such an abundance of speculative ideas to draw on, there is an ever-constant danger of overwhelming the reader: of inflicting, as I think of it, 'world whiplash'. To help with navigation, the first time a world appears, you will find its world number highlighted in bold and an explanation of its key characteristics, as relevant to the point being made, plus a note crediting the contributor(s) and, where relevant, a link to further detail on the project website. Where a world appears in more than one chapter or chapter section the same highlighting and explanation is provided, along with signposting to earlier mentions of the world. This signposting is intended only to facilitate connections between the chapters; you are not expected to remember details from the earlier discussion. Where I think it would be helpful for you to refer back, a page number is provided. If you would like to look at all mentions of a specific world, you can use the World index at the start of the book to identify the relevant pages.

Ready? Let's explore.

131
THE CLOTHES
ON YOUR BACK
100%
ORGANIC
COTTON
LUCKY
PERFECT
BETTER
untill hands
years later

3

Stories and language

Fashion stories

I had a vivid imagination as a child: I was forever making up fictional, often rather fantastical, propositions. Later, I channelled my creativity into design and making. I have not felt, as an adult, any particular desire to have a go at writing fiction – until I started to develop the first Stage 1 fictions. But I found great satisfaction from engaging, even in a modest way, in the ancient practice of storytelling: 'the recounting of a particular series of events that occur in a particular place and time'.[1] In more theoretical terms, a story is 'a cognitive construct that concerns certain types of entities' – including a world, characters, objects, physical and mental events and consequent changes – 'and relations between these entities'.[2] The backstories that form part of many of the Stage 1 fictions, which explain how the worlds came to develop differently from our own, fit these descriptions well. Consider just one example: in **World 178**, professional footballers staged a protest against consumerism by symbolically donning old strip and demanding that their clubs release new merchandise just once a decade, triggering changes not only in fashion culture but also in the wider economic system.[3] While some of the Stage 1 fictions omit an explicit backstory, all give some sense of the storyworld: the context in which events take place, often described in terms of cultural values and everyday fashion practices.

The word story – like the related term, history – can be traced back to the Greek *histor*, meaning 'having seen, hence knowing' and beyond that to the Indo-European *ueid*, meaning 'look at; see; an object of vision'.[4] Today, we commonly associate stories with fiction, distinguished from historical fact. Yet it was only in the sixteenth century that *history* and *story* began to develop these distinct meanings in English: before that time, the words were used almost interchangeably.[5] Furthermore, the boundary between these seemingly simple categories is far from clear. As Rob Pope explains, 'The

Figure 3.1 *In the real world, greenwashing skews our understanding; in fictions such as World 131, words are used to imbue clothing with meaning.*

problem … is precisely how far we can actually distinguish fiction from fact and story from history in any particular instance.'[6] Indeed, many of the stories we tell are firmly rooted in lived experience, rather than wild imagination. Barbara Benjamin notes that the internet, for example, 'is a repository of virtually endless stories, from gossip and urban legends to case studies'.[7] Personal stories, meanwhile, are understood to be crucial to our sense of self.[8]

It is widely acknowledged that stories and storytelling are a fundamental part of human life. Richard Kearney, for example, describes stories as 'an indispensable ingredient of any meaningful society'.[9] Stories give meaning to the world, help us to understand our place within it and enable knowledge to be transferred from person to person and from one generation to the next. As a result, as Benjamin puts it, 'everyone has access to the wisdom of the past as they live in the present and move toward the future'.[10] In Chapter 1 I noted the role of fantasy in providing a useful sense of distance between the reader and the fiction, which enables us to think things through in a space of safety. The same can, in fact, be said of all stories: Kearney describes a 'curious conflation of empathy and detachment which produces in us – viewers of Greek tragedy or readers of contemporary fiction – the double vision necessary for a journey beyond the closed ego towards other possibilities of being'.[11] The Fashion Fictions stories allow us to 'try on' fictional fashion systems without commitment, and thus think through how our dress practices might be otherwise. We get up close, but can step back at any time.

Social and environmental justice activists are interested in the narratives that underpin individual stories, and the role of these narratives in shaping societal attitudes. US-based project Narrative Initiative explains that:

> Narratives are often described as a collection or system of related stories that are articulated and refined over time to represent a central idea or belief. Unlike individual stories, narratives have no standard form or structure; they have no beginning or end. What tiles are to mosaics, stories are to narratives. The relationship is symbiotic; stories bring narratives to life by making them relatable and accessible, while narratives infuse stories with deeper meaning.[12]

Narratives affect the ways in which we understand and navigate the world. As Bridgit Antoinette Evans suggests: 'We are all swimming in a kind of ocean, except instead of water swirling around us, there are narratives … these narratives are influencing everything about how we think about, live, and see ourselves in the world.'[13] One widespread narrative frames fashion and sustainability as being in opposition, or even as a paradox. Mathilda Tham points out that this narrative taps into a longstanding tendency in Western thought to construct dichotomies, especially as a way of coping with emergent phenomena. This framing is problematic, for it positions fashion as 'the extreme and almost perfectly decadent pole to sustainability's wholesome proposition' – which hardly invites constructive change.[14] Furthermore, it is inaccurate. When Tham invited fashion stakeholders to describe key characteristics of fashion as part of her doctoral research, their list included 'creativity, story-telling, visuality, tactility, zeitgeist-intuneness, emotion and vision' – characteristics that are far from incompatible with the qualities of sustainability.[15]

The most intractable and pervasive narratives can be described as deep or meta-narratives – or, to use the terminology of social science, social imaginaries. Sacha Kagan describes a social imaginary as 'a patterned set of shared images, forming a matrix that affects our access to the world'.[16] These imaginaries are shaped by all of us, en masse, and they in turn shape each of us. They underpin our experiences of the world; they inform what we understand as common sense; they tell us how to act and what to value. It is from the 'cognitive and cultural *humus*' of imaginaries, Kagan explains, that narratives and stories grow and take root.[17]

I have already discussed some imaginaries in Chapter 1: the imaginaries of progress and of economic growth. That chapter also touched on what Sheila Jasanoff describes as sociotechnical imaginaries: 'collectively held, institutionally stabilized, and publicly performed visions of desirable futures, animated by shared understandings of forms of social life and social order attainable through, and supportive of, advances in science and technology'.[18] A collaborative European research project is currently investigating cultural imaginaries of sustainable futures, with a focus on food, clothing and transport.[19] Jon Alexander identifies the most powerful imaginary of our times as the 'Consumer Story'. This imaginary frames us primarily as individual consumers, expressing ourselves through the choices we make about what to consume and competing in pursuit of our own self-interest.[20] Indeed, this way of understanding ourselves and each other is produced and required by capitalism. Although such freedom may seem appealing, Martin Parker and his co-authors argue, 'The competitive drive for money, status and material things leads to anomie, alienation and addiction, while undermining our capacity to build connections with others'.[21] Alexander suggests that the Consumer Story has developed over the past eighty years in the global North, becoming 'a foundational narrative that shapes every aspect of our world' in practical, physical, metaphorical and even moral terms.[22] Harold Glasser makes a similar proposition, describing four dominant metaphors that have shaped the modern world: 'anthropocentrism, individualism, exploitation of humans and nature, and unfettered economic and technological growth'.[23]

The dominance of these imaginaries means that lifestyles that are inherently unsustainable – those with demands that are far beyond fair shares of the earth's resources – are readily perceived as positive and progressive.[24] These embedded ways of thinking fly beneath our day-to-day awareness and are typically unaddressed by sustainability initiatives. As Dan Lockton and Stuart Candy explain, 'Much design which aims to have an effect on social or environmental issues becomes itself constrained by or locked into assumptions about those issues, becoming part of the system it seeks to affect'.[25]

Particular stories of past, present and future, then, nestle within narratives and social imaginaries that reflect and shape our understanding of the world – and constrain the possibilities we tend to envisage. Both sociotechnical imaginaries, with their assumptions of technological progress, and the

Consumer Story, with its emphasis on neoliberal markets and competition, are rooted in the troubled paradigm of modernity/coloniality discussed in Chapter 1. If we are to shift our course away from this paradigm, away from environmental collapse, then we must disrupt these entrenched narratives and replace them with what Glasser describes as 'life-affirming guiding metaphors'.[26] This work is already underway. Manjana Milkoreit, for example, discusses 'socio-climatic imaginaries': a set of future-oriented imaginaries that place an emphasis on future relationships between natural and social systems, rather than technological progress.[27] Alexander, meanwhile, encourages us to turn away from the Consumer Story and instead step into the Citizen Story, a powerful alternative meta-narrative: 'We must see ourselves as Citizens – people who actively shape the world around us, who cultivate meaningful connections to their community and institutions, who can imagine a different and better life, who care and take responsibility, and who create opportunities for others to do the same.'[28]

The stakes are high. As Narrative Initiative proposes, 'Narrative work, the shifting of consciousness and values, is not just a long game, it is *the* long game.'[29]

* * * * * * * *

What stories and storyworlds have we created in Fashion Fictions? I will focus first on the Stage 1 fictions: the 100-word outlines of fictional parallel worlds in which people live differently with their clothes. As I explained in Chapter 1, these are playful visions rather than fully considered propositions and vary in their relationship to the real-world fashion system: some worlds feel fairly close, while others are – intentionally – highly implausible. Intrigued to identify common themes in the Stage 1 worlds, a couple of years ago I undertook an interpretive content analysis of the fictions available at the time: the first 120 worlds.[30] This form of analysis involves 'narratively describing the meaning of communications, in specific contexts', considering both the content that is literally present in the text and the content that is implicit or implied within it.[31] Focusing my analysis on the descriptions of contemporary storyworlds rather than the invented backstories, I worked through the repository of fictions, identifying the topics mentioned in each one and highlighting those that I considered to be central to that world.[32]

Overall, I identified 632 topics in the collection of fictions, with a 'long tail' distribution: 63 per cent of the topics are only mentioned once and less than 1 per cent are mentioned more than ten times. I organized the topics into sixty-seven dimensions, and in turn clustered the dimensions into fifteen groups. The topic map in Figure 3.2 highlights the broad span of the fictions, from areas that are clearly closely relevant to fashion systems, relating to the clothes worn and means of production and consumption, to those that are much broader, including nature, economics and global issues. The analysis offers useful opportunities for navigating the collection of worlds: I can review the variety of ideas that have been shared within a particular dimension, or identify all of the fictions that mention, or centre, a particular topic.[33] The topics gathered within the *Domains* dimension of the

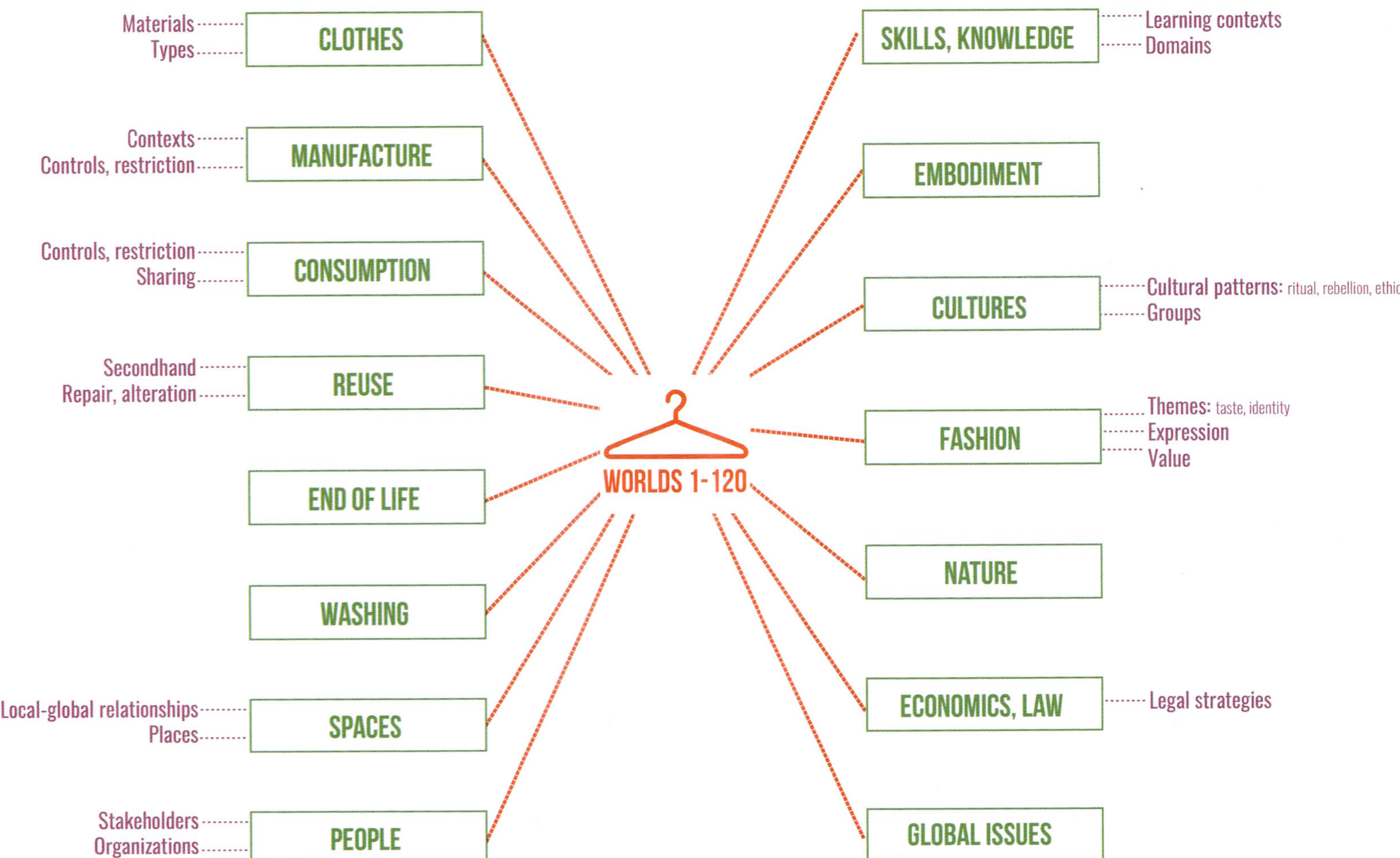

Figure 3.2 *My analysis of the first 120 Stage 1 worlds generated a list of 632 topics. I organized these topics into sixty-seven dimensions, which were in turn clustered into fifteen overarching groups. The groups and some of the more frequently mentioned dimensions and topics are shown here.*

Skills, knowledge group, for example, articulates many different areas of knowledge that are valued in the fictional worlds, from sewing and styling to body flora, agriculture and theatre.

The analysis also enables a comparison between the themes that arise frequently in the fictions and those that dominate mainstream sustainable fashion narratives. Some topics that are established as mainstays of sustainable fashion discussions, such as organic fibres, are largely absent from the fictions. There is also a notable lack of interest in shops and shopping within the fictions: this central feature of the mainstream fashion system is barely mentioned. Intriguingly, this absence mirrors Tham's research: in the list of characteristics of fashion identified by her participants, neither 'shopping' nor 'consumption' were present.[34] Perhaps the most exciting use of the Stage 1 analysis is the identification of common themes that look beyond the familiar territories of sustainable fashion, including language, ritual, rebellion and spirituality. These themes, enriched by the ideas that I identified through analysis of the Stage 2 and Stage 3 data, informed the ideas explored within this book – and have the potential to form valuable new fashion narratives and imaginaries.

At Stage 2, the 100-word fictions are 'fleshed out': the storyworlds are embellished, adapted and even reinvented, according to the interests of those involved. A participant at one of the Stage 2 workshops that I ran, Sally, reflected on the experience of picking up and adding to the fiction that her group had selected: 'I think it became richer as we talked about the many different ways that this could manifest … there were lots of different elements to it, and it started to feel quite … really very different from here.' The documented workshop conversations reveal a rich tapestry of ideas being constructed, with a vibrant interplay between the Stage 1 fiction, the contributors' individual thoughts, collective decisions made by the group and the logical implications of how these various factors would play out in the world. On occasions, I saw this interplay become even more complex when participants borrowed an element of another fictional world being explored at the same workshop and wove it into their own vision.

An important element of Fashion Fictions, presented as part of the guidance at Stage 1 (see Activity 2.1) and also relevant to Stages 2 and 3, is the emphasis on positive and enticing, rather than dystopian, worlds. To support this orientation, towards the end of the world-building process at Stage 2 I often ask participants to identify who might be disadvantaged in the world they are imagining, and discuss how this disadvantage might be addressed within that culture. The prompt was well received at the workshops; various groups whose interests had not been initially considered were identified and the world was reconfigured accordingly.

In the process of fleshing out and enacting worlds, then, we try to notice shortcomings in specific visions: contexts in which the world's culture would be experienced negatively, rather than positively. Zooming out to consider the project as a whole, shortcomings and gaps can also be observed. The analysis of the Stage 1 worlds exposes absences in the stories we have told together.

Some of these absences, such as shopping, have already been mentioned. Laundry, too, is largely absent. This is an important topic when considering the sustainability of fashion, which is frequently overlooked in favour of less mundane practices. There are some surprising gaps. Mental health, for example, is notably underexplored in the fictional worlds, considering its visibility in contemporary culture. There are also, arguably, gaps in terms of the fictions' appeal. Rachael, a participant at a Stage 2 workshop, wondered whether the fictions that had been explored would excite a mainstream audience. As she wrote, 'I can relate each story to different people. There is almost something for everyone – BUT perhaps that says something about the people I know. There is nothing here for my Aunty Sue.'

There are certainly gaps in terms of the diversity of contributors taking part in the project. I set up Fashion Fictions with the ambition of an international reach. I hoped to create a platform for voices that are often excluded from fashion and sustainability discourse, which tends to be dominated by people in the global North. I am delighted that fictions, prototypes and enactments have been gathered from contributors across six continents: the diverse perspectives inherent in these visions strengthen the project immeasurably. Yet there are notable biases that must be acknowledged. A significant proportion of the fictions have been created by contributors based in the UK, reflecting my own location and network.[35] The Stage 2 and Stage 3 activities conducted for the research, which generated a significant proportion of the data used in this book, also took place in the UK – although I was pleased that the groups included international participants, who brought their experiences of growing up in countries including India, Korea and Czech Republic, and several participants with dual heritage and lived experience of further cultural contexts. Diversity at the Stage 2 and Stage 3 activities was somewhat limited, being dominated by women and – at Stage 3 in particular – by participants in their thirties, forties and fifties. Looking beyond the activities that I ran for the research, many of the international project contributions have been generated through university activities, primarily engaging participants from another limited demographic group. Furthermore, most participants have rooted their contributions in experiences of wearing and designing clothes, rather than hands-on experience of manufacturing.

As a whole, then, Fashion Fictions is missing many storytellers and many stories. There are, of course, other spaces for people to imagine and to tell stories. My knowledge is enriched by exploring such spaces, and particularly those that explore territory that is underrepresented in Fashion Fictions, such as the Cripping Masculinity project led by Ben Barry (Figure 3.3). I continue to seek ways to extend the invitation to participate in Fashion Fictions beyond the groups it has reached so far – with this book as part of that invitation.

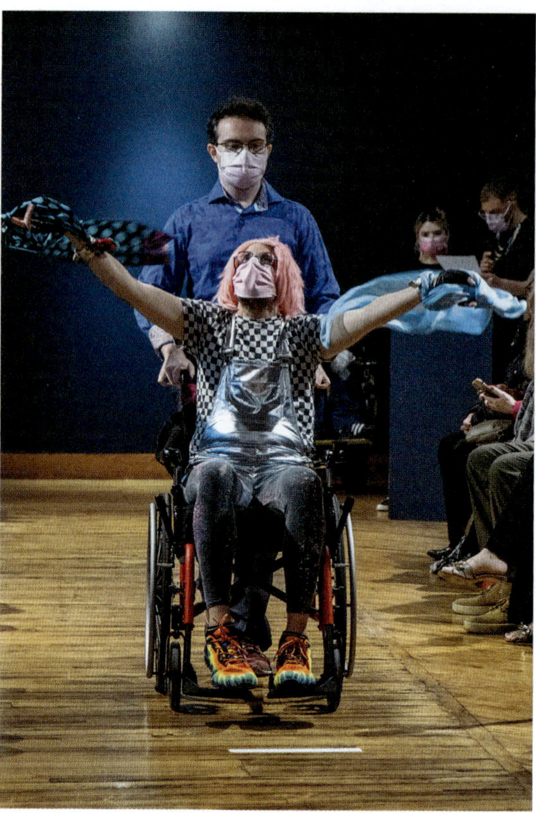

Figure 3.3 *The Cripping Masculinity project is a journey into the fashion worldbuilding of Disabled, Deaf and Mad-identified men and masculine people.*[36] *Here, collaborator CX is wearing an 'outside' designed by CX and Jonathan Dumitra in* Fashion Utopias: A Cripping Masculinity Fashion Show, *Tangled Art and Disability, 29 April 2023.*

Telling stories

For some Fashion Fictions contributors, creating a fictional world is not enough. A second layer of fictions, quietly woven through various worlds, prototypes and enactments, reveals a thirst for stories *within* the stories. A common format for these secondary fictions is the fashion magazine, created as a Stage 2 prototype. (The magazine shown in Figure 4.4, for example, parodies media tropes to provide an insight into **World 19**, in which the fashion system is entirely in service of nature.) A magazine cover works well as a representation of a parallel world: it showcases the icons and ideas that have cultural currency and draws on established conventions that can be easily imitated. Furthermore, despite the proliferation of digital media formats that have broadened the scope for fashion journalism in recent years, the print magazine endures as a readily recognizable cultural product.

Rosie Findlay and Johannes Reponen explain that fashion journalism 'seeks to position fashion within culture, to evaluate its contribution and meaning, and emphasize its importance as a product but also as a belief and a system'.[37] Straddling commerce and culture, journalism has been linked with the fortunes of the fashion industry since its emergence in France in the seventeenth century and rapid expansion in the nineteenth century.[38] Mainstream fashion magazines rely on brands for the revenue generated by advertisements and on designers for access to the shows that they report; brands and designers, meanwhile, rely on the magazines to give visibility and meaning to their products.

How do these industry–media relationships play out in terms of sustainability? A study by Katie Baker Jones, which examined coverage of sustainable fashion in *American Vogue* between 1990 and 2015, sheds light on this question. As Jones explains, *Vogue* is worthy of investigation: it is a powerful institution that has for a long time 'held a disproportionate amount of power in the industry in terms of information molding and dissemination'.[39] Her research found that in the early 1990s, *Vogue*'s coverage of sustainability engaged, to some extent, with the topic's complex political and social dimensions. Sustainability then receded from view for a decade from 1995 to 2005. When it returned to prominence, Jones explains, it was primarily explored via 'lifestyle segments that turned serious public issues into infotainment articles illustrating the good life informed by environmental or social conscientiousness'.[40] Over time, then, *Vogue*'s treatment of sustainability shifted: from a political issue requiring collective effort, to an opportunity for individual consumerism. Jones observes that this latter position 'neutraliz[ed] most negative considerations of fashion consumption' and sidestepped deeper issues including the growth-focused economic system and associated overproduction.[41] And no wonder. If the magazine were to engage with these deeper issues, it would 'undermine the fashion system *Vogue* has helped build and within which it thrives'.[42]

Jones draws on the work of Italian philosopher Antonio Gramsci to frame *Vogue*'s treatment of fashion and sustainability as a 'passive revolution'. Gramsci famously developed the concept of hegemony: 'a state of consensual predominance of the powerful group or class in a society or social system over the ruled'.[43] A passive revolution occurs when challenges to a powerful hegemonic system are absorbed and neutralized, meaning that the status quo is reinforced, rather than dislodged. In making the connection between her *Vogue* study and Gramscian theory, Jones references political economist Thomas Wanner. Wanner frames green growth – as discussed in Chapter 1 – as a passive revolution in relation to the hegemony of capitalism. He argues that green growth, which is deeply embedded in the capitalist economy, works to subsume more radical approaches to sustainability. As such, it 'divert[s] the counter-hegemonic challenge of environmentalism' and ensures that the underlying system – and its imaginary – continues untouched.[44] As Jones points out, this is a striking mirror to the passive revolution of *Vogue*'s coverage of fashion and sustainability.[45]

Considering this critique of fashion media, we might wish to be wary of regurgitating established tropes in our Fashion Fictions prototypes. It is possible that we could inadvertently perpetuate a culture of individualized consumerism – the Consumer Story – while trying to communicate an alternative message. But glossy magazines such as *Vogue* are not all that fashion journalism can be. Consider, for example, *Display Copy*, a media platform featuring secondhand-only clothing[46] (much like a magazine imagined in the fictional **World 24**[47]); *London Review of Looks*, an email newsletter described by Rosie Findlay as 'a kind of literary non-fiction that attends to the ways mood intersects with fashion and dress';[48] and *A Magazine Reader*, a workshop that invites participants to physically and metaphorically deconstruct a mainstream fashion magazine and use the material to create a new, critically engaged, zine, as a way of 'becom[ing] aware of our position to shape and create fashion' (Figure 3.4).[49] And there could be so much more; as Morna Laing points out, independent fashion media could be a highly effective network for 'social dreaming'.[50] *Future Fashion Media*, an online exhibition organized by members of the Atlas of the Future, Makerversity and Colèchi communities, explored this potential by presenting prototypes of media intended to contribute to positive change

Figure 3.4 *The A Magazine Reader workshop was devised by Femke de Vries and Hanka van der Voet. Participants work together to 'critically read and literally dissect one specific existing mainstream fashion magazine … surfac[ing] dynamics in fashion media that are often overlooked when casually browsing through it'.*[51] *The material is then translated into new imagery and text and compiled to form an alternative zine.*

in the fashion system.[52] One prototype was *The Slo-Down,* a weekly e-newsletter of enticing non-shopping-based fashion activities; *OFF (Our Fashion Futures)* was a local clothes-focused platform with content created by young people for young people, supported by fashion, media and climate mentors; and podcast *Back of the Wardrobe* aimed to engage a more mature audience through entertaining discussion of clothing quandaries.

＊ ＊ ＊ ＊ ＊ ＊ ＊ ＊ ＊

Having considered fashion media as a space for sharing fashion stories, let us now focus on stories themselves, and specifically those that are attached, as if by invisible threads, to the garments in our wardrobes. Such stories are sometimes found within fashion media but are perhaps more often encountered in everyday life. We share them naturally: when someone compliments you on an item, the response is often, like a reflex, to share something about it: where and when you got it, when you wear it, how it has aged, whether it was a bargain or a considered investment. In fact, there is much that could be told. Clothes are, after all, deeply entwined in our lives, collaborators in the construction of identity. In the bestselling books *Worn Stories* (2014) and *Worn in New York* (2017), artist and editor Emily Spivack compiled such stories from notable contributors including writers, artists and designers; in 2021, the concept was extended into a Netflix series. As Spivack writes in the introduction to the first book: 'The clothes that protect us, that make us laugh, that serve as a uniform, that help us assert our identity or aspirations, that we wear to remember someone – in all of these are encoded the stories of our lives. We all have a memoir in miniature living in a garment we've worn.'[53]

Similar ideas are at work in the fictions. In **World 120**, miniature garment stories are recorded in written notes, attached to borrowed clothing:

> A brainchild of two ground-breaking entrepreneurs, the Clothing Library stores clothing articles of different fabrics, uses, decades, and styles. They also host a network of guilds who help with customizing and repairing the articles. The 'borrowers' are encouraged to leave behind notes which explain how they used the clothes and pictures of the outfits they put together.[54]

A workshop group exploring **World 3**, meanwhile, imagined the circulation of verbal, rather than written, anecdotes. In this world, community laundries are vibrant social hubs, where people enjoy spending time together.[55] These spaces, the group thought, would generate rich seams of gossip – some prompted by items inadvertently left in the machine drum. The **World 87** fiction goes further (and, in a pleasingly subversive manner, challenges the Fashion Fictions 'rule' of physical possibility) when the garments themselves start to narrate stories:

> People always came together to tell each other stories and to listen to each other. But in 2020, because of the pandemic, this sitting together and travelling around was no longer possible. The clothes realised that people, sitting lonely at home, not able to travel, were getting sad. Therefore,

in World 87, the garments took over and started to tell their stories. They narrated what they experienced travelling around the world during the production process. Thus, people found out that their garments were very precious storytellers and from then on, they dreamed to hear in future different fashion stories.[56]

An alternative take on garment stories is offered by **World 182**, in which material shortages lead to a culture in which fashion is primarily experienced not by wearing, but by reading evocative accounts of historical dress practices:

In World 182, the production of Parisian haute couture abruptly ended in 1932 due to a disastrous economic crisis, combined with extreme shortages of raw materials, and strong political will. Yet the craving for high fashion grew but stronger. Fashion producers began to pen accounts of new clothing, which customers read avidly. Evolving from the mere description of garments, these stories soon narrated transacting acts and wearing experiences. Over time, narratives based on historical fashion grew more popular than fictional accounts. Consuming historical garments vicariously became the norm. Fashion historians became key workers of the French fashion system.[57]

Figure 3.5 *In World 50, people exchange sewn signatures on clothing as a sign of social connection. This customized garment, created by a group exploring World 50 at a Stage 2 prototyping workshop, features various signature styles.*

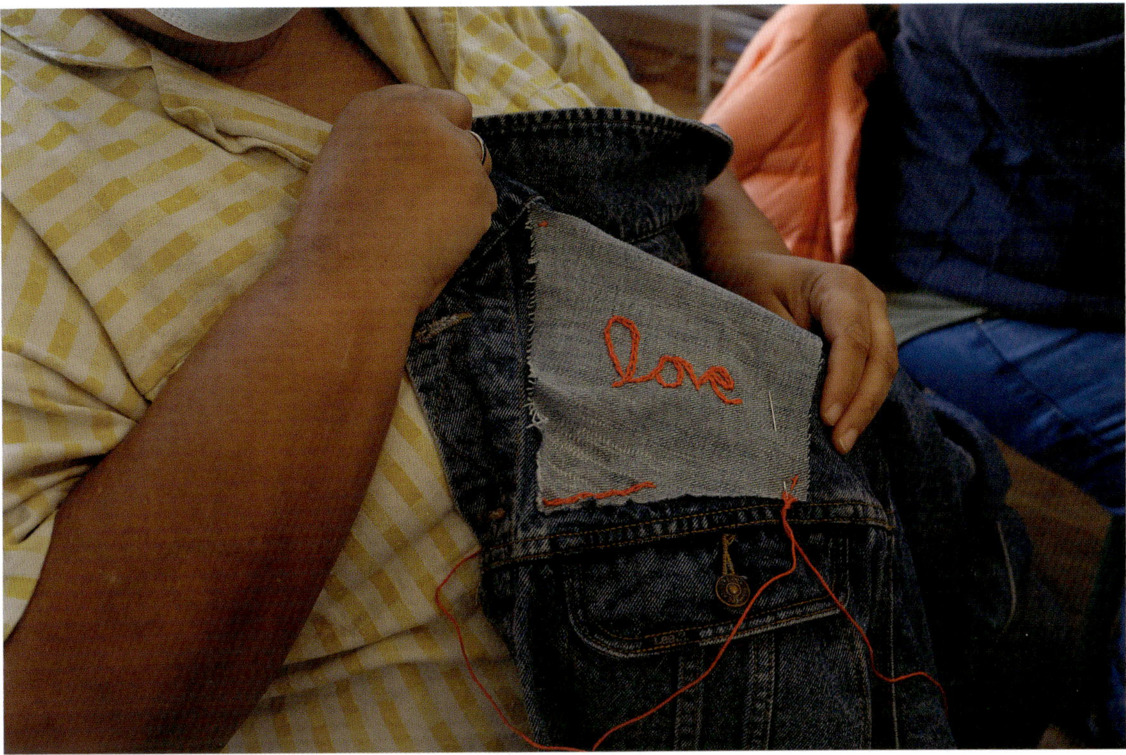

Figure 3.6 *It is common in the fictional World 131 to embellish clothing with mantras, ideas, thoughts and feelings.*[58] *At this enactment, held at Curiosity Studio in Minneapolis, participants experienced life in World 131 for a couple of hours, using embroidery and screen printing to add words to their own garments.*

The **World 50** fiction offers another vision in which clothes are carriers of stories. In this world, garments are used to record their wearers' social connections and experiences:

> In World 50 each person has a unique, sewn signature with which they adorn each other's clothing. The more signatures a garment 'holds' the more it's prized. This reciprocal embellishment produces a culture which values longevity and creative exchange, and produces communities.
>
> The practice began as a way for a resistance group committed to preserving 'material communities' to recognise each other (the origins of the group are unclear, but it's believed they first emerged in response to Nixon closing the US gold window in 1971), becoming widespread after a series of popular uprisings inspired by the group in the early 1990s.[59]

The group that formed to explore this world at a Stage 2 workshop were attracted by the notion of reciprocal textile signatures.[60] They spent time during the world-building phase thinking through how this practice would work. Would all garments carry signatures, or just one particular item? If a single item, would it be worn every day, or saved for special occasions? What would trigger the act of embellishment: would every chance meeting be recorded, or would the process be respected as a special ritual? As they talked, they described how clothes would document and communicate the wearer's 'personal story'. They imagined subcultural groups locating their signatures in a particular position as a sign of belonging – or rebelling through extreme minimalism or abstinence. When the group's work in progress was shared, one of the other workshop participants wondered about inheritance: whether a wearer would be buried in their embellished garment, or the item would be passed down – and, if so, what the ramifications would be:

> If everybody has got one garment like this, and everyone is passing them on … I'm wondering what happens, like, a hundred years down the line. Is there a really new way that we decorate our homes, and we don't put pictures on the wall any more, we hang garments up?

* * * * * * * *

Garment stories were placed at the heart of the **World 27** fiction:

> In World 27, post-pandemic consumption and lifestyle shifts force a re-examination of value systems: closets full of empty clothes no longer articulate with day-to-day experience.
>
> Textile histories become central to the way we value garments, with Cuba as global leader in the post-capitalist heirloom-chain economy.
>
> Value shifts to that based on palimpsestic load: the greater the number of associated histories, the greater a garment's desirability. Garments are traded and gifted within the framework of performative activities such as mending circles, where storytelling plays a significant role. A new, unscarred, non-storied garment is of little appeal; lived-in, mended, altered garments are in highest demand.[61]

This evocative outline was picked up and developed at a Stage 2 workshop.[62] One member of the group presented their finished prototype (Figure 3.7) by speaking in the first person as a traveller who had visited this unfamiliar world: 'The people there were astonished by the blank emptiness of our unstoried clothes, and how clean and unstained our outfits were. They found our style hilarious, as we found theirs extraordinary and strange. A cacophony of prints, textures and colours and shapes.' The group's discussions were not limited to the aesthetics of the clothing in World 27; they talked in detail about the day-to-day experience of a culture in which people are custodians, rather than owners, of garments. After a couple of hours they suddenly realized that concepts such as commercial exchange and even the cultural preservation of clothing would be absent in World 27: 'There are no clothes shops, not even charity shops, nor museums or private collections, as preservation of clothing is frowned upon. Clothes need a life, and multiple owners are revered as part of the exchange.'

Figure 3.7 *These jeans from World 27 are accompanied by a set of 'deeds': three oral stories, recorded by former wearers over a period of fifty years.*

Further discussion focused on ways in which the stories would be shared and documented. The group felt that some stories would be inherent in the items themselves, implicitly recorded in the ways the textile had worn and the clothes had been repaired and altered. Other stories, though, would not be evident in the garments, and the group thought carefully about how such stories might be shared and recorded for future reference. They came up with the idea of 'clothing deeds', inspired by the written deeds that accompany a house when it changes ownership. This meaning of *deed* is defined in the *Oxford English Dictionary* as 'An instrument in writing … purporting to effect some legal disposition, and sealed and delivered by the disposing party or parties'.[63] The group also had in mind another meaning of the same word, defined as 'Action generally; doing, performance'. Clothing deeds, then, are records that document the 'doings' of a garment over time; each owner adds to the deeds at the point of exchange. The group reflected on the trustworthiness, or otherwise, of these records: when created, they would reflect a subjective perspective and, additionally, might be subject to misinterpretation or mistranslation over time. Like any other historical record, they could be carefully kept or could easily go astray. Lost deeds might be rediscovered through a process of 'garment genealogy'.

The prototype that the group presented as their souvenir of World 27 was a repaired and altered pair of jeans, with a hand-stitched QR code label that, they explained, would allow the wearer to access the garment's deeds. While some clothing deeds are textual or visual, in this case they are oral: three digital audio recordings of stories, recorded – we were informed – at intervals over the past fifty years. The recorded stories told not only of each wearer's experience of possessing the jeans but also of their desire to offer the jeans for exchange, knowing that this process would enable the garment to gather more stories and therefore maintain its value. The audio stories were played to the other participants at the Stage 2 workshop and were enthusiastically received. As one person commented, 'the telling of the stories was … quite magical to listen to. It felt more real, and it felt like an experience that I wanted to get involved in.' Another participant agreed that the stories enabled her to engage with the logic of the fictional world: 'It does make it very convincing. It makes you go, oh yeah, maybe you don't want to just hang onto them forever. You want to imbue them with more stories. Where previously I'd think, but why would you want to do that?'

The Stage 2 group also spent time discussing the World 27 events at which garments would be exchanged. I drew on their discussions when I designed the Stage 3 enactment for this world: an intimate garment exchange that took place in an atmospheric wooded quarry. The eight participants were asked to bring a 'story-full' garment from their wardrobe, in order to experience the process of offering it to others. I will discuss the event itself in detail in Chapter 5; for now, I will focus on the stories that were generated there.

During the afternoon, each person was invited to document their garment's story in a format, or formats, of their choice. Their responses included audio recordings, handwritten stories, typed narratives, image collages and mind maps. These stories provide enticing insights into the life of each garment: they relate how the item came into the person's possession, their experiences while wearing it, and interventions – both intentional and accidental – they have made. We learn about their feelings towards the garment, how they have felt while wearing it and how it has suited their needs. Participant Wendy, for example, made an audio recording to document the tale of an adventure-scarred outdoor jacket, while Eleanor wrote about an embroidered dress, purchased on a whim and worn to events that called for a folkloric vibe. Each of the precious 'deeds' was handed over in exchange for a garment label printed with the URL of a unique space on a digital repository; the label was then stitched into the garment (Figure 3.8). Next, the group gathered in a circle to share an oral version of their stories, one by one, and place the items on a washing line as a way of symbolically offering them for exchange. Following the workshop, the deeds were uploaded to the digital repository, for access by curious future custodians.[64]

Figure 3.8 *Any future custodian of this dress will be able to follow the URL on the label to read the associated 'deed' recorded at the World 27 enactment by Talia. She wrote the story from the perspective of the dress itself; it describes being purchased in Bangalore and worn to parties and restaurants there before being brought to the UK and languishing in a cold, damp closet.*

Wording stories

The Fashion Fictions Stage 1 fictions, Stage 2 prototypes and Stage 3 enactment discussed so far in this chapter include various instances of participants playing with words. Consider, for example, the double meaning of *deeds* and the notion of clothes as *empty* or *full* in World 27. At workshops I have enjoyed seeing groups come up with engaging words and phrases that provide a strong taste of their world's culture – such as the group exploring **World 80**, in which it is normal to wear clothes continuously for a month.[65] They coined the memorable phrase 'stealth washing' to refer to a temptation that would, presumably, be ever-present in World 80 culture.

Mathilda Tham, drawing on the influential work of biologists Humberto Maturana and Francisco Varela, discusses the concept of *languaging*: 'the continuous and co-dependent process of understanding through saying and defining, and by saying and defining in turn shaping our world'.[66] Language enables us to not only describe our thoughts and actions, but also express novel ideas – and, by doing so, influence the world in which we think and act. This capacity for open-ended invention through words is powerfully exploited in fantasy literature. As Brian Attebery explains, the fantasy author can 'name objects we have never seen' and 'narrate events that never happened',[67] calling them into existence by using the factual *this is* rather than the conditional *this could be*. The same happens in Fashion Fictions. We might start the world-making process by asking 'what if' but for much of the time we talk about the world in factual terms and draw on what Attebery terms 'the past tense of historical assertion' in outlining its past events.[68] The authority of the resulting story is reflected in a comment by a workshop participant who had been wrestling with an apparent contradiction in their group's fiction: 'We sort of went with the cop out of, well this world exists, so it must be possible!'

Language matters, too, in terms of how we understand things that are going on beyond our direct experience in the world – such as climate change – and how we make sense of and respond to these phenomena. Norwegian linguist Kjersti Fløttum reports that 'the meaning people ascribe to climate change (e.g., their understanding of the phenomenon, their perception of the risks involved, the value judgments they make, and the emotional reactions they experience) is closely related to how climate change is portrayed in various contexts of climate communication'.[69] The same observations could be made regarding fashion and sustainability. Tham explains that 'When environmental issues first entered fashion organisations – usually assigned to or championed by quality control staff and sometimes buyers – they carried with them the heritage of a scientific and quantitative language, and were typically regulated through tick-box-lists'.[70] This approach, Tham argues, still dominates today – contributing, like the framing of fashion and sustainability in paradoxical terms, to a one-dimensional view of a complex and multifaceted system. The language used in other common narratives is similarly problematic. As Fletcher and Tham note in *Earth Logic,* for example, 'the

Figure 3.9 *This magazine prototype was created to represent a version of World 12 in which regional cultures thrive and the North African region has particularly influential fashion and music scenes. The title,* Because you're a Girl, *is written in Amazigh, an indigenous North African language.*

pairing of the terms "production" and "consumption" as polar opposites … create[s] arbitrary and problematic separation between practices which are more fluid'.[71]

Fletcher and Tham, like many other environmental thinkers, see language as a powerful lever for change. They suggest that a strategy for working with language could involve bringing certain words to the fore and eliminating others to create new systems of thought:

Imagine a vocabulary without consumption. Instead we would use a diversity of words to define a diversity of practices – nurturing, stewarding, growing, mending, borrowing, relating, sharing. Imagine a dictionary without the word waste, because it was no longer relevant. Imagine when the words for being with fashion, are as rich and nuanced and scented as the plants of a wild meadow.[72]

Another strategy could involve learning from the vocabulary and grammar of different languages. In *Braiding Sweetgrass,* botanist Robin Wall Kimmerer shares the words of one of the last native speakers of Potawatomi, the language of Kimmerer's First Nations tribe: 'The language is the heart of our culture; it holds our thoughts, our way of seeing the world. It's too beautiful for English to explain.'[73] A 2019 book, *An Ecotopian Lexicon,* presents words from languages that could be loaned to English 'as conceptual tools for reckoning with the environmental, political, social, and philosophical challenges of the Anthropocene, today and in the decades to come'.[74] *Ghurba,* for example, is a word borrowed from Arabic that the authors use 'to describe a sense of longing for home that we apply to the ecological undoing of climate change, with all that we stand to lose'.[75] Other entries in the lexicon present words invented by fiction writers and philosophers. The Bureau of Linguistical Reality, a participatory artwork by Heidi Quante and Alicia Escott, generates new words 'to express what people are feeling and experiencing as our world changes as climate change accelerates' – such as *wormdazzle,* a verb used to describe a point of positive transformation evident in both compost heaps and societies.[76] Back in the sphere of fashion and sustainability, the neologism *defashion* has been defined by Sandra Niessen as a process that aims to 'dismantle the fashion system and replace it with a pluriverse of local, sustainable, historically and culturally relevant systems'.[77]

A new word was coined in the Stage 2 exploration of **World 91**, in which mushrooms are widely recognized as spiritual guides. After some in-depth discussions about the ramifications of this widespread belief system, the Stage 2 group came up with a vision of a service that offers bespoke shoes made from mycelium (the connective strands of fungi).[78] The bespoke footwear would be grown to order in a couple of months; when ripe, the customer would come along to harvest their shoe. When the shoe was worn out, the group explained, it would be returned to the biosphere. They searched for some time for an existing word for this return that would capture a sense of positive regeneration. Rejecting any options they could come up with, they eventually invented their own term, a variation on harvest: *revest.*

The use and invention of words was a central theme in the Stage 2 exploration of **World 4**, which envisioned a society in which the thriving of nature has become the foremost concern for humanity. I wrote the original World 4 fiction: a lighthearted vision of a culture in which people dress up for nights out using foliage, grown in community gardens, rather than fast fashion.[79] Benji, who worked solo to explore the world at Stage 2, created a striking and radical interpretation of this text.[80] In their vision of the world, a catastrophe prompted humans to recognize themselves as entirely dependent on other species and the earth's systems. The calendar was reset and *homo sapiens* was renamed as *homo marginem*: a species on the edge. As Benji explained in the voice of a World 4 citizen, 'We're starting again from this point; we're going to change everything.'

Intentional shifts in the use of language, one aspect of this changed worldview, were recorded in the prototype: a fragmented memoir reportedly created by an elderly citizen of World 4 (Figure 3.10; see also detail in Figure 6.9). Old and new definitions of words are documented: the new meaning of *alive*, for example, is 'possessing the quality of naturalness', while *dead* is 'possessing the quality of spuriousness'. *Beauty* is 'a combination of qualities … that pleases the moral soul' – rather than, as in the previous era, qualities that please the senses. In a satisfying example of fiction-to-fiction transfer, Benji also incorporated the term *revest* to the memoir, having heard about it when I shared the story of the World 91 group's inventive use of language. These aspects of the fiction resonate with *Earth Logic*'s encouragement for 'naming that which we wish to cultivate'.[81] Following Benji's vision, we might explore new meanings for familiar words to reflect the practices and values we wish to nurture.

Figure 3.10 *This fragmented memoir was created by an elderly citizen of World 4, known as a 'high fashion witch'. The memoir documents the changes in language and culture the author has seen during their lifetime, as humans have shifted from* homo sapiens *to* homo marginem: *the species on the edge.*

* * * * * * * *

Another of the worlds explored at Stage 2 and Stage 3, **World 62**, enables us to dig further into the theme of language:

> In World 62 the Dot-Com NSDAQ crash ends attempts to commercialise the internet. The deaths of Princess Diana and a handful of malnourished super-models leads to strict legislation controlling the publication of images of people. To reach customers at home, fashion brands turn to Teletext.
>
> Buying clothes based on text-only descriptions of garments means customers develop a complex vocabulary and literacy around colour, fibre, and fabric. Descriptions of texture are particularly important. People's discussions and engagement with fashion centres around rich verbal descriptions, tactility, story-telling and provenance.[82]

The World 62 outline was picked up at a Stage 2 workshop by two participants, Wendy and Jana, who were attracted by the contrast with the endless flow of seductive imagery in the real-world fashion system.[83] They talked in depth about the implications of the image ban and, for their prototype, mocked up a World 62 magazine that used carefully selected typography to visually represent garment forms and fabric textures. I built on their Stage 2 exploration to design a Stage 3 enactment, guided by a new outline:

> In World 62, the distribution of images portraying clothes is outlawed; fashion mail order is based solely on descriptive texts. Despite well-developed garment-related literacy, the arrival of a new purchase inevitably involves some collision of mental picture and material reality.
>
> Many have grown to appreciate the anticipation inherent in this process and set up round-robin fashion groups to mirror and amplify the experience. A group member writes a garment request; another selects a secondhand item in response. It is then passed around the collective, with each person adding to a tantalizingly cryptic description before the recipient enjoys the eventual 'reveal'.

Fifteen geographically dispersed participants took part in this three-month enactment, organized into three five-person circles. Each participant requested a garment; purchased a secondhand item in response to another person's request; contributed to several written descriptions; and, finally, received the garment that had been purchased in response to their request. Each item was passed round the circle by post, with every person adding to the collaborative garment description, before reaching its intended recipient.

The requests that kicked off this process were notably varied. One was a single line, while others were much longer; some were pragmatic, others poetic; some specified requirements in terms of size, garment type, fibre, shape, colour, pattern or purpose, while others were much more open. I commissioned poet Teo Eve to create three video tutorials to provide inspiration for the 'cryptic' descriptions that the groups would construct for each garment.[84] Under Teo's influence, the descriptions flourished into a compelling mix of matter-of-fact descriptions, whimsical statements from the garment's perspective and various, sometimes rather surreal, forms of poetry (Figures 3.11 and 3.12).

The original Stage 1 text indicates a widespread fashion-focused literacy in World 62. At the Stage 2 workshop Wendy and Jana talked of people finding joy in the creative use of language. This certainly played out at Stage 3: many of the participants said they enjoyed the creative garment-description process. Jade commented, 'I felt I was given permission to engage with clothing in a new and thrilling way'; while Sarah noted, 'I liked being able to just let the words do whatever they needed to do in relation to what I had in my hands.'

Several participants described the enjoyment they gained from reading a garment description before seeing the actual item. Charlotte framed the texts as 'the perfect puzzle; not too hard to decipher but not literal nor obvious either'. Alison noted that the impression she gained from a

Filmy, gauzy, fine, sheer, light, lightweight, thin, flimsy, see-through, diaphanous, chiffony, gossamer, delicate. Drift, glide, sail, slip, slide, waft, flow, stream, move, travel, be carried. Banded, stripy, barred, lined; streaky, striated, variegated wrinkle, crease, pucker, furrow, line, corrugate, MEDALLION crimp, crumple, rumple, ruck up, scrunch up, ruckle. Be carried, be carried (away/along), be borne, be wafted; float, bob, move slowly, go with the current, coast, meander. Drift, float, glide, whirl, travel, be carried, be borne, be conveyed, be transported. Thin, fine, feathery, flyaway, straggly. Gauze, gossamer, chiffon. Bark, ridged, striated.

Figure 3.11 *This is an extract of a collaborative description of an item purchased for Jade. She wrote her request from the perspective of her desired garment: 'I evoke something of Kings Road, London in the late 60s, early 70s (although I could have been made at any time). I give off mystic vibes. Some may call me hippie, but I prefer to consider myself esoteric.'*

LAST NIGHT I DREAMED OF RIPE BANANAS SURROUNDED BY BUMBLE BEES. I ISOLATED THE AREA WITH HAZARD TAPE. DESPITE THIS, A YELLOW-BELLIED SISKIN SWOOPED ONTO THE SCENE. I WOKE IN A JAUNDICED MOOD AND RUBBED THE SLEEPY DUST FROM MY EYES SO HARD THAT I SAW STARS.

Figure 3.12 *This text is part of the collaborative description of an item purchased for Vanessa. Her original request concluded, 'My pattern should say: feminine-ish; assertive, yet entertaining; with a hint of the recluse. Just like me.'*

written description was rarely correct – although when she reviewed the description *after* seeing the garment, she could see how they fitted together. In her reflections, Annebella made reference to the writing of visual studies scholar W. J. T. Mitchell, pointing out that while a picture may be worth a thousand words, 'a thousand words can never make a picture'. She also referenced influential cultural theorist Roland Barthes. In his 1967 book *The Fashion System* Barthes describes opening a fashion magazine and seeing an image of a garment, along with the same item described in words:

> In principle these two garments refer to the same reality (this dress worn on this day by this woman), and yet they do not have the same structure, because they are not made of the same substances and because, consequently, these substances do not have the same relations with each other: in one the substances are forms, lines, surfaces, colors, and the relation is spatial; in the other, the substance is words, and the relation is, if not logical, at least syntactic; the first structure is plastic, the second verbal.[85]

Continuing, Barthes analyses the differences between image and text – and the material substance of the garment itself. As he suggests, 'Written clothing is carried by language, but also resists it, and is created by this interplay.'[86]

At Stage 2, Wendy and Jana noted the potential for misinterpretation in a text-only fashion system and wondered about the need for a shared understanding of specialist terminology. A common language was indeed important during the era of text-based fashion promotion. Stage 3 participant Sarah, who has academic expertise in fashion history, explained that 'Fashion historians have to learn a vast vocabulary of textile types and colour names in order to understand Victorian and Edwardian women's magazines, which would have been common "expert" knowledge for readers/fashion consumers of the time.' When Wendy and Jana sought to imagine how the text-only system might be exploited by unscrupulous operators, they made reference to the euphemisms used in real-estate listings: *compact* to describe a cramped space, *an opportunity to make it your own* to describe a derelict wreck. Would the same happen in garment descriptions, they wondered?

In the enactment, gaps in understanding were typically appreciated rather than condemned. Elly, for example, noted that 'When the descriptions were written factually it was easier to realize where details were missing … a more poetic approach gave me a clear idea of colour and a vague sense of shape, but suddenly the specific details didn't seem to matter.' This appreciation was likely due to context: the participants were engaging in a playful collaborative initiative rather than the 'serious' purchase of clothing. Yet there was certainly a shared sense that an evocative description could make a garment more enticing. As Alison noted, 'Describing something as "loose" isn't the same as "floats around you as you walk, like a halo".' In an essay for *A Magazine Reader,* Femke de Vries and Ruby Hoette make similar comments about the emotive texts found in fashion magazines: 'These phrases are collections of words that speak to our imagination, a form of suggestive poetry rather than facts

Figure 3.13 *This item was purchased in response to a request inspired by a much-loved scarf, which had recently been lost. The writer noted, 'All the garments in my closet have asked me to make this request, as they miss it and I do too.' The first part of the descriptive text portrayed the newly purchased scarf as 'not so much a replacement … more a response in spirit'.*[87]

Figure 3.14 *This Zara jumpsuit was purchased as a resourceful response to a request from Elly for a flamboy-ant floral-print maxi dress. The collaborative description created by the other members of the group included factual observations, styling suggestions and a poetic interpretation of the colour palette as 'thoughts of water on a hot day'.*[88]

or rational arguments in a logical order.'[89] One of the project participants, Charlotte, suggested that the garment descriptions the groups had created 'animate the garments, imbuing them with life', while another participant reflected: 'the use of poetic descriptions and describing the "feeling" of a garment has proven more inspirational to me than images'. Annebella agreed that 'imagistic writing … can … trigger the imagination in productive ways … A lot of clothing's power exists in the mind rather than solely in the body, in fantasy and anticipation.'

The participants' reflections also highlighted the fact that images, like text, can be misleading. As Vanessa mentioned, 'the photographic brings with it information which may not be necessary, and which can be misunderstood as important'. Elly observed that while there would be potential for disappointment and deception in a text-based fashion promotion system, the same is true with images, for 'even the most basic fashion shoot is a fantasy world'.

Back at the Stage 2 workshop, Wendy and Jana saw the potential for positivity in the fictional vision, in comparison with the real world. Wendy, in her initial thoughts, suggested that World 62 would be 'quieter, more thoughtful and maybe (hopefully) a more creative fashion world. It would feel less pressurized as there wouldn't be the constant visual bombardment.' A little later in the workshop, sharing her duo's discussions with the wider group, she suggested that this parallel-world culture might involve 'different types of ways of dressing … because if everything is written, everyone's going to interpret that in a slightly different way' and suggested a possible positive impact on body image. The pair also compared the instant impact of visual images with the time and effort – and, therefore, the implicit consent – involved in reading a text. Or, as Jana evocatively put it, 'rather than plunging yourself in, it's like walking slowly into the water'. De Vries and Hoette see value in this slowness: 'there is the potential for text, counter to fast and "easy" imagery, to play a role in slowing down our frenzied consumption: reading word by word as a reaction to fast fashion'.[90]

While the Stage 3 participants did not see the round-robin arrangement they had tested as a viable real-world setup, some participants expressed enthusiasm for activities that could follow a similar – if less logistically complex – path. They also saw value in enhancing and deepening the text descriptions that accompany clothes at the point of sale or exchange. Charlotte thought such descriptions 'could really add to the value and "picture" built up', while Sally suggested that texts crafted with care could help to communicate the material qualities of clothing.

A final insight into the value of working with words came from Sarah. When writing her garment request at the start of the project, she found herself writing in negatives. Realizing that this 'felt all wrong', she shifted to a more positive approach. During this process, she experienced

one moment that has had a profound and lasting impact on me. I was afraid that someone would buy me something lacy, so I wrote quite a strong statement that I don't want lace. Then I thought, why am I being so violently opposed to lace? What is the feeling of fear that has bubbled up in my articulation of self?

These thoughts revived the distant memory of a classmate criticizing a lace-embellished costume created for a school play, prompting Sarah to wonder whether the lingering embarrassment of this long-ago incident could have caused her vehement rejection of lace today. She then challenged herself to experiment, buying and wearing a secondhand lacy top – and receiving many compliments. On reflection, Sarah felt that this process of examining her preferences and aversions through writing had been beneficial: 'at the risk of being melodramatic and oversharing, there could even be some personal healing and development in the exercise of requesting garments and experimenting with buying.'

Activity 3.1: Take action – garment-description game

Want to visit **World 62**, in which images portraying clothes cannot be distributed? Try this collaborative activity, in which garments are exchanged and creatively described in words.[91] The activity is designed for a group of five participants, but can be adapted for more or fewer people. You could do it slowly, as described in the World 62 enactment text presented on page 68, or speed it up.

1. Write a request for a garment and pass the request to the person purchasing for you. (An adaptable template is available online to help you plan who purchases for who.[92]) Your request might be very specific or much more open. Reflect on your wardrobe and think about what it needs. Your request might include details of colour, garment type, size, fibre, texture, weight, aesthetic, mood … or something else!

2. Select a secondhand item in response to the request written by the person you are purchasing for. Start a description of the purchased garment and send the item to the next person in the circle. (Again, use the template to help with these arrangements. Note that each garment will be passed around the whole circle before reaching its intended recipient.)

3. Open the package you receive and add to the communal description of that specific garment. (You could watch the clothing poetry videos created by Teo Eve for the original enactment for inspiration.[93]) Send the item to the next person in the circle.

4. Repeat Step 3 two more times.

5. Before you open the package containing your garment, prepare by re-reading your request and the collaborative garment description; consider your mental picture of the item. Open your package and enjoy the 'reveal'.

6. Following your World 62 round-robin fashion game, reflect on the experience (see Activity 2.4).

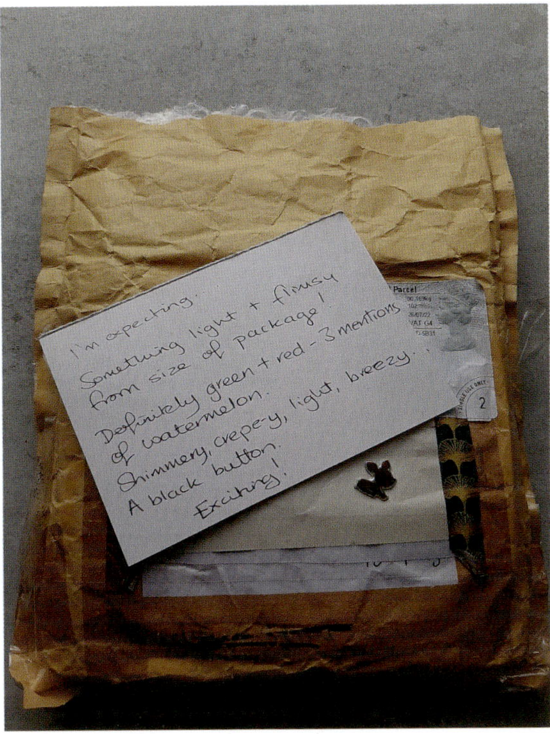

Figure 3.15 *Before opening the package containing the mystery item purchased for her, one participant in the World 62 enactment noted her expectations.*

Performing stories

At Stage 3 of Fashion Fictions we bring our stories to life through embodied action. I have already discussed two Stage 3 enactments in this chapter: the **World 27** garment exchange and the **World 62** round-robin fashion game. In this section I will discuss two more: a weekly task devised to explore mushroom-centric **World 91** and a dressing-up event based on the resourceful culture of **World 54**. All of the Stage 3 activities were designed as ways to step inside the fictional worlds, moving from abstract concept to participatory performance. I wrote the short texts that guided these four enactments, combining ideas from the groups that prototyped the worlds at the Stage 2 workshops with my own creative intentions and various practical considerations.

Fashion Fictions enactments ask participants to take action, putting their identity – and occasionally their dignity – at stake. By doing so, we seem to discover insights that would not otherwise be accessed: *doing* reveals things that *thinking about doing* does not. Natalia Eernstman and Arjen Wals point out that while we may have visions and plans of possible sustainable systems, 'until we start animating, walking, the plan, it essentially does not exist'.[94] Embodiment is a crucial aspect of this experience, for – as Torkild Thanem and David Knights observe – 'it is through our bodies that our actions, subjectivities and relations with others are realized, materialized and made visible'.[95] Thanem and Knights draw on the work of philosopher Maurice Merleau-Ponty, who recognized the body as 'the vehicle of being in the world'[96] and sought to 'establish the body as an active and intentional medium of learning, habit, skill and knowledge'.[97] We learn about alternative possibilities for fashion practices by experiencing our stories with our sensing bodies.

Perhaps the most obvious references for the Fashion Fictions enactments are *reenactments*: performances that recreate events from the past. The term likely brings to mind performances of notable battles, whether iconic scenes from the US Civil War[98] or, in the case of an event created by artist Jeremy Deller, a historic 1984 clash between striking miners and police in the north of England.[99] Charlotte Canning argues that embodied reenactments can offer accessible understandings of the past, encouraging 'considerations of the gestural, the emotional, the aural, the visual, and the physical in ways beyond print's ability to evoke or understand them'.[100] Reenactment organizers vary in their desire for historical accuracy. Some venerate authenticity, focusing on details such as the exact button used on a uniform from a particular year. Others wilfully ignore such concerns, instead focusing on 'creating a space of potential and community in the present'.[101] I am interested in the latter approach, and particularly in inclusive reenactments that focus on participation. In the early stages of Fashion Fictions I was influenced by a reenactment practice that I encountered via a 1970s BBC documentary about the Devon town of Totnes, in which dozens of locals dressed up in Elizabethan costume every Tuesday while going about their everyday business: serving in the post office, shopping in the market, vacuuming the stairs.[102]

Another key influence lies in participatory activities that seek to bring possible futures to life in the present. These 'experiential futures' projects, installations and encounters enable participants to experience and reflect on speculative propositions. As Stuart Candy and Kelly Kornet explain, 'Experiential Futures (XF) is a family of approaches for making futures visible, tangible, interactive, and otherwise explorable in a range of modes'.[103] Tobias Revell, Justin Pickard and Georgina Voss describe how these approaches 'collapse the wall between the speculative and the present and allow us a glimpse of the experience of being in the world'.[104] Activities vary widely in terms of scale, duration and fidelity, from highly polished immersive experiences to rough-and-ready improvisations. A large-scale public project led by Jake Dunagan and Stuart Candy in Hawaii took the form of 'a gubernatorial debate, a citizenship ceremony, an environmental education workshop and a business pitch for human enhancements'.[105] Participatory enactments facilitated by design researchers in Denmark, in contrast, involved groups generating and enacting their own speculative propositions using accessible materials such as foam, cardboard and tape, along with ready-to-hand props.[106]

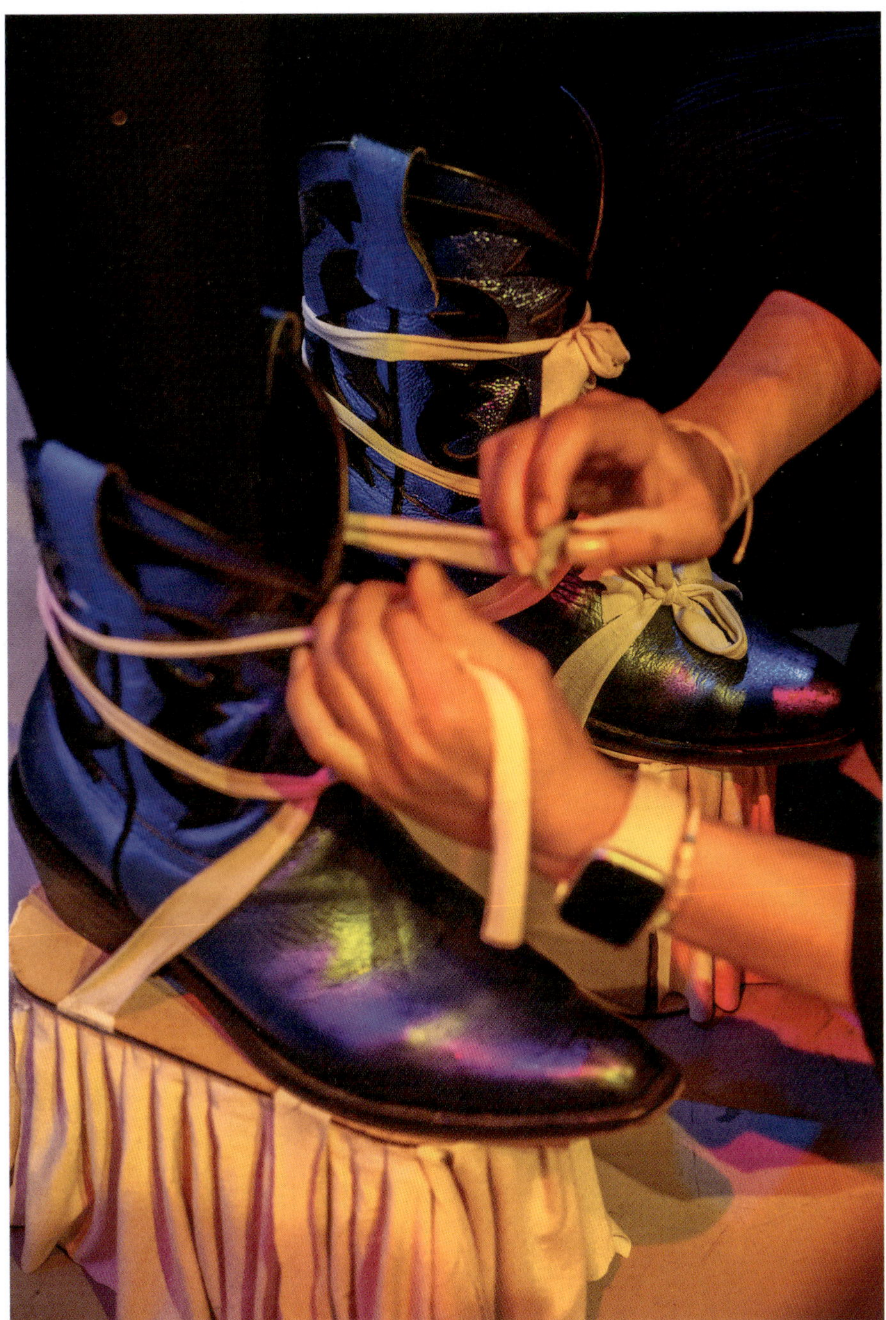

Figure 3.16 *In World 221, people connect with mythical beasts through dress.[107] At this intimate Stage 3 enactment, which took place at a gallery in Bogotá, visitors were invited to take part in the Ceremony of Inoxiva. Each person selected a card associated with a specific beast, adorned their body with a relevant artefact, and explored the embodied wearing experience. These tie-on platforms link to the beasts of the Corpusia family.*

The performances discussed so far may appear to be very different: some recreate historical events, while others are expressions of imagined futures or alternative presents. Some draw extensively on tangible props such as tools and costumes to 'persuad[e] the experiencing body of the reenactor',[108] while others are much leaner in their use of such items. Yet all involve what Richard Schechner calls 'restored' or 'twice-behaved' behaviour. He describes restored behaviour as 'living behavior treated as a film director treats a strip of film', which 'can be rearranged or reconstructed'.[109] This reconstruction of behaviour, in Schechner's view, is the basis of all performance.[110] He argues that 'so-called new behavior is really the rearrangement of old behavior or the enactment of old behavior in new settings. … Experimental performance thrives on these rearticulations masquerading as novelties.'[111]

Historical reenactments that aim for authenticity seek to replicate the behaviour of the past in the present day. Authoritative evidence of this behaviour is, however, elusive, for – as already noted – the distinction between fact and fiction, story and history, is far from stable. In historical reenactments, then, people draw on their knowledge of human behaviour to *imagine* the behaviour that would have happened in the past and restore it in the present. The same happens in enactments of futures and parallel presents: people draw on their lived experience to imagine what would happen there. Just as we use real-world ideas, language and resources to generate fictional worlds, we use real-world embodied behaviours to enact them. This experimental process, Schechner explains, creates an 'in-between' space of possibility, a space that 'is precarious because it is subjunctive, liminal, transitional: it rests not on how things are but on how things are not; its existence depends on agreements kept among all participants … The field is the embodiment of potential, of the virtual, the imaginative, the fictive, the negative, the not not.'[112]

* * * * * * * *

To examine the experiences of those taking part in Fashion Fictions enactments in more detail, let us focus on **World 91**. Its origins lie in a Stage 1 fiction:

> In World 91 in 2010 Caroline Lucas became the UK's first Green Prime Minister. Lucas redefined STEM [science, technology, engineering and maths] subjects in schools. Through the new 'Sewing, Theatre, Ecology, and Mindfulness' curriculum an ecologically minded generation of thinkers emerged who adopted mushrooms as their nonhuman spiritual guides.
>
> Every Friday a Mushroom-themed Mardi Gras fills the streets. Fantastical costumes made from fungi fabrics adorn floats. Headdresses are shaped like giant puffballs; wings are coloured in shades of green by shingled hedgehog mushrooms and fans shaped like oyster mushrooms are waved at spectators. A magical night of festivities follows paying homage to Lucas and the mushroom guides.

Figure 3.17 *A pilot Fashion Fictions enactment explored World 2, in which chemical dyes have been banned for fifty years.*[113] *The geographically dispersed group enacted the world each Thursday by wearing undyed items from their wardrobe and exploring coloration using natural dyes. As part of the enactment, participant Amanda visualized her World 2 'look'.*

The fiction was developed by a group at a Stage 2 workshop. Earlier in the chapter I mentioned how this group invented a word, *revest,* to describe the process of returning mycelial shoes to the soil. After the workshop I picked up some ideas that arose in the group's discussions and carried them forward to a Stage 3 enactment. The enactment drew on the format of the pilot I had organized a couple of years earlier, in which geographically dispersed participants engaged in a fictional-world practice once a week for six weeks and shared their activities via a WhatsApp group. (In the pilot the participants enacted the fictional **World 2**, in which chemical dyes have been banned for fifty years, by dressing as if in that world each Thursday; see Figure 3.17.) For the World 91 enactment I invented a specific fictional-world practice for the participants to explore: I reported that in World 91 people present themselves to the mushroom spiritual guides (whether visible fungi or hidden mycelial networks) once a week, taking great care over their dress. The invitation to participate went out to all those who had attended the first two Stage 2 workshops. Twelve people – mostly the previous participants, along with a few of their friends who were enticed to join in – came forward. The setup was flexible: some participants took part every week; others dropped in and out as circumstances allowed; a few were unable to join in at all. Occasionally, others – friends, partners, family members, dogs – were involved in the week's mushroom visit. These varied activities were documented in the WhatsApp chat via a steady stream of photographs, written comments, short videos and voice notes.

In his writing on restored behaviour, Richard Schechner describes the process by which finalized theatrical performances emerge. This process often involves a workshop phase: 'a deconstruction process, where the ready-mades of culture (accepted ways of using the body, accepted texts, accepted feelings) are broken down and prepared to be "inscribed" upon'.[114] The World 91 participants played with these deconstructed elements as they started to create their interpretation of the enactment text and the world that it represented. Their ideas were sometimes expressed as tentative statements about the world's spiritual guides; at other times they were phrased as questions. Talia, for example, mused, 'I wonder if people in MW [mushroom world] cultivate mushrooms and how? Is it active or through benign neglect that makes room for them?' Some comments used more definite language, when a participant reported a decision about their interpretation of the world or simply shared a statement of fact. Writing in this mode, Talia reported cycling to visit the mushrooms on one occasion 'because cycles of all kinds are at the heart of life in our society'. One week Tamar was unable to venture outdoors due to illness. She improvised by connecting with a carved wooden mushroom and noted in her WhatsApp post that 'On days that the spiritual guides are not physically present, an idol is used to focus the reflection.'

Schechner explains that the fragments of behaviour generated in a workshop are typically selected and refined through rehearsal into a performance.[115] In the World 91 enactment, however, we remained in workshop mode. Even in the few examples I have shared, we can see that interpretations of the world varied within the group; in fact, the WhatsApp chat shows the interpretations shared by a single individual varying from post to post. The group's visions of the fictional world, therefore, were multiple, fragmented and contradictory. At Stage 2 workshops participants usually attempt to resolve inconsistencies in their collective vision; in this Stage 3 enactment there was no need for, or even attempt at, consensus. Each iteration of the enactment – each visit, even each comment – was, in a way, accepted as a new adaptation of the fiction: a new version of the story, reshaped for a specific context or set of preferences.[116] All of these adaptations, all of these stories, comfortably coexisted. This multiplicity of possibilities is reminiscent of 'pluralized knowing' in Theatre of the Oppressed, a form of theatre developed by Brazilian playwright Augusto Boal that represents an instance of oppression and invites the audience to step in and influence the action, proposing and trying out possible interventions. As Frances Babbage describes, 'As each new intervention takes place, forcing the other actors to improvise and realign themselves in relation to the changing action, the narrative is unmade and remade before our eyes.'[117] The approach thus 'invites multiple interpretations … without collapsing meaning down to one "right" answer or meaning'.[118]

This workshopping process was also present, albeit in a different form, in the enactment of **World 54**. The original fiction described a world in which all adults were restricted to owning ten garments at a time.[119] At Stage 2 the group took the idea in a new direction, developing a vision of a world in which people have become highly resourceful in their dress. I took the idea and ran with it to create this text to guide the Stage 3 enactment:

> For environmental reasons, production of new textiles is severely limited in World 54. A resourceful yet opulent fashion culture has arisen in which people dress using sheets of cloth combined with cardigans for warmth, secured using ingeniously versatile straps and button arrangements. Assorted objects, often not originally intended as adornments for the body, are used as a form of oversized jewellery.
>
> Dressing in this culture requires time, effort and creativity. Trends typically focus on the way in which fabric is draped, the arrangement of fastenings and the careful selection of colour and decoration. Intensive swapping enables further novelty and opportunities for self-expression.

I described the enactment to the nineteen participants as 'a dressing-up activity that is one part party game, one part art installation, and one part creative thinking workshop (with bonus cake)'. I hoped to focus attention on the experience of dressing in World 54 via two activities: *performances* and *scenarios*. We started with the performances. After exploring the affordances of the sheets and straps, the group was invited to use a randomly assigned set of instruction cards – inspired by Fluxus artist George Brecht's *Motor Vehicle Sundown (Event)*[120] – to experience a speeded-up version of dressing in World 54 (Figure 3.18). One person's set of cards might include the instructions *Make your outfit longer*; *Take everything off and start again*; and *Look at others' outfits. Select one and imitate*

Figure 3.18 *In the World 54 enactment, participants took part in an experimental participatory performance. Each person followed a randomly assigned set of instruction cards to experience a speeded-up version of dressing using just a buttoned sheet and versatile strap.*

it in some way. In following these instructions, the participants drew on their experiences of dressing in conventional garments while responding to the particular affordances of the items provided. The group threw themselves into this activity with gusto. One participant, Jay, reflected: 'It was a great way of thinking through doing. It felt playful in the best way.'

In the second part of the workshop, I wanted to slow down and dig deeper into the imagined cultures of World 54. The participants were split into small groups; each group was given a scenario to devise and act out. One group, for example, enacted a World 54 scenario in which a rare item is brought into a swap meet and several people are desperate to take it home. Time was tight, with only a few minutes allowed for workshopping before embarking on the informal performance. (Before the World 54 workshop, I was concerned that this 'acting' task might push some participants out of their comfort zone, but in fact they engaged with great enthusiasm – perhaps helped by the fact that all of the performances happened simultaneously, with no audience.) As in the World 91 mushroom-visiting activities, world-building arose alongside enactment: the participants asked questions about the world and developed their own personal interpretations.

Figure 3.19 *Participants in some Fashion Fictions enactments seem to dwell in two worlds. Their both/and position is evident when things they encounter in the real world are interpreted through a fictional-world lens. This dilapidated football, located during a weekly mushroom search by Talia, was interpreted as 'a decaying artefact from the synthetic before times' in fungi-centric World 91.*

The structure of the **World 27** enactment – the garment exchange in the woods discussed earlier in the chapter – was somewhat different. I guided the participants through a series of activities; the event unfolded like a performance without any rehearsal, with an interpretation evolving along the way. In the **World 62** enactment – the round-robin fashion game also discussed in this chapter – the sense of enacting a fictional world slid into the background. The participants focused on the task of describing and passing on garments; there was no script beyond the text guiding the activity, no rehearsal, no story beyond each participant's experience. The activity thus perhaps felt more like playing a game than workshopping a performance.

Let us return to mushroom-centric World 91 to consider a final characteristic of the Stage 3 enactments. The initial guidance I created for this activity invited participants to post in two voices: as their real-world self or as their World 91 alter ego. I was inspired to try this approach by participatory design enactments that have involved participants stepping in and out of character, 'shifting between immersion and commentary'.[121] I imagined a binary distinction between these two positions: immersed in the fictional world or standing in the real world, acknowledging the artifice of the activity. Yet in the participants' accounts – and in my own experience, when I had a go at visiting the mushrooms myself – the worlds actually seemed to blend. They become overlaid realities, making the position not *either/or* but *both/and*. The participants were simultaneously in the real world *and* in the fictional world – or perhaps even, at times, in the multiple interpretations of the fictional world that they had constructed. Furthermore, the fiction lingered between the weekly visits, simmering in the background of day-to-day life. This blending was not so apparent in the other enactments; the fiction sometimes dominated and sometimes receded. Yet it was always at work to some extent. The *both/and* experience corresponds with Augusto Boal's ambitions for Theatre of the Oppressed, in which – as Frances Babbage explains – participants 'experience [a] form of dual existence, with no one either entirely outside the drama or wholly immersed within it'.[122] Perhaps this is the power of the enactments: the opportunity to dwell in a story *and* in the real world. To access an alternative culture we need not drop out of everyday life entirely; instead, we can add a new way of doing things, overlaid on top of the familiar.

Stories and language: ideas for the real world

Five themes from this discussion of stories, storyworlds, language and performance suggest avenues for further inquiry:

1. Narratives

What are the narratives and imaginaries that underpin fashion stories? How can we reveal, challenge and reshape these narratives?

2. Gaps

Which stories and storytellers are missing from Fashion Fictions? How can we learn about the dreams of people who have not yet been reached by the project?

3. Language

How can we expand the language of fashion and sustainability? What new concepts and practices could we name and thereby cultivate into being? Could the creation of new meanings for familiar words offer a tool for change?

4. Text over image

If we were to challenge the centrality of images in fashion culture, what possibilities would open up? How could we use text to slow down, to imagine, to reflect on our relationships with our clothes?

5. Reconfiguring reality

In Fashion Fictions, we draw on real-world experiences, behaviours and materials to construct our fictional stories. There is latent potential in the most unexpected of places. What can we reconfigure to make new stories? How can we shuffle the familiar to create new possibilities?

* * * * * * * * *

The discussion has also identified missteps we may make when trying to work for change. Issues to bear in mind include:

Continuing harmful narratives

We must beware of inadvertently perpetuating harmful narratives and imaginaries. Many of these narratives, such as the Consumer Story, are so embedded in our experiences of the world that they can easily creep in to our conversations.

Passive revolution

Some initiatives that present themselves as helping towards sustainability lead only to a passive revolution: they actually serve to reinforce the unsustainable status quo. It is important that we think critically about the initiatives we encounter and create.

Not stepping in

Embodied action can, for some, feel a little intimidating. Yet vital discoveries are made when we step in to the space of speculation with our bodies and commit to experimental action.

91

4

Nature and spirituality

Fashion and nature

Walking through the centre of Nottingham, I am on the search for nature. My quarry is not the pigeons and weeds that scratch a living on the streets nor the glorious planters cared for by the city gardener, but visual depictions of the natural world. I am confident that high-street clothing stores will be a fertile hunting ground. Indeed, when I step inside and scan the rails, I encounter an array of visions. Flowers abound: ditzy petals, glitchy bouquets, cartoonish blooms. The animal world is similarly well represented: leopard-esque patterns in clashing colour combinations, zebra stripes of all scales, the tactile quiver of freshly made fake-fur trims.

Representation of the natural world in textile form has a long history, extending back to ancient times. Fragments of textiles that have survived for over 1,500 years in Egypt, Syria and China demonstrate the creation of animal motifs via embroidery and weaving in diverse historical cultures.[1] In Renaissance Europe, a new approach emerged: highly refined illustrative textile patterns representing plants and animals. This innovation was driven by developments including: the scientific study of nature; exploration and colonization that brought unfamiliar species to European consciousness; and the distribution of this knowledge in visual form via novel printing technologies.[2] In the seventeenth and eighteenth centuries, close connections between naturalists, botanical painters, embroiderers and weavers strengthened the associations between natural imagery and fashion textiles – particularly floral designs – that endure today.[3] The eighteenth century also saw the first fad for animal-patterned textiles: although we might think of leopard- and zebra-print fabrics as a phenomenon emerging in the twentieth century, in fact they have enjoyed periods of popularity since the 1760s.[4] Fake fur, meanwhile, was developed alongside other synthetics in the first half of the twentieth century, becoming widespread in the postwar era amid ethical concerns about real fur.[5]

Figure 4.1 *While the real-world fashion system is responsible for devastating deforestation, the culture of World 91 nurtures connection between humans and other species.*

Considering this history, fashion's aesthetic connection with the living world is readily apparent. Perhaps less obvious is the fact that fashion is utterly dependent on the earth's resources. Many of our textiles are made from plant and animal fibres: cotton, linen, hemp, wool, alpaca, cashmere, silk. Some people also wear the skins of animals in the form of leather and fur. All of these resources ultimately depend on functioning ecosystems, fertile soil and favourable climatic conditions. While manmade fibres such as viscose and lyocell go through intensive chemical processes to be turned into textiles, they are likewise derived from a natural material: wood pulp. Even the synthetic fibres that form the majority of clothes sold today[6] – polyester, nylon, acrylic – come from the earth: they are made from oil and therefore were once, millions of years ago, living things. At one time, all dyestuffs were organic materials derived from plants, animals and minerals. In the nineteenth century, it was discovered that a byproduct of the gas industry, coal tar, could be used to manufacture manmade dyes.[7] Their vibrant colours quickly attracted fashion-conscious wearers and today chemical dyes dominate industrial production.

While the contemporary globalized fashion system relies on the natural world, its activities contribute to ecological devastation. Consider biodiversity loss: leather production has been linked to deforestation of the Amazon,[8] while it was revealed in 2014 that a third of the trees cut down annually to make manmade fibres such as viscose come from ancient and endangered forests.[9] Impacts related to water use are similarly shocking. The dramatic shrinking of the Aral Sea in Kazakhstan and Uzbekistan is one famous example, caused by the diversion of major rivers to provide irrigation for cotton production in an area already suffering from water scarcity.[10] The industrial pollution of water is a further issue. The textile industry has a long history of releasing hazardous chemicals into waterways, with implications for the health of ecosystems and human communities alike. Regulation is inconsistent and while voluntary initiatives to 'detox' the fashion supply chain have had significant success in recent years, poor practice persists.[11] Another form of water pollution is the shedding of microfibres from synthetic clothing during washing. Small enough for organisms to ingest and often contaminated with harmful chemicals, these fibres are believed to be damaging ocean ecosystems[12] and have even been found in human blood.[13]

The huge quantities of clothing that are incinerated or sent to landfill also have considerable impacts. To give an idea of the scale of this problem: it is reported that in the UK 300,000 tonnes of clothing is discarded in household waste every year, of which 20 per cent goes to landfill and 80 per cent is incinerated.[14] On top of this domestic disposal is the issue of waste colonialism: 'the practice of developed countries exporting their waste to developing countries … [with] a devastating impact on the environment and the health of people in these often struggling communities'.[15] This practice is widespread in the fashion sector: for example, fifteen million secondhand items are imported to Ghana from countries including the UK, US and China every week.[16] Finally, the fossil fuels used throughout the garment lifecycle drive up the concentration of carbon in the atmosphere and thus

Figure 4.2 *In this Stage 2 interpretation of World 1, a debate is taking place about the ethics of the fashion industry. A powerful campaign proposes that commercial exchange of clothing should cease, highlighting fashion's role in the destruction of the earth.*

contribute to the warming of the climate – and the manifold consequences of that warming. It is clear that fashion's enduring passion for the aesthetics and materials of nature coexists with activities that, whether directly or indirectly, plunder natural resources and disrupt the ecological systems that sustain life.

* * * * * * * *

The link between the garments on the rails of shops in the global North and the devastation of natural systems has been highlighted by activists for generations, most recently in the form of hard-hitting campaigns by organizations including Greenpeace, Extinction Rebellion and Fashion Act Now. As awareness increases, it is common for material choices to be brought into focus. The questions seem simple: what should my clothes be made of? Is bamboo better than cotton? Is it bad to wear polyester? What about the waterproof coating on my raincoat? These questions can be difficult to answer: the environmental impacts of fibres depend on multiple contextual factors and misinformation is rife.[17] Moreover, an overly narrow focus on materials can direct our attention away from fundamental questions about the volumes of garments being produced and the mindsets that drive consumption.

An interest in materials is evident in the fictions generated for the Fashion Fictions project – often with a notably inventive edge. In one group of worlds, outlandish material innovations have occurred. In **World 118**, for example, jellyfish have mutated into parasitic tree pests.[18] The pests cause major problems but are also harvested to create a new fabric made from mesoglea, the animal's gelatinous flesh. This notion may seem fanciful but is nonetheless reminiscent of real-world innovations such as a bioengineered fibre based on spider silk proteins, created through a fermentation and spinning process.[19] In **World 142** a new metal, 'transmentum', is discovered deep in the roots of every tree – and, thanks to its amazing flexibility in colour and texture, comes to be used for all clothing.[20] This story brings to mind the versatility of graphene, discovered by scientists in 2004, or perhaps the powerful vibranium of science fiction film *Black Panther*.

In these fictions I sense a weariness with the intricacies of real-world fibre choices and a wish for a magic solution that would overcome the difficulties of navigating them. I also sense a hint of what Paul Wapner describes as the 'dream of mastery': an attitude that sees nature as a raw material for humans to use, manage and control.[21] From this position, he explains, 'humans will realize their highest potential as individuals, societies, and species to the degree that we can manipulate the natural world as we see fit'.[22] While the dream of mastery can be traced back to the time of Socrates,[23] it flourished within the Enlightenment mindset that saw natural resources as 'limitless and inexhaustible'.[24] Today, it is evident in techno-optimist thinking: the conviction that climate change and other global challenges will be overcome through technological innovation alone. This position underpins the pursuit of green growth, as discussed in Chapters 1 and 3, and can be observed in the fashion industry's sustainability initiatives. These initiatives aim to mitigate specific impacts of production, use and disposal through incremental changes to established processes, rather than addressing the relationship between fashion and the earth's systems in the expansive and ambitious way that is urgently needed.

Another group of the project's fictional worlds focus on fibres linked to food production. In **World 112**, fabrics are made from rice stalks (Figure 4.3); in **World 96**, straw from cereal crops is used, along with other byproducts from the production of food and medicines. The World 96 fiction explains that the emergence of this approach dates back to 1799, when a global agreement was reached to abandon cotton farming.[25] Fibre production in **World 130** – a world in which petrochemicals have never been used to make products of any kind – is also based on the scraps left by agricultural food production.[26] The ideas within these fictions correspond with the real-world development of materials made from agricultural waste. A new cellulosic fibre has been made from wheat straw, for example,[27] while an innovative nonwoven textile made from waste pineapple leaf fibre is used as a substitute for leather.[28] This is just the latest iteration in a long history of pineapple fibre use: textiles made from the leaves in Asia were exhibited at the Great Exhibition in London in 1851, while pineapple cloth was produced in South America and the Caribbean before the Spanish conquest of the sixteenth century.[29]

In this crop of fictions I identify a shared yearning for coordinated and forward-looking strategies that integrate farming for food and fibre. In them, the ethos of mastery is not evident. Instead, the common thread is a willingness to question established real-world systems. In the fictions fashion is shifted down the agricultural pecking order, becoming secondary to the production of food. This speaks to a recognition of the limited land and water resources available for farming. Perhaps more fundamentally, it indicates a wish for the mainstream fashion system to embrace a degree of humbleness. Such humbleness would represent a major change in culture: the industry typically presents itself as a space of boundless power and possibility, while 'coolness' – an elusive quality highly valued in the fashion context – is often linked to a sense of superiority and aloof detachment.[30]

* * * * * * * *

If a single-minded focus on materials is limiting, there is great value in shifting our gaze to consider the fashion system in a much more holistic way. In the real world, a holistic view prompts us to question volumes of production and the underlying drivers of overconsumption, rather than focus only on the impacts of particular materials or processes. In the language of education for sustainability, a holistic perspective is part of the systems thinking competency: the ability to recognize and understand 'how systems are embedded within different domains and different scales'.[31] Systems thinking exposes the staggering scale of change needed to create fashion systems that respect planetary boundaries: as discussed in Chapter 1, in high-income countries this means a 70 per cent reduction in resource use and a 91–5 per cent reduction in carbon emissions. Without doubt, dramatic shifts in production and consumption patterns are needed.

Figure 4.3 *In World 112, Thailand's self-sufficiency philosophies have gained global influence. Fabrics are made from rice stalks; clothes are made from the fabric in an unbleached state and wearers are encouraged to dye and customize each piece.*[32]

A holistic view, coupled with a yearning for a positive fashion–nature relationship, can be identified in another set of the Stage 1 fictions. In **World 16**, for example:

preservation and regeneration of the biosphere is now the centre of every fashion activity … clothes are now seen as a key conduit to interconnected living. Human attempts to 'put a price on' and control nature and to exploit natural resources for short-term human benefit, have been consigned to the same category of shameful and unconscionable past practices as racism and genocide.[33]

This fiction evokes what Wapner describes as the 'dream of naturalism': the idea that humans should 'harmonize ourselves with, rather than impose ourselves on, the natural world'.[34] It is the dream of naturalism that inspires us to preserve and protect natural wilderness and to live in balance with the earth's biophysical limits. The idea of 'living according to nature to protect one's health and safety, and as a means to a good, fulfilling life',[35] has a long, even ancient, history. Marius de Geus identifies this urge in a series of ecological utopian visions, from Henry David Thoreau's famous retreat to the woods, to William Morris's pastoral socialism and Aldous Huxley's novel *Island*.[36] The mindset also underpins the deep ecology movement, which argues for the intrinsic value of all life on earth.[37]

The dream of naturalism feels present in many contributions to the Fashion Fictions project. A clear-cut example would be **World 13**, in which a radical rewilding strategy sees land masses left fallow, on rotation, for decades, to allow for the restoration of natural ecosystems.[38] We might also trace its influence in fictions where the human body itself is seen as a kind of natural material. In **World 111**, for example, people have no need for physical protection from clothing and instead use their bodies as a canvas,[39] while in **World 75** humans have evolved to absorb natural pigments, injected under the skin.[40] In **World 40**, body and textile are intriguingly integrated: 'Weaving and plaiting "technologies" using hair and other fibrous materials are integrated with the body; in effect, the composition of body contours, textures and hair become the proto-warp'.[41]

The dream of naturalism has a strong presence in **World 19**:

The 2009 H1N1 influenza virus in World 19 succeeded in dismantling capitalism more efficiently than any environmental activist could have dreamed.

The purpose of the fashion 'season' is turned on its head. Fashion 'capital' is driven by collectives exploring sensitive ways to promote the health of insects, rivers, weather. Communities compete to demonstrate imaginative responses to seasonal knowledge through clothing intimately connected to the requirements of the other-than-human. Success is judged by the way knowledge is shared and embodied, habitats are ameliorated and harmful practices replaced.

Fashion producers unanimously adopt the environmental Hippocratic oath – 'first do no harm'. Climate summit goals are strengthened – and met.[42]

This fiction was one of five put forward for exploration at the first Stage 2 workshop. Jade, who picked it up, was immediately attracted by the intertwining of fashion and nature – and the prospect of rethinking the fashion season.[43] At first glance, the meaning of this term is straightforward: the selection of clothing appropriate for the climate at different times of the year. Yet for over 150 years it has been used as a means of marketing fresh collections of garments, typically months in advance of the season for which they are designed.[44] The emphasis has thus been on the regular provision of novelty, rather than catering for temperature and weather conditions: as Malcolm Barnard comments, 'the point of seasons is that they pass and are replaced by another season'.[45] The advent of fast fashion has seen an amplification of this novelty, with the tradition of two collections per year replaced by fortnightly, weekly and even daily updates to fashion product ranges.[46] The World 19 fiction, while ambiguous in its exact meaning, suggests a recalibration of fashion's relationship to natural seasonal rhythms.

For her prototype, Jade collaged images from real-world fashion and gardening magazines to create a series of pages from the leading World 19 fashion magazine, 'Séasúr' (Figure 4.4). By incorporating

Figure 4.4 *Ecology and seasonality guide all fashion choices in World 19, as shown by these layouts from the leading fashion magazine, 'Séasúr'. The 'who are you wearing' page identifies the three species that the featured garment benefits.*

real-world references, juxtaposing images and playing with common media tropes such as the 'must-have', she constructed a window into a familiar-but-strange fashion experience. During the earlier world-building phase of the workshop Jade had considered a rich array of implications of the central 'what if', contemplating ideas such as 'road kill couture' and the use of discarded garments as habitats for wildlife.

The notion of textiles providing support for other species is the focus of the **World 74** fiction:

In World 74 seeded, knitted textiles first used for food-growing are upcycled into clothes, the textures initially knitted to benefit the seeds becoming the textures of the cloth … The origin of this culture can be traced back to the accidental sprouting of seeds being transported in knitted cloth – around 11th century BC. This evolved into a complex technology that became the basis for loops of fiber-food-clothing-compost biomass-based societies where clothes are a collaboration between landscape, plants and people.[47]

Figure 4.5 *In World 74, knitted textiles are used for food-growing and later upcycled into clothes. The fiction is based on the real-world research of the author, Alice-Marie Archer, who is exploring the creation of knitted structures for soil-less farming.*[48]

In World 74, textiles are used first for growing crops, and only later for clothing. Like those discussed earlier, the fiction offers a vision in which fashion is secondary to food production. But it goes further, outlining a thriving culture in which people, food, fibre, soil and place are deeply integrated. In Worlds 19 and 74 I perceive a culture of negotiation and connection: between people, the need for food, the need for fibre, the needs of the soil, the needs of the ecosystem. These ideas bring to mind the real-world Fibershed movement, which supports the development of regional fibre systems. As founder Rebecca Burgess explains: 'Similar to a local watershed or a foodshed, a fibershed is focused on the source of the raw material, the transparency with which it is converted into clothing, and the connectivity among all parts, from soil to skin and back to soil.'[49] Fibershed's inspiring work encompasses both deep understanding of soil health and deep consideration for the person-to-person connections that are needed for a thriving local textile system.[50]

Post-nature communities

The dream of mastery wants to control nature and exploit it as a resource; the dream of naturalism wants to protect and preserve it. Both depend on a common understanding of nature as, in Paul Wapner's words, 'the world acting by itself … the way of things beyond the human realm'.[51] The last few decades have seen this understanding being challenged, through discussion of the 'end of nature'. One strand of this discussion focuses on human impacts on nonhuman life. It recognizes that human activity has affected every ecosystem, even the most remote, whether directly via extraction or indirectly through the changing climate – and argues that, therefore, there is no longer any place in which the natural world is acting independently of human interference. In this context, the argument goes, efforts to preserve or restore nature will inevitably be outdated and ineffective.[52]

The second strand of the 'end of nature' discussion is conceptual and proposes that nature, while appearing to be a straightforward reality, is actually a jumble of ideas, an unhelpful social construction that obstructs a deep ecological understanding.[53] Lisa Garforth draws on the work of social theorists Bruno Latour and Jane Bennett to explain that we have long mixed up natural, cultural and technological elements to create diverse hybrid entities. These hybrids highlight the falsity of the perceived boundary between humans and nature that underpins the dreams of both mastery and naturalism. Garforth helpfully summarizes the theorists' position:

> [Latour and Bennett] argue that we need to let go of nature to find appropriate ways of attending to a complex and fully interconnected world, one that includes nonhuman others as agents … The end of nature would be the death of modernity's most absurd and dangerous illusion, one that prevents us from recognizing the mixed-up human/nonhuman worlds we inhabit.[54]

I find these conceptual ideas provocative but engaging: the notion of human/nonhuman worlds feels relevant to the fashion system's intense entanglements of the material, the natural, the social and the personal, and, as someone instinctively drawn to the dream of naturalism, I am intrigued by the argument that our perceptions of nature are getting in the way of meaningful action towards sustainability. Yet the notion of the end of nature can be critiqued: as Wapner explains, some feel that it simply represents the dream of mastery, dressed up in new clothes. Furthermore, for many the demise of nature as a concept would represent a moral, emotional and spiritual loss. Wapner argues that the social construction of nature has value: 'Yes, we humans tell ourselves stories about the more-than-human world, but there also seems to be something genuinely revealing about those stories.' Helpfully, Wapner suggests a middle path that embraces the sensibilities of both naturalism and the end of nature. He sees this path as a post-nature age, 'in which neither nature nor humanity has a singular essence'.[55] The concept of nature is not abandoned, but nor is it used uncritically. Post-nature thinking acknowledges the complexities of living in a world full of human/nonhuman hybrids; it explores ways of supporting the health of ecosystems and people that recognize these complexities.

This nuanced approach feels relevant to many of the ideas explored in the Fashion Fictions project: it resonates with the ethos of negotiation and connection that I have identified in the fictions discussed earlier in the chapter. Wapner sees the post-nature era as an age of ambiguity that celebrates and learns from uncertainty regarding the right way forward in response to the climate, biodiversity and related global crises. An embrace of ambiguity contrasts with a desire for certainty, which is identified by Sharon Stein as one of eight patterns of thought and behaviour embedded within modernity/coloniality. As Stein explains, this pattern 'denies that all knowledge is situated and contextually (rather than universally) relevant, and that all solutions are partial, imperfect and may reproduce the problems they seek to address, or create new ones'.[56]

To bring our fashion systems into balance with the earth's capacity to support life, we need to let go of deeply embedded ways of thinking and move towards new social, cultural and economic arrangements. But what form these alternative arrangements could take is not yet known. In Fashion Fictions we explore not convictions but tentative proposals, not single visions but plural fragmented suggestions. Uncertain of the right path, we feel our way through the possibilities together.

* * * * * * * *

The Stage 2 workshops are a fertile site for examining the complexities of post-nature thinking. As the participants flesh out their chosen fictions and encapsulate a world's culture in a representative artefact or image, they negotiate between multiple elements of human and nonhuman systems and try to resolve contradictions and inequalities. Let us briefly consider two examples: World 28 and World 124. In both cases, an event some decades ago has led to a close relationship between people and other species. The first is **World 28**, in which this relationship is based on dyeing:

Synthetic dye shortages in World 28 during WWII prompted growth of dye plants in the 'dig for victory' movement and natural dyeing skills were taught in 'make do and mend' pamphlets. As the war ended this appetite for self-sufficiency continued and became an integral part of British culture.

Home gardens, allotments and community gardens are hubs of growth and creativity. Wearing naturally dyed clothing is now normalised and dyeing skills alongside sewing, mending and upcycling are taught in schools. The food and fashion systems are now more entwined, localised, seasonal & community efforts.[57]

Two Stage 2 workshop participants worked together to explore World 28.[58] Building on the initial fiction, they envisaged a society in which nature is 'rooted into our lives'. They noted the cultural importance of growing crops for food, fibre and dyeing, imagining these practices to be highly regarded, widely practised and fully embedded in the education system. Though they questioned many aspects of real-world life in their construction of the fictional world, they decided that some elements should continue – such as the convenience of machine washing. A particular concern throughout their discussions was the health of the soil, both for its own sake and in growing food for human consumption. As they explained, 'If you start using chemical dyes, or fertilizers, that's a big no. You are in trouble then; you're ostracized from the town.' Their conversation turned to the mordants needed in natural dyeing to create a bond between dye and fibre. While organic materials, including soy milk, can be used as mordants, the more common approach is to use metallic salts. The group felt that those in World 28, like many real-world dyers, would be wary of metallic mordants making their way into the soil and, potentially, into their food. They settled on the exclusive use of organic mordants and, aware that this might mean that some dyes would fade more quickly, came up with a novel idea for their prototype. They devised and mocked up a coloured soap block, made using the remnants of a natural dye, that could be added to the washing machine to simultaneously clean the garments and renew the intensity of their colour (Figures 4.6 and 4.7).

A similar negotiation between a nature-centric culture and modern conveniences can be observed in the Stage 2 exploration of **World 124**:

Due to the publishing of Rachel Carson's *Silent Spring* in World 124 in 1962, bans on herbicides and pesticides were introduced nationwide. Unable to cope with the sudden overgrowth of pavement weeds, councils were inundated with mobility complaints. City farms took the problem into their own hands, herding their flocks through the streets to graze on overgrown grasses and weeds.

As city sheep populations grew, their wool became an abundant byproduct of weed management, freely shared amongst the community for use in knitting projects. Different cities and towns favour their individual sheep breeds which has led to distinctive local fashions.[59]

Figure 4.6 *In World 28, natural dyeing is an integral part of British culture. Ivy soap – a combined soap and colourant made from natural materials – is a popular way to brighten up naturally dyed clothes that may otherwise fade quickly.*

Figure 4.7 *World 28's ivy soap is distributed wrapped in a printed newsletter that includes do-it-yourself instructions.*

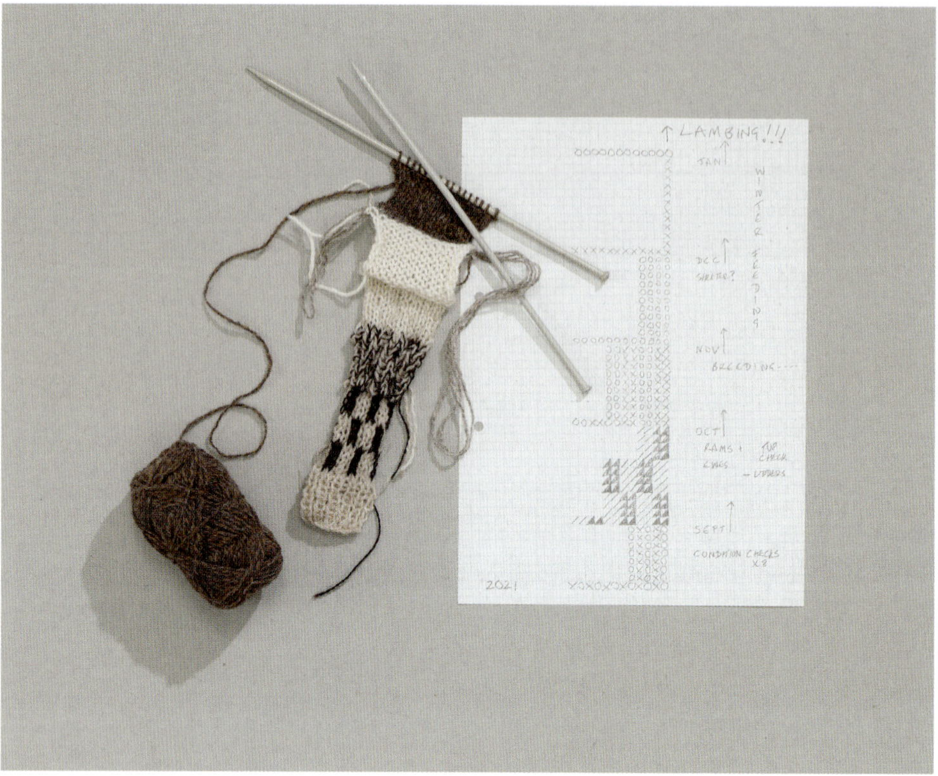

Figure 4.8 *In World 124, knowledge of how to care for the sheep that roam London is embedded throughout the community, learnt by children as young as four. This knitted calendar (with diagrammatic equivalent) represents the shepherding almanac, showing jobs that need to be undertaken each month.*

In this fiction we see human decisions and nonhuman responses combine to develop a distinctive culture. The duo who explored this fiction picked up on this interplay.[60] Focusing their speculation on London, they spoke about the city as a biodiversity-focused 'managed landscape', with people using patch grazing and moving herds around from season to season to avoid the impacts of overgrazing. This approach, they explained, is needed for 'a proper ecosystem, and particularly bird life'; when successful, it has a significant impact on biodiversity. The participants debated the impacts of the World 124 system in climate terms, weighing the benefits of the carbon storage offered by the city's deep-rooted grasslands against the methane produced by the sheep. The practical and scientific aspects of these discussions were delivered with such conviction that to the casual observer it was impossible to tell where real-world knowledge slid into whimsical speculation.

Another important characteristic of the World 124 culture, as discussed at the workshop, is a widespread willingness to relinquish some control over day-to-day life. It is common in World 124 for scheduled grazing to limit access to certain parts of the city, while escaped sheep frequently cause

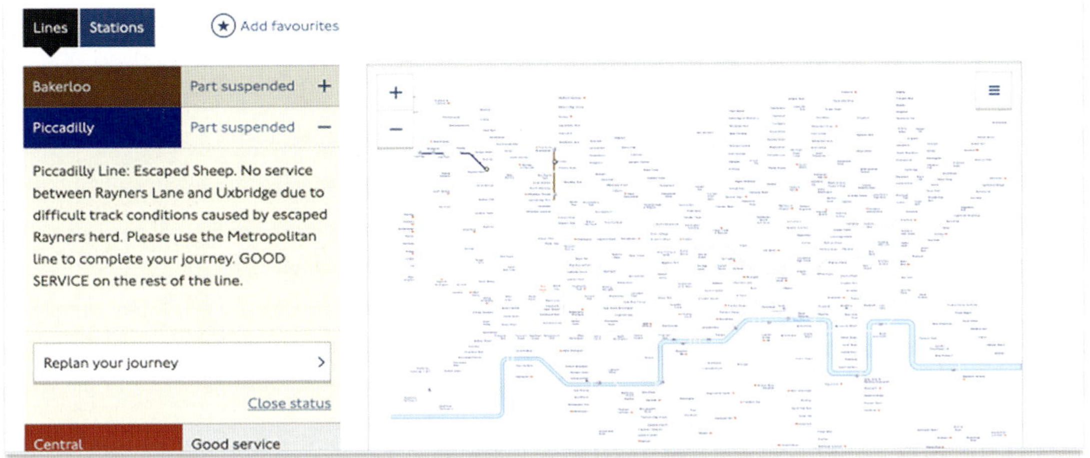

Figure 4.9 *The sheep-centric culture of World 124 affects every aspect of life – such as causing delays to the underground train service, as shown here. This is one of several prototypes created for this world that played with familiar media formats.*

delays to the underground train system (Figure 4.9). The need to protect sheep, meanwhile, has led to the culling of the urban fox population and a significant decline in dog ownership. In World 124, as in World 28, we thus see visions of post-nature negotiation in action, as people find ways to live alongside nonhuman others in thriving communities, working through the tensions and trade-offs that inevitably arise. Donna Haraway's book *Staying with the Trouble* offers a valuable lens through which to view this negotiation. Acknowledging the scale of the ecological devastation we are living through, Haraway explains that she is not interested in the restoration of wilderness. Instead, she is 'deeply committed to the more modest possibilities of partial recuperation and getting on together'.[61] She sees this 'getting on together', which is a context-specific, situated process, as involving multiple species: 'We are all responsible to and for shaping conditions for multispecies flourishing in the face of terrible histories, and sometimes joyful histories too, but we are not all response-able in the same ways. The differences matter – in ecologies, economies, species, lives.'[62]

Haraway's concept of 'response-ability' involves kin of different species finding ways to survive, coexist and even thrive in unexpected and contingent collaborative relationships.[63] Such relationships can be identified in other fictions generated within the project. In **World 63**, for example, lockdown restrictions prompt people to start recognizing the plants they rely upon for food and fibre as fellow community members, leading to a culture of interspecies collaboration and kinship.[64] In **World 146**, a ban on insecticides leads to the spread of clothes-eating insects, the proliferation of holes in clothes and a consequent increase in mending practices. As people embrace this shift, wardrobes come to perform a dual role: 'garments with insects' holes gain value as they contribute [to] insects' safeguard. … Subcultures appear around the planet where communities create common interspecies closets. They become biodiversity and fashion hubs.'[65]

People in World 146 are not aiming to restore a pure and authentic vision of nature; they are finding ways to live alongside insects that were previously seen as pests. This vision of human–insect communities resonates with Haraway's idea of companion species: 'ordinary beings-in-encounter' that come into contact in the spaces of day-to-day life.[66] The theme of companionship and collaboration is taken into a more fantastical space in **World 126**:

> After the collapse of Western human centred civilisation in the 2020's heatwaves in World 126, a panpsychist approach to clothing spread from the global south. To survive the increasing climate crisis, garments took control, collaborating with humans to form assemblages of beings. Layers of sentient bio-clothing formed on humans as complex collaborative communities.
>
> Each living community made decisions for the good of the whole. The growing and adapting fibres steered human decision making to ensure survival. Clothing selected their human – the most sustainably aware humans flourished. Materials collaborated to balance ambient temperatures with their human. A consensus across fibre/human communities formed governments.[67]

Earlier, I mentioned fictions in which fibre production for fashion became secondary to food production. In comparison, the visions discussed here envisage a more fundamental recalibration of the relationship between people and other species. Humans become less dominant and embrace the intertwining of their lives with nonhuman others. This corresponds with Haraway's vision of an era in which 'the order is reknitted: human beings are with and of the earth, and the biotic and abiotic powers of this earth are the main story'.[68]

The Stage 2 exploration of **World 4** introduced in Chapter 3 envisioned a society in which the thriving of nature has become the foremost concern for humanity: people have consciously stepped away from being 'the main story'. In a decisive shift from an ethos of mastery, humans have come to recognize themselves as entirely dependent on other species and the earth's systems. This version of World 4 presents a narrative of partial recuperation in a post-nature era, as outlined by Haraway: humans and nonhumans establishing new relationships, appropriate to specific contexts. Biodiversity is venerated and human scientific knowledge is used for the benefit of all. In the fashion context, comfort, smell and imagination are valued, along with the diversity of species that an outfit supports. As time passes, however, a more extreme, even dystopian, culture emerges. This culture, manifested in increasingly restrictive rules, seems to be driven by an understanding of humans as innately destructive, even poisonous. This notion is present in the real world; for many, it is the implicit meaning of the

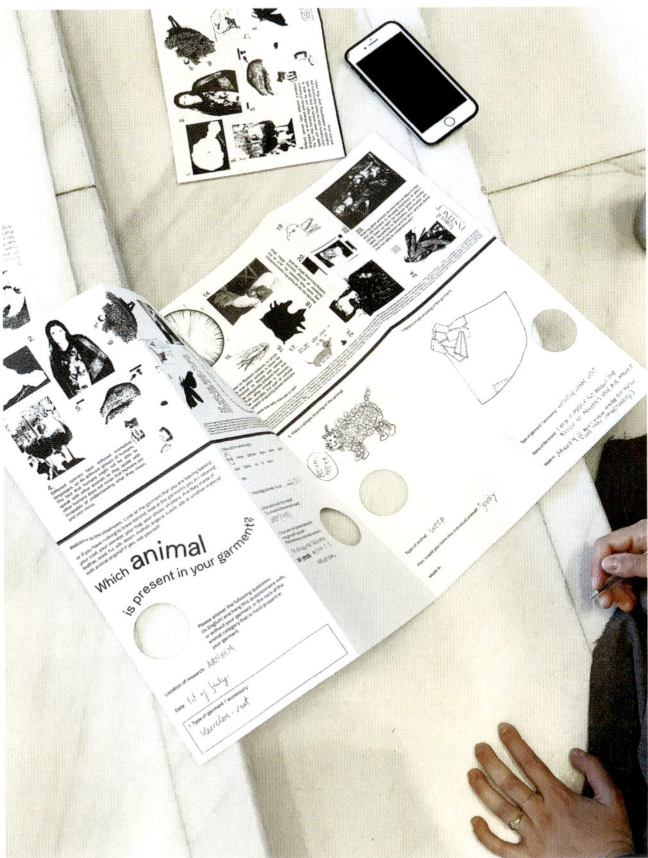

Figure 4.10 *Which Animal is Present in Your Garment?, created by Femke de Vries, is 'a cloakroom interven-tion that invites participants to take into regard the nonhuman animals that are present in their garments'.*[69] *When handing over their coat or bag for storage, each visitor is invited to consider which animal-derived materials are present in their item and to reflect on their understanding of those animals. When they pick up their item later, a label is attached that offers an insight into the life of the animal, such as 'how a cow uses a range of different sounds to greet others, how rabbits take care of their young, how birds have dialects and fall in love'.*[70] *Overall, the research aims to open up critical discussion about relationships between humans and nonhuman animals in the fashion context.*

naming of our present geological epoch as the Anthropocene. This term indicates 'the time during which humans have had a substantial impact on our planet';[71] yet it is not *all* humans who have wrought this impact. An understanding of humans as innately destructive is a deeply problematic view, for it wilfully ignores the many historical and contemporary societies that have thrived on earth without causing irreversible changes to the climate. Furthermore, it limits the scope of our thinking about sustainable transitions. As Evan Berry points out, 'it is difficult to imagine environmentally benign economies or to envision a sustainable future while clinging to a pessimistic anthropology'.[72]

Meeting the mushrooms

If the Stage 2 prototyping process helps us to think a world through in practical terms, the Stage 3 enactment allows us to experience it from the inside. One of the first Stage 3 enactments was the ecocentric – or, more precisely, fungi-centric – culture of **World 91**. This world was introduced in Chapter 3: I discussed the use of language in the Stage 2 prototype and outlined the Stage 3 enactment. By considering the development of the fiction and examining the embodied experiences of the enactment participants, we can take a deeper look at the theme of nature, and draw in the related theme of spirituality.

The original World 91 fiction (see page 78) paints a highly engaging picture of a world in which fungi are deeply respected and celebrated. I was not surprised that this vision caught the imagination of participants at the Stage 2 workshop. Fungi, although often treated as part of the plant kingdom, actually form a vibrant biological category of their own. These organisms are hugely diverse, including the microscopic yeasts that thrive in our gut and the mould that grows in the damp corners of our homes alongside the mushrooms that land on our plates. Mushrooms are the fruiting bodies of fungi, producing spores that act like seeds and help the fungi to spread.[73] Long overlooked in both popular culture and scientific research, fungi are currently enjoying a period of increased visibility. Merlin Sheldrake's bestselling book *Entangled Life: How Fungi Make Our Worlds, Change Our Minds, and Shape Our Futures* has brought the complexity and intrigue of these fascinating organisms to a wide audience. 'Fungi are taking over fashion', declared *Vogue* in 2021;[74] the following year, *Elle* observed that 'From clothing and jewellery to music and microdosing, Fungi are having a moment'.[75] Practical initiatives are seeking to apply the power of fungi to various pressing problems, from reducing colony collapse disorder in honeybees to breaking down waste and filtering heavy metals from water.[76] Fungi are also being used to create innovative biomaterials such as mushroom 'leather'.[77] These varied uses build on a staggeringly long history of humans using fungi for medicinal and other purposes.[78]

While some contemporary applications hum with the dream of mastery, interest in fungi extends deep into the dream of naturalism: many people are keen to learn from these unfamiliar lifeforms. Fungal networks, known as mycelium, are a common source of fascination. The networks, some stretching over kilometres, allow water and nutrients to flow through ecosystems and enable plants to share resources, and even communicate, via the fungal connections.[79] The Stage 2 workshop group were keen to explore the wider implications of a culture guided by mushrooms, and considered how mycelial thinking would affect day-to-day interactions. As part of this conversation they speculated on the potential influence of mind-altering psilocybin ('magic') mushrooms. As Merlin Sheldrake explains, psilocybin induces feelings of love, joy, awe and interconnection, the loss of sense of self, and 'profound intuitive understanding about the nature of reality'.[80] How would culture and creativity in

World 91 be affected if mushrooms were used in place of other intoxicants? Would the traits of World 91 people be very different to people in our world? The group wondered whether mushrooms would be used for mental health, or – in a thought-provoking reflection on the real world – whether mental health problems might be less prevalent in an ecocentric culture, compared to a society driven by capitalist competition. It seems certain that World 91 would be shaped by very different imaginaries to those that dominate in our world.

The idea of spirituality, mentioned in the Stage 1 fiction, was picked up in the Stage 2 discussions. One member of the group described 'this idea of the mushroom … almost as a form of spirituality, connecting you with the regenerative nature of the natural world'. Spirituality is a term used so freely in popular discourse that its meaning can be difficult to pin down. Philip Sheldrake (no relation, to my knowledge, to the author of *Entangled Life*) provides a useful definition. He explains that spirituality concerns every aspect of a person's life, rather than an isolated element of human experience, and involves a quest for both meaning and the sacred – which might be found in nature or the cosmos, as much as a divine being. In contemporary contexts, spirituality is often contrasted with a materialistic approach to life. The rise of spirituality – which Philip Sheldrake describes as 'a striking feature of our times'[81] – has been linked to the questioning and decline, in many Western contexts, of traditional religion during the late twentieth and early twenty-first centuries. This distinction, between organized religion and personal spirituality, was reflected in a conversation about the culture of World 91 at the Stage 2 workshop. When I asked whether the mushrooms represented a belief system, a member of the group responded: 'more like [a] mindset'.

Other Stage 2 explorations already mentioned in this chapter made reference to ecocentric forms of spirituality. The people of **World 28**, in which natural dyes are widely used, were described as 'worshipping nature', while **World 124**, in which sheep herds roam city streets, was acknowledged as a 'wool-worshipping society'. When I wrote a text to guide the Stage 3 enactment for World 91, I built on the original Stage 1 fiction in describing mushrooms as the world's 'spiritual guides'. Philip Sheldrake suggests that those who see themselves as spiritual but have rejected traditional religion search for alternative sources of self-orientation.[82] By enacting World 91, the participants were able, for six weeks, to try out a life in which fungi provide this guidance. While the premise of the world was an unfamiliar, even amusing, novelty for those taking part, the notion that fungi might play a spiritual role has real-life precedents. Mind-altering mushrooms have a long history of use in spiritual practices,[83] while yeast – the apparently magical fungal ingredient that conjures wine from grapes and beer from grain – has, historically, been considered as a 'a divine energy, a spirit, or a god'.[84] Fungi certainly seem worthy of worship, given their role in some of the most fundamental elements of the biosphere: nine out of ten plants depend on them, soil would be sluiced away without the dense fungal tissue that gives it structure and fungal spores in the atmosphere trigger the formation of rain.[85] Furthermore, fungi are rendered implicitly mystical by a lack of human understanding. It is estimated that there are between 2.2 and 3.8 million species, and just 6 per cent have been described.[86] As Merlin Sheldrake states, 'We are only just beginning to understand the intricacies and sophistications of fungal lives.'[87]

* * * * * * * *

My short text outlined the weekly World 91 task that the Stage 3 group were to undertake:

> Once a week in World 91, people undertake a quiet ritual: they present themselves to the mushrooms that are widely understood as spiritual guides.
>
> For most, this practice involves a fleeting visit to a wooded area to enable a few minutes' connection with either visible fungi or the hidden mycelial network, and reflection on cycles of decay and regeneration.
>
> As a sign of respect in this nature-centric culture, people take great care over what they wear for the mushroom visits. Aesthetics vary: some adopt celebratory flamboyant styles, while others opt for a more subtle approach.
>
> The mushrooms see it all.

The enactment participants hunted out mushrooms – often alone, sometimes with a canine or human companion – in a variety of locations: parks, gardens, wild areas, edge land, cemeteries, dunes. The mushrooms were not always easily found. As Jade noted, 'I noticed the most mushrooms when I stopped looking. I was transported back to years of rummaging in charity shops. It's always when we stop looking and wanting when we find a gem.' Whatever the strategy, the participants were often rewarded: photographs shared in the group chat showcased an impressive array of species. Sometimes, however, no mushrooms were forthcoming. I had anticipated this issue, hence my encouragement for the participants to focus their attention on unseen mycelial networks if needed. This seemed to work for them: as Jade said in her World 91 voice, 'I know they see me.'

The participants presented themselves to the mushrooms in a variety of ways. Sometimes, they stood or sat quietly in a form of salute. At other times they took the opportunity to relax in the natural environment: drinking, eating, knitting, listening. They often documented their activities, and the mushrooms that they came across, in photographs and videos. One week, Kate improvised a ritual:

> I made circles of sticks and twigs to honour the holy ground where the mycelium revealed the mushrooms to me, and I took off my shoes so that I could better commune with the mycelium underground, through the soles of my feet … I spent some time with my eyes closed, reaching out with my senses to the mycelium underground and to the elements above and around me.

The Stage 3 text was intentionally ambiguous regarding what to wear when visiting the mushrooms. Interpretations varied. Colour and pattern were recurring themes: mushroom colours, mushroom-print

Figure 4.11 *On Annebella's first visit to the fungi she took a pair of red flamenco shoes, selected for their resemblance to spotted fly agaric mushrooms.*

Figure 4.12 *The enactment participants searched for and discovered mushrooms in a wide array of places, including – to my surprise – sand dunes.*

fabric, spots and dots – and animal prints, selected by Julie to be 'disguised as a woodland creature'. Kate focused particularly on natural fibres and dyes. Inspired by the maxim 'everything you make returns to the earth as either food or poison', she wanted 'to show respect for the mushrooms who will be fed by our garments when they decompose'. On one occasion, Jade framed her observation of the mushrooms in the language of fashion media: 'It seems this season is all about stacking, frills and multiples for the mushrooms. I'm pondering my existing wardrobe and materials. How can I pull together an outfit for next week's presentation?'

In the participants' weekly updates we occasionally saw flamboyant 'dressing-up' clothes and, more frequently, hats. A couple of people made or adapted items: a mushroom-themed necklace, a spotty beret. One participant wore a hand-knitted jumper: 'I feel like offering them a piece I have made shows my personal respect for them, thought and effort in every little stitch.' Some outfit choices reflected human connections. Ruhee wore beautiful handloom sarees to express her identity as an Indian woman living in the UK. Others wore items that had been given as gifts to acknowledge the importance of family – and 'to acknowledge the gifts we are given by the natural world'.

The weather was an important consideration when dressing for the mushrooms. The six weeks of the enactment saw the mixed-up weather that comes along as winter slides into spring. On some occasions the participants found themselves swathed in too many layers; at other times, they were shivering. Elly advised that someone joining the ritual for the first time should prioritize weather-appropriate clothing, explaining that 'it's harder to hear the mushrooms if you are distracted by cold hands or wet feet'. In an example of the organic extension of the fiction that happens at Stage 3, she went on to indicate that some in World 91 'like to immerse themselves in the natural world more fully' – suggesting that embodied discomfort would be, for some, part of the spiritual experience. (These people would surely be kindred spirits of real-world cold-water swimming evangelists.)

Beyond clothing choices, interest in the changing seasons ran throughout the enactment. Talia, for example, reported, 'Knowing that I was going out to see the mushrooms cued me to think about and notice other seasonal cycles – the bulbs that are coming up and a few early tree blossoms.' Elly enjoyed observing changes from day to day: 'It's interesting to see how a fairly small environment can change as the weather does – which plants are thriving, which animals and birds are out, and

Figure 4.13 *Elly documented each week's visit to the mushrooms in a composite image posted in the group's WhatsApp chat, along with some written notes about her experiences and reflections.*

which hide, or close their flowers.' One week, she translated insights from the natural world into her outfit choice:

> Today I'm giving thanks for the regrowth and rejuvenation we see in nature at this time of year by wearing clothes I haven't worn for at least a year. After lying dormant during the winter, the natural world reminds us that if something needs a rest, that doesn't mean it's come to the end of its life.

Cycles of growth and death were prominent in discussions about World 91. The Stage 2 workshop group talked about fungi's fundamental role in the decomposition of other organisms, bringing nutrients back into circulation in the ecosystem. The group felt that a fungi-centric culture, in comparison to the real-world culture they live within, would be accepting of death. As Elly put it, 'Death has become less of a taboo and more just a fact of life.' As the Stage 3 enactment unfolded, this theme was developed by forager and mushroom expert Fergus Drennan, who I had invited to contribute to the WhatsApp chat. Through a series of video posts, Fergus shared firsthand stories of the varied uses of fungi, along with associated folklore. In one of his messages he focused on the decomposition of dead wood, explaining that when a tree is dying, 'the fungi take on the life force … they start breaking the tree down'. The end of one life enables another to flourish. Therefore, he explained, 'In the kind of world I inhabit, there is no real distinction between life and death.' Appreciation of decay was evident in the Stage 3 enactment. Jade reflected on the beauty of mushrooms populating dead wood and wondered about its equivalent to fashion. 'Who or what feeds on dead trends and dead clothes?', she asked. 'How can this be harnessed in the flourishing mushroom world?'

The participants enjoyed looking, as one person put it, 'through mushroom-tinted spectacles' for the duration of the project. Several were reading *Entangled Life* and found great inspiration in its pages. One person learned 'how the mycelium network only grows towards positive stimuli' and decided, 'I'm going to let that be my intention for the week – growing towards the positive things in life.' More than once, participants commented on the commonalities between the mushroom visits and attending church: focused reflective activities, taking place every weekend, for which outfit choices may be critical. After her first visit, Annebella – an atheist brought up as a strict Catholic – reflected that 'it did feel, sort of, strangely religious. As I stood there … I definitely felt like I was worshipping. I thought about my Catholic background, of sort of genuflecting, or standing up at certain points in the religious service.'

Further links with organized religion arose from time to time. Participants gave thanks to the mushrooms for good news; left offerings to the unseen mycelium; and, once, used an idol – a wooden mushroom – in place of connection with living beings. Ruhee brought real-world religion into her weekly mushroom visit by marking the beginning of the Hindu new year and Navratri, the nine-day festival of the avatars of Durga, the goddess of power, strength and preservation. She presented herself

Figure 4.14 *Participant Charlie interpreted this structure that she discovered on her weekly mushroom visit as 'a temple to the mushrooms'. As she explained: 'Each year at spring equinox, mushroom worshippers gather in the woods to build structures from branches and dead wood, hoping to build a new habitat for the mushrooms.'*

wearing a yellow and red handloom saree, selected because yellow is the colour of Shailputri, Durga's avatar who is worshipped on the first day of Navratri. Kate wondered whether different approaches to dressing for the mushrooms might develop into 'different factions of mushroom worship', as arise in real-world religions.

The participants, then, made various connections between the fiction and religion. But did the fiction ever start to blur into reality? Did the enactment support a quest for meaning and the sacred? Perhaps, at a few special moments. One such moment was captured on video by Elly after her second weekly visit, when war was breaking out in Ukraine. The devastating destruction unfolding on the other side of Europe led her to seek reassurance from nature. She reported on the experience:

> I don't know if I found a profound answer to any of my worries this morning. But yeah, it's been interesting to realise that this has kind of gone beyond … just participating in this project. I genuinely felt like I was seeking some answers this morning. And I don't know if I found them, but I did find nature asking me questions about my perceptions.

Annebella, meanwhile, shared her sense of uncertainty about the potential significance of the mushroom spiritual guides:

> I shift between quite happily taking a flippant view of this activity which is completely anthropocentric and makes the mushrooms into metaphors and, on the other hand, a slightly unsettled different position, more humble but also slightly circumspect, that thinks the mushrooms might be more complex and knowledgeable (in some non-normative non-conscious way) than we mostly allow …

To conclude this reflection on spirituality in World 91, I would like to consider a recurring theme that caught my attention: *ground, soil, earth.* At the Stage 2 workshop, a participant described World 91 as 'a literally grounded world: there's so much more thought about the ground and under your feet'. Kate's Stage 3 ritual, described earlier, created a connection between her bare feet and the soil. Julie shared her own reflections about looking down:

> As I walked, I reflected on the last few weeks and how my focus on a Sunday, and really, on most of my near daily wanders with my dog, was on ground level, looking out for mushrooms. Prior to my immersion [in World 91] I think I looked more ahead. The same is probably true on a metaphorical level: I tend to always have a plan on the horizon and am seldom satisfied and content with the ground beneath my feet.

Tamar, speaking in her World 91 voice, likewise focused on the ground:

> My family have always used their footwear worn on a Saturday to channel the spirit guides. Representative of knowledge coming up through the ground and energising the soul, we reflect on

how we travelled through the week. What energies took us there. The signs noticed (the signs are always conveyed – whether you notice them is down to you). The journey this particular Saturday footwear took to reach their current destination.

This interest in the ground contrasts, in simple terms, with religions that guide our attention beyond the material realm, upwards to the heavens. It feels more at home with forms of spirituality discussed by Bron Taylor in *Dark Green Religion: Nature Spirituality and the Planetary Future*. Gaian spirituality, for example, 'understands the biosphere (universe or cosmos) to be alive or conscious'.[88] This perspective prompts a focus on connecting through the ground with the earth as a whole. Animism, meanwhile, relates to 'the perception that spiritual intelligences or lifeforces animate natural objects or living things'.[89] From this position, the soil and its inhabitants could be considered as sentient beings, animated by the same spirit as people. Robin Wall Kimmerer observes that 'In English, you are either a human or a thing'.[90] In contrast, Native American languages reflect an animist perspective. This difference in thinking affects how we act. As Kimmerer notes, 'If a maple is an it, we can take up the chain saw. If a maple is a her, we think twice'.[91]

When considering the ground-oriented ethos of World 91, I am reminded of the theme of humbleness discussed earlier in the chapter. The etymological root of the word *humble* is the Latin *humus*, meaning ground or earth.[92] To be humble is to lie low to the ground, to be with the earth. Humbleness is mentioned in Annebella's contemplation of the mushrooms quoted above, and feels present in this comment made by Elly in her World 91 voice:

> Sometimes I feel that the attention of the mycelial network is focussed elsewhere, which can make me feel insignificant or unimportant. But I think it's occasionally important to be reminded that we might be the main character in our own story, but we aren't the main character in an ecosystem.

If Fashion Fictions indicates what the community of contributors are collectively wishing for, a desire for *the humble, the earthly, the grounded* would appear to be one vital element.

＊ ＊ ＊ ＊ ＊ ＊ ＊ ＊

What might we take from the exploration and enactment of World 91? It has generated, for me, some insights about the space we make – or do not make – for other species. Enacting an ecocentric culture within the real world has brought this issue, usually hidden, into the light: the participants' experiences reveal how, in Talia's words, 'we force nature into corners and groom it within an inch of life, and how resilient the mushrooms are nevertheless'. One of the most memorable stories was a report from Annebella. Visiting a local high street full of pest control shops and beauty parlours seeking 'to add artificial gloss and to counter human decay', she noted how unwelcome the mushrooms would be – but then found the fungi thriving anyway, in the form of mould on a restaurant wall (Figure 4.15). Kate, meanwhile, gained a visceral insight into the disconnect between people and nature by taking part in the project. She reflected that although she had spent a lot of time outside as a child, she had not made time in her adult life for being in nature with no agenda. The impact she felt was profound:

> I've been finding with this project, it's been really … it's quite staggering how much it is changing the way I feel about nature and being part of nature. And how it's making me feel … making the discomfort of our disconnect from nature with fashion, more real. … [I'm] just feeling … on the cusp of something different, a different way of thinking.

My eyes have certainly been opened to the importance of understanding and respecting fungi. As Merlin Sheldrake explains, these diverse organisms 'provide a key to understanding the planet on which we live, and the ways we think, feel and behave … The more we learn about fungi, the less makes sense without them.'[93] Fungi play a crucial role in ecosystems and offer compelling new metaphors for

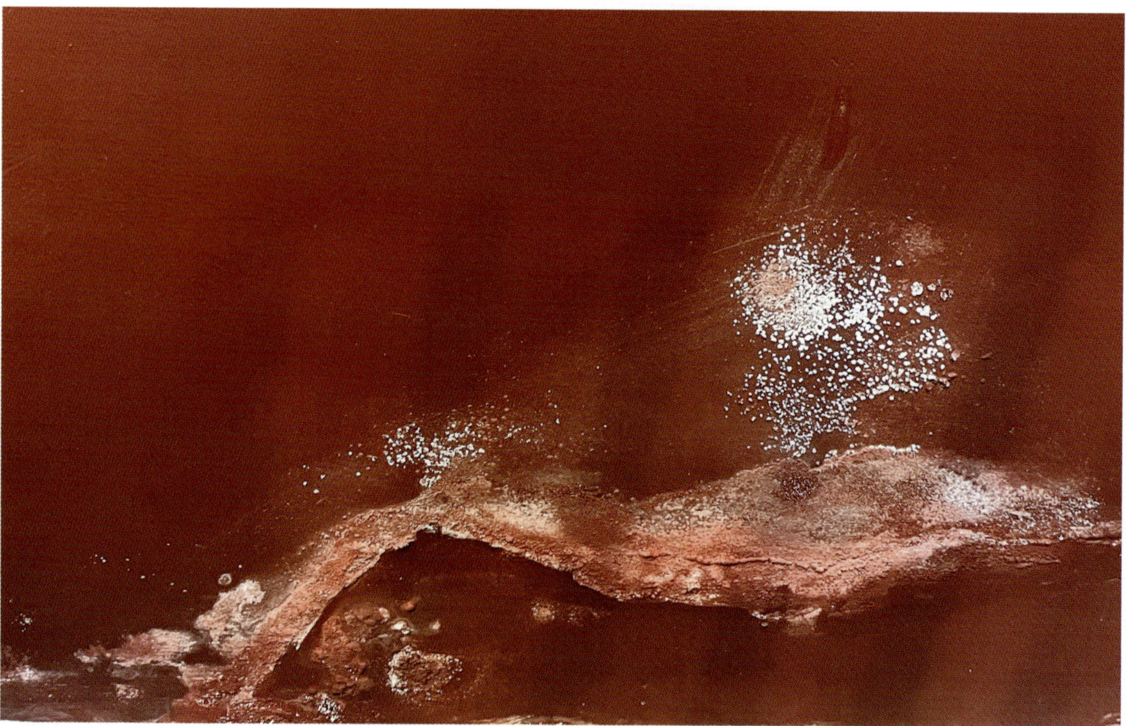

Figure 4.15 *Annebella encountered fungi in an unexpected setting, in the form of fungal blooms on a restaurant wall.*

understanding the social world – including the fashion system. As agents of interspecies connection, they feel particularly ripe with insights about human/nonhuman communities finding ways to live together, as discussed earlier in the chapter. Anna Lowenhaupt Tsing's book *The Mushroom at the End of the World* is valuable in exploring these ideas more deeply. Tsing explores the 'interspecies entanglements' of matsutake, a highly sought-after mushroom that grows in human-disturbed forests, to build an understanding of how we might live in a deeply uncertain post-nature world.[94] Given their role in decay and decomposition, fungi could also help us to think about deconstructing the mainstream fashion system. What systems and mindsets do we want to decompose? How could we break them down from the inside? Could we create new habitats for other species in the process, as fungi do when breaking down a dying tree?

While we have much to learn from fungi, there is danger in lazy interpretations. As an illustration, we can consider the fungi-inspired Alexander McQueen autumn/winter 2022 collection. Taking inspiration from the ecological role of mycelium, designer Sarah Burton described the collection as a celebration of 'community and interconnectedness'.[95] Yet the influence was purely conceptual: no mycelial materials were used, leaving the collection open to allegations of greenwashing – or, perhaps, mushroom-washing. As Annebella suggested, it could be described as 'a new mycelial spin on commodity fetishism'. Furthermore, Burton's framing is rather romantic. In notes accompanying the catwalk show, she described mycelium as 'a magical underground structure, allowing trees to reach out to each other when either they or their young need help or are sick'.[96] Mycorrhizal networks do indeed allow plants to share resources, but the interactions are far more complex than Burton's words indicate. The networks facilitate competition as well as cooperation, and the distribution of poisons as well as nutrients.[97] As Merlin Sheldrake explains, we frequently fall into the trap of projecting human values onto nonhuman systems; symbiotic relationships such as those between plants and fungi act 'like a prism through which our own social values are often dispersed'.[98]

The tendency to think of mycelial networks as altruistic is as problematic as the notion of nature as sacred, which underpins much environmental thought. Both restrict our thinking. They prevent us from fully engaging with the weirder, darker, more mixed-up realities in which we rub along with each other and our nonhuman kin. Merlin Sheldrake challenges us to understand ecosystems on their own terms, without projection: 'Are we able to stand back, look at the system, and let the polyphonic swarms of plains and fungi and bacteria that make up our homes and our worlds be themselves, and quite *unlike* anything else? What would that do to our minds?'[99]

Activity 4.1: Take action – meet the mushrooms

This activity invites you to experience **World 91**, in which mushrooms are hailed as spiritual guides, via the enactment discussed in the chapter (see page 106).[100] You are invited to present yourself to the mushrooms, once a week, for six weeks; you can do this individually or alongside others.

1. For your first visit, decide how to dress to present yourself to the mushrooms. Don't buy anything new – use what's already in your wardrobe. What do you think the mushrooms want to see? There are no right or wrong answers!

2. Locate some mushrooms. You might need to hunt a little: wild areas with fallen trees are a good place to look. If you struggle to find any visible mushrooms, find a place where you can think about mycelial networks hidden in the soil.

3. Present yourself to the mushrooms! It's up to you whether your visit is brief or lingering, and what 'presenting yourself' will involve. You might want to reflect on cycles of decay and regeneration.

4. If you wish, record your experiences in some way. You might want to record your experiences as yourself in the real world, or 'in character', i.e. as the World 91 version of yourself.

5. Repeat the previous steps every week for six weeks. Your approach to dressing and presenting yourself might evolve over the weeks, or it might stay the same.

6. After you have completed your six-week taster of World 91, take some time to reflect on the experience (see Activity 2.4).

Figure 4.16 *When considering how to dress for the mushrooms, you might focus on your entire outfit or a particular detail. Explore the potential in your wardrobe, and your surroundings.*

Figure 4.17 *Students at Universidad de los Andes in Colombia participated in an enactment adapted from the World 91 recipe. They were invited to select a 'being' or aspect of nature – tree, flower, river, sky – to spend time with and then reflect on the experience through writing, drawing, audio recording or photography.*[101]

Fashion and spirituality

Spirituality in fashion, as expressed in the visions generated for the Fashion Fictions project, extends far beyond the ecocentric culture of World 91. In the Stage 2 explorations of **World 12** and **World 27** featured in Chapter 3, for example (see Figure 3.9 and page 60), clothes were described as 'sacred' and 'talismanic'. These passing mentions reflect an awareness of deep connections between dress and spirituality in the real world. Consider the 'no frills' dress of Christian Anabaptist communities such as the Amish,[102] the yarmulke worn by Jewish men[103] or the robes worn by Buddhist monks and nuns.[104] These varied items give just a taste of the countless ways that people adorn, cover and reveal their bodies as part of their religion. Lynne Hume summarizes the diversity of the meanings of dress in this context:

> when it is coupled to religious beliefs, dress itself becomes a sacred item, a statement of ideologies and mores, a contestation of power, a reflection of the spirit world, an active agent in transformation,

an access to the supernatural and even a form of punishment. It can be a bridge between the world of the living and the world of the dead.[105]

Clothes can be used to signify adherence to a particular religious belief or rebellion against it;[106] they can distinguish between the sacred and the profane.[107] They can also be used as a tool of violence, such as in the forced conversion of Indigenous people to the religious practices of colonizers and the control of female sexuality by men exercising patriarchal power in the name of religion.[108] Given the significance of these varied and powerful connections, it is notable that there are almost no references to specific religions – as opposed to spirituality more generally – in the Stage 1 worlds. The only exceptions are **World 248**, in which Buddhist principles shape fashion practice and wider society,[109] and **World 128**, which mentions 'ShamanWear' as part of a world 're-centered on prior and current global shamanic material culture practices to pursue wonder, insight, and multi-generational design processes'.[110] Shamanism is an ancient form of religion,[111] encountered in societies across the Arctic, Asia, Oceania and America.[112] Within these societies, shamans are believed to have the power to heal the sick and to communicate with the world beyond;[113] shamanic dress varies from culture to culture, but often plays an important role.[114] Western interest in shamanism developed in the second half of the twentieth century and continues today.[115] Native American spiritual practices in particular have appealed to environmentalists for decades, as they seek to learn how to live in harmony with nature. The situation has become highly contentious: while, as Bron Taylor notes, cross-cultural exchange can be positive, the appropriation of Indigenous spirituality without proper attribution or understanding ultimately represents a continuation of extractive colonial practices.[116]

Making and repair, as well as practices of dressing, can form part of the expression of religion. Edwina Ehrman, for example, describes how the thrifty reuse of garments was widespread in Europe until well into the twentieth century, because 'to be wasteful was against the laws of God and nature'.[117] Several of the Stage 1 fictions highlight making as a spiritual practice. In **World 10**, for example:

> creativism is akin to a world religion and making by hand is a quasi-devotional act … Making your own clothes is regarded as an act of observance, a communing with materials and ancient knowledge, and a path to 'enlightenment'.[118]

The notion of hand stitching as a spiritual act is reminiscent of practices linked to the making of monks' robes in some real-world lineages of Buddhism: sacred texts specify that a bowing gesture or incantation should accompany every stitch.[119] The **World 132** fiction, which was influenced by the life and work of British self-taught artist and medium Madge Gill, takes a more open-ended approach to spirituality and making:

Figure 4.18 *This prototype presents an alternative vision of World 152 to that shown in Figure 1.7. In this interpretation, daily gratitude to clothing is commonplace. Found in homes on personal clothing altars and in community making spaces, the device – akin to a sundial – honours the collective energies of the universe and acknowledges that all garments are sacred.*

Clothing manufacture begins healing. High speeds of hand stitching enable trance-like states. Spiritual guidance requested from imaginary worlds is received through the work, and manifested in automatic embroidery on free-willed clothing shapes.[120]

* * * * * * * * *

The Stage 2 exploration of **World 45** offers a final case study for this chapter, and a valuable opportunity to consider in more depth a fictional vision that connects spirituality and clothing. I wrote the original fiction:

In World 45, window coverings – rather than personal wardrobes – are the focus of fashion. Since the development of power looms in the Industrial Revolution, people have been superstitious about cutting newly woven cloth; consequently, all textiles are initially used as curtains. It is considered bad luck to make a curtain into garments or other items until it has been hung for at least a year.[121]

World 45 was picked up by a group of three participants in a Stage 2 workshop.[122] Under their stewardship, the world's superstition grew into a sense of spirituality. The group initially toyed with ideas that referenced organized religion: they discussed weavers' homes as temples and the weavers themselves as revered, even 'God-given' figures. Inspired by long-established rites, they wondered whether new fabrics would be created to mark key events such as birth, marriage and death. These ideas receded as a more distinctive interpretation of World 45 spirituality unfolded. In this interpretation, fabric became 'a material which represents your spiritual wellbeing'. As group member Gautham explained at one point: 'We were thinking of the fabric as a medium of spirituality, where they imagine the whole world … We could see the materiality of objects, especially fabric, to understand ourselves.' The group saw the culture as spiritual rather than religious, with 'no imposed institutionalism', and inherently inclusive: 'I mean, everyone needs clothes'.

The group outlined a set of spiritual practices linked to the hanging and cutting of the curtain, which – in a further reference to real-world religious practices – they described as 'baptism'. When the curtain is hung, a ritual is carried out to give thanks for the precious cloth: 'You take a sample of the material and, depending on what feels right, you might set fire to it, float it away, bury it.' The spirituality of World 45, as well as being material-focused, is nature-oriented – hence the ritual offering to soil, water, wind, fire or light. After a year, a second ritual marks the transition of curtain into garment. At this event, the household reflects on the past year and discusses how the curtain cloth will be used. This event is clearly spiritual, as well as practical. As Rachael, another member of the group, described, the family members 'let everything that the curtain has witnessed over the last year move into the past, and then allow for the creative potential of the household to just give thanks for what it's about to receive'.

There was a sense in the group's discussions that the curtains were, to some extent, sentient. An early conversation was influenced by *The Book of Form and Emptiness*, a novel by Ruth Ozeki in which objects can express emotion. Carrying this animist idea into World 45, the group wondered whether a fabric not ready to be cut might make a noise when approached with the scissors, or a fabric made into an inappropriate item might respond by coming to pieces. While the notion of the vocal and active curtain receded as the world-building process continued, the idea that the textile would observe and even care for life within the household remained: 'You want a curtain that can look out for you and understands the place it's in.' The cutting of the fabric represents a shift in form and nature, which the group saw as a material rite of passage: the fabric 'grows up, in a sense'.

The two rituals – hanging and cutting – interconnect. In the period preceding the sacred cutting of one curtain, there is discussion not only about the use of that cloth, but also about the ideal fabric, colour and pattern of the replacement curtain, with consideration for the materials that will be needed for clothing in a year's time. The Stage 2 group felt that this could be a difficult process, with the collective decisions requiring trust within the household. There may be conflicting ideas about how the fabric should be used, and some people may find it easier to envisage the possibilities than others. The group saw a role for a 'baptism expert' who comes to the home and helps with the rituals, resolving tensions by facilitating positive choices about the design and use of the cloth. The expert also supports the creation of visual material that links the two ceremonies. The offering of the sample to nature is documented as a short film clip in the first ritual. The clip is automatically sent as a digital notification to the phones of the household after a year, to mark the start of the second ritual (Figure 4.19).

Another element of the curtain rituals constructed by the Stage 2 group was the family dictionary, which is handed down from generation to generation (Figure 4.20). As they explained: 'This volume is used to aid expressive conversations, as the household plans their transformation of curtain fabric into clothes, and to replace the curtain. The dictionary contains a rich language to describe the material and spiritual qualities of transformation.'

The group created the dictionary as one of their prototypes, alongside a collection of digital notifications. Perhaps influenced by the French–English dictionary that they used as the basis of their prototype, the book provides two-way translation between material and spiritual dimensions. An interest in language, as discussed in Chapter 3, is here extended into the material and visual realm. The group felt that each family's copy of the dictionary would evolve over time, with notes and memories

Figure 4.19 *Still from a Transformation Notification Gif, created in World 45 when a new curtain is hung and sent to the phones of the household after one year to indicate that the fabric is ready to be cut into new clothing.*

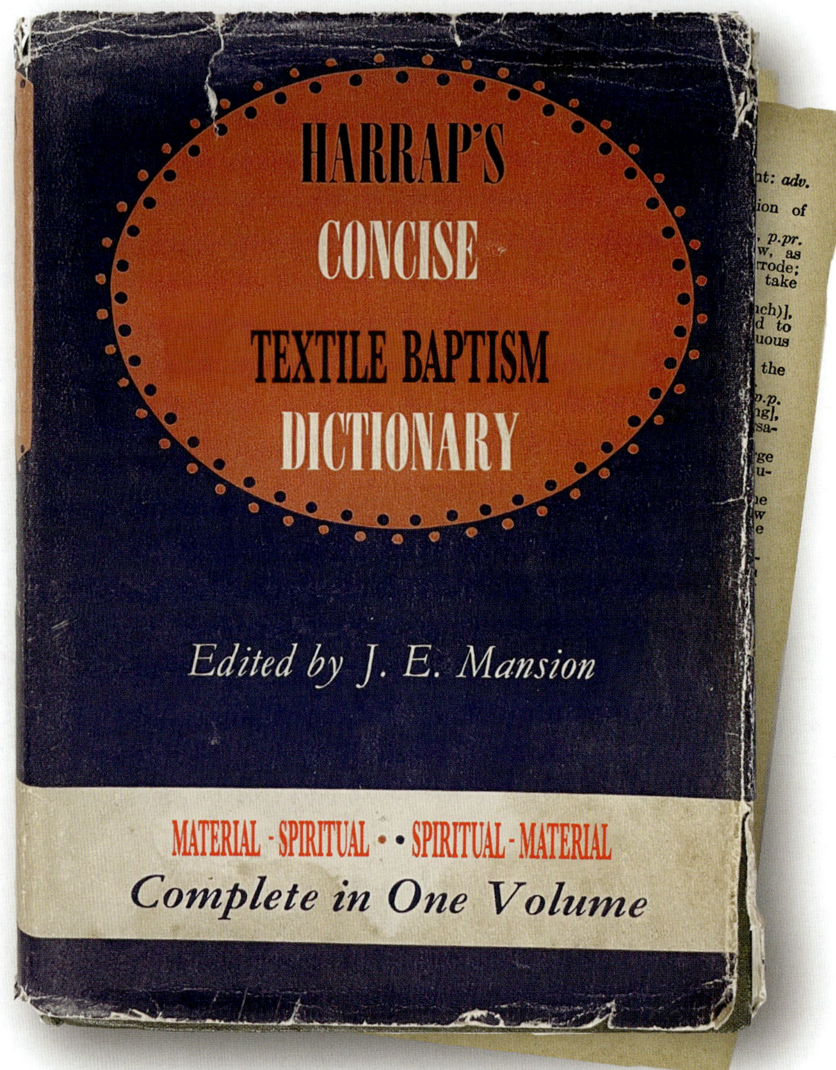

Figure 4.20 *The* Textile Baptism Dictionary (Material–Spiritual / Spiritual–Material) *contains detailed knowledge about the spiritual dimensions of fabric in World 45. Notes and alterations are added to each family's copy over time to ensure the positive growth of the household over generations.*

being documented and new interpretations and ideas emerging. Their discussion gave an enticing glimpse into the nature of the specialist knowledge embedded in World 45 culture:

> There's a lot of in this psychology in the dictionaries, an awful lot about the mathematical patterns that happen in repeat patterns in curtains, and how they relate to different parts of our soul. And some of us can handle polka dots and some can't. All of that is definitely a much more developed language that they can just talk about.

It is evident that the spiritual dimension of World 45 culture shapes every aspect of its clothing-related practices. If we compare the world to our own mainstream fashion system, fashion occupies a very different position, bound up within spirituality rather than a capitalist economy. Interestingly, similar ideas about the influence of spirituality on the material aspects of fashion arose in the Stage 2 exploration of fungi-centric **World 91**. Elly compared the group's vision of World 91 with her real-world experiences:

> I found it really interesting … to think about the idea of a spirituality that informs your global choices in a way your clothes are made. Because I don't consider myself religious, and so a belief system is not in any way … well I suppose a belief system is involved in a slight way, in the way that I buy my clothes, trying to shop ethically and sustainably, and I don't buy from high street stores … going from that, which is very much like fiddling around the edges of the current system, [to] suddenly this spirituality is part of the manufacturing process, the buying process and the wearing process.

The distinction that Elly makes is crucial. In the mainstream globalized fashion system we are directed to express our ideas, even spiritual ideas, through our consumer choices. The visions of Worlds 91 and 45 are different: not an ethical set of options sitting within a wider culture, but rather a widespread, even universal, spiritual knowledge that underpins everyday fashion practice. These visions speak to the concept of 'dressing deeply' proposed by Otto von Busch and Jeanine Viau in their book *Silhouettes of the Soul*, where fashion is understood 'not as a cover but as a membrane between imaginal realities, surface and depth, body and soul, temporal and contextual domains of aspiration and devotion'.[123]

* * * * * * * *

What drives the interest in spirituality that can be identified across many Fashion Fictions worlds? I see three potential reasons. The first is that our fictions are shaped by contributors' interests – and particularly those that they might not have space to fully express in the real world. Given the recent rise of interest in spirituality, it is hardly surprising that this dimension of human experience has found its way into the collective imaginings. The second reason is that spirituality is a useful narrative tool in envisioning unfamiliar cultures. A belief system shapes what is acceptable and what is taboo: as creators of worlds, it gives us a warrant to frame specific practices and attitudes as being unquestionably normal – even those that would be ridiculed in the real world. The third and final reason is because, I suspect, people are yearning, whether consciously or unconsciously, for a different way of approaching sustainability in the fashion realm. Industrial sustainable fashion initiatives have taken a technical path: the substitution of one material for another, the use of blockchain technology to aid transparency in the supply chain, the development of recycling technologies to tackle the 'monstrous hybrids' of blended-fibre fabrics.[124] Fictions that focus on spirituality, whether linked to the awe of the natural world or another source of the sacred, challenge this dominant culture. They bring emotion, instinct and desire into play and create powerful new spaces for the imagination.

Interest in spirituality, then, is strong – but it would be a mistake to assume that Fashion Fictions contributors wish to bring these forms of spirituality directly into the real world. In reflective discussions following the workshops and enactments, I have heard time and time again that the participants would not like to actually live in the worlds they have explored together; none offer a straightforward solution or blueprint for the ideal fashion system. The value of the speculations lies not in the outcome, but the process: not in the beliefs that are imagined, but in the fact that a different belief system can be imagined at all. Each vision helps to push at the boundaries of the thinkable, to dislodge our minds from the comfort of familiar structures, and thereby to expand the possibilities for real-world action.

Nature and spirituality: ideas for the real world

From the diverse ideas and visions relating to fashion, nature and spirituality, five themes feel ripe for investigation:

1 Humbleness

How can we embrace humbleness, both in our fashion systems and as a species more generally? What would it mean to design, make, wear, care for and dispose of our clothes in an earthly, grounded, humble way?

2 Time

How can we reconnect fashion with the time and rhythms of the biosphere, whether the earth's seasonal cycles, the rhythms of our bodies or the time required to grow, harvest, process and decompose the materials used in our clothes?

3 Multi-species life

How can we learn to embrace the hybrid, complex and uncertain post-nature age in which we are living? How can we live in community with other species? How could fashion enable us to connect with other living things?

4 Decomposition

If we were to take inspiration from natural systems, we would think about decomposition as much as growth. What systems, mindsets and institutions do we need to decompose? How can we break them down and what new habitats could we create along the way?

5 Spirituality

How could spiritual thinking infuse our fashion practices? What different modes of thinking and being can we draw into the frame of fashion and sustainability? What if spirituality and materiality were deeply entwined?

* * * * * * * * *

There is much for us to explore together. But we must be wary of seeing nature and spirituality as convenient routes to more considered consumption, for there are many potential pitfalls we may encounter. Here are three to consider:

Dualism

Modernity/coloniality thrives on dualistic thinking, such as the separation of humans and nature. This separation underpins both the dream of mastery and the dream of naturalism, and can lead us to think of nature as sacred and humans as poisonous. These ideas stop us from fully engaging with a complex, hybrid, uncertain world and limit our ability to find ways of living that enable all species to thrive.

Extraction and projection

In our search for new ways of thinking about humans and the natural world, we often seek to learn from the spiritualities of cultures other than our own. While these cultures may have much to teach others, there is a danger of harmful appropriation if practices and ideas are taken without proper attribution or understanding. On a related note, the tendency to project human values onto natural systems prevents us from learning deeper (and perhaps weirder) lessons from our nonhuman kin.

Commercialization

The fashion industry, like capitalist business more generally, is adept at commercializing ideas that emerge in the margins, neutralizing their transformative potential. Indeed, the contemporary enthusiasm for spirituality is often manifested in new consumer products, rather than non-consumerist practices. How can we connect nature and spirituality with our fashion systems while evading this process? How can we nurture life at the margins?

NEW YORK
PARIS
MILAN
LONDON
17
S/S
A/W

5

Place and togetherness

Locations and localism

As I write, my gaze occasionally wanders from my computer screen. It typically falls upon a flat-roofed edifice visible from my window that today houses a bed and sofa shop – but was, I recently discovered, a dress factory in decades past. Intrigued, I checked the archives of the *Nottingham Post* and found job advertisements: for experienced dress machinists to work the factory's evening shift in 1951; for a manageress in 1966; for lockstitchers, overlockers, examiners, folders and pressers in 1974. The business survived until the early years of this century, following a period in which garment manufacture in Nottingham – a city built upon the textile trade – rapidly declined.[1] The only remaining trace of the factory's activity is the company's garments that circulate on eBay and Vinted. This story, replicated across the city and in many other former centres of garment manufacture in the global North, is a microcosm of the shifts in the geographies of fashion that have unfolded in recent decades, since production started to shift offshore in the 1970s and 1980s.

In comparison with heavier forms of manufacturing, garment production is mobile: there are low barriers to entry in terms of workforce training and the installation of equipment, meaning that factories can be set up in new locations with relative ease. In the US in the late nineteenth and early twentieth centuries, textile and garment production shifted from mills and factories in the northeast to new locations in the southern states, to take advantage of lower labour costs and a lack of trade union representation.[2] A 1925 publication discussed the trend of manufacturers leaving New York: 'The chief motive for moving … is the desire to escape from the union, and to secure cheap and docile labor'.[3] These motives remained relevant later in the twentieth century, when the clothing industries became the first 'to take on a global dimension'.[4] In fact, insiders have observed that the fashion

Figure 5.1 *The real-world dominance of fashion weeks, air travel and globalized production contrasts sharply with the grassroots culture of World 17, in which sewing is enthusiastically embraced by young men.*

industry 'follows poverty', readily shifting 'from Latin America to China, to Bangladesh – wherever costs are lowest'.[5]

For several decades, the Multi-Fibre Arrangement (MFA) regulated world trade in textiles and clothing. Set up in 1973, this international agreement set limits on the quantity of textile goods that could be exported from one country to another and aimed to balance the interests of countries with established garment industries and those in which industries were developing. Peter Dicken explains that the MFA's 'provisions and their implementation – and their avoidance – were major factors in redrawing the global map of these industries'.[6] In 2005 the MFA was abolished; with import quotas no longer imposed, trade in clothing and textiles opened up. In the following years, production increased significantly in the countries that are familiar today as major clothing exporters.[7]

Another crucial factor in the growth of globalized trade was the introduction of the shipping container in the 1950s. Before this point, the transport of goods was expensive and complicated; as Marc Levinson explains, 'the world was full of small manufacturers selling locally'.[8] The container, which came to dominate in the following decades, made shipping incredibly cheap and highly efficient. By the start of the twenty-first century, Levinson continues, 'purely local markets for goods of any sort were few and far between'.[9] As a result of this shift, supply chains – particularly in the fashion and textile industry – have grown longer and more complex. The process of turning fibre into yarn, then into fabric, then into garment, and finally transporting the finished item to the retail store, often involves multiple journeys totalling thousands of miles.[10] The shipping container made these journeys possible. As Levinson argues, it 'changed the shape of the world economy'.[11]

The fashion system, then, is global; its supply chains form networks that span the world. These networks intersect with those that connect 'fashion cities': urban centres recognized as hubs of fashion business, media, culture and commerce, including the influential locations of Paris, New York, London, Milan and Tokyo alongside others including Antwerp, Kuwait City, São Paulo, Melbourne, Shanghai, Cape Town, Mumbai and Copenhagen.[12] Christopher Breward explains that, in recent decades, the notion of the 'fashion city' has been used 'as a form of protectionism, as a promotional tool, or as a mechanism for rebranding and regeneration'; in the twenty-first century, these cities have increasingly been portrayed as aspirational shopping destinations.[13] Yet the connection between fashion and the urban environment runs much deeper than the fashion city notion might suggest. In fact, the development of the entire Western fashion system is bound up with urbanization and the experience of modernity, of seeing and being seen in the bustle of the metropolis. Breward traces these connections back as far as the fourteenth, fifteenth and sixteenth centuries, arguing that European cities during this period 'offered spaces where crowds might congregate, classes of people intermingle, and individuals compete for attention through the modishness of their attire'. As he summarizes, 'To be fashionable was to be urban and vice versa'.[14] Fashion theorist Elizabeth Wilson also discusses the relationship between fashion and the city, drawing on the work of German sociologist Georg

Simmel. At the start of the twentieth century, Simmel wrote about the shift from rural to urban life, arguing that the chaos and social complexity of the city led to a growing emphasis on the individual. In the urban environment, Wilson explains, 'the individual constantly interacts with others who are strangers, and survives by the manipulation of self. Fashion is one adjunct to this self-presentation and manipulation. It is the imposition of this newly found self on a brutally indifferent and constantly fluctuating environment.'[15]

Intriguingly, the longstanding connection between Western fashion and the city is not replicated in Fashion Fictions: the expressions of location in the fictions, prototypes and enactments are much more diverse. When I created the interactive world generator, which people can use to create a skeleton outline of a fictional fashion system by exploring combinations of pre-written phrases (see Figure 2.2), I created one element of the text to describe where the fiction is set – and included *mountain, forest and island wildernesses* and *one ostensibly sleepy village* alongside *a notably cosmopolitan city*. Further options suggest larger geographical regions, from *one forward-looking nation* to *countries across the world*. This non-specific phrasing is echoed in many of the Stage 1 fictions submitted to the project: they take place in, simply, 'a country': somewhere with a sense of place but no specific location. With no further clues, we might assume that it is the country with which the writer is most familiar – or interpret it within our own cultural context.

Plenty of Stage 1 fictions, though, are placed in particular locations – from Denmark[16] to Rwanda[17] to the Middle East.[18] (Some world-writers even invent a new place in which to situate their fiction. In **World 92**, for example, a small land mass drifts off the coast of Northern Scotland for 500 years; forgotten by those on the mainland, the community develops great expertise in textile mending and remaking which is then shared when their floating home is rediscovered in the 1970s.[19]) Stage 2 prototypes, too, are often situated in specific places. Contributors Nobukhosi Ncube and Nancy Coulson, for example, grounded their interpretation of the **World 36** fiction – in which mending studios are widespread[20] – in Johannesburg, where they are based.[21] Several of the groups at the Stage 2 workshops in Nottingham chose to locate their prototypes in parallel-world versions of the city, including that shown in Figure 5.2.

Regarding Stage 3, my overwhelming sense is that the fictions are situated wherever the enactment is happening. That might seem obvious: *things happen where they happen* is hardly headline news. Yet given that the Stage 3 enactments are, essentially, a game of let's pretend, the pretending *could* have extended to an imagined location. But in the enactments I have organized, the participants have focused firmly on the here and now of what they are doing. The wood, wasteland or rehearsal room in which the action is happening is, for the duration of the enactment at least, as much a centre of fashion as anywhere else. This embrace of diverse fashion places resonates with the Fashion Ecologies project led by Kate Fletcher, which explored the potential for fashion culture grounded in localism (Figure 5.3). As Fletcher notes, 'Everything happens somewhere. The fashion industry is often

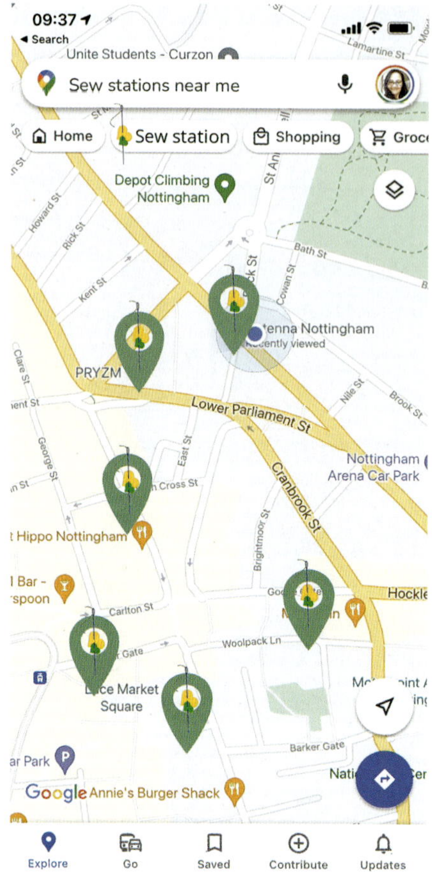

Figure 5.2 *In World 50, people exchange sewn signatures on their clothing as a sign of connection. The group who explored this world at Stage 2 imagined 'sew stations' that would provide space and supplies for this process. Their Google Map shows the sew stations in Nottingham city centre.*

described as a global sector. Yet this overlooks the fact that the one fashion experience that we all have in common – the wearing and maintaining of clothes – takes place locally.'[22]

* * * * * * * * *

Many fictions focus not on particular places but rather on connections between locations, imagining altered patterns of trade. One common fantasy is the termination of all global supply chains in the fashion and textile industry: a cancellation of the highly efficient transportation networks that have been established in the last fifty years. A companion fantasy is the radical re-localization of production, from fibre through to garment. On the surface, this idea connects with real-world interest in 'reshoring': moving production to the country in which the goods will be offered for sale. Yet

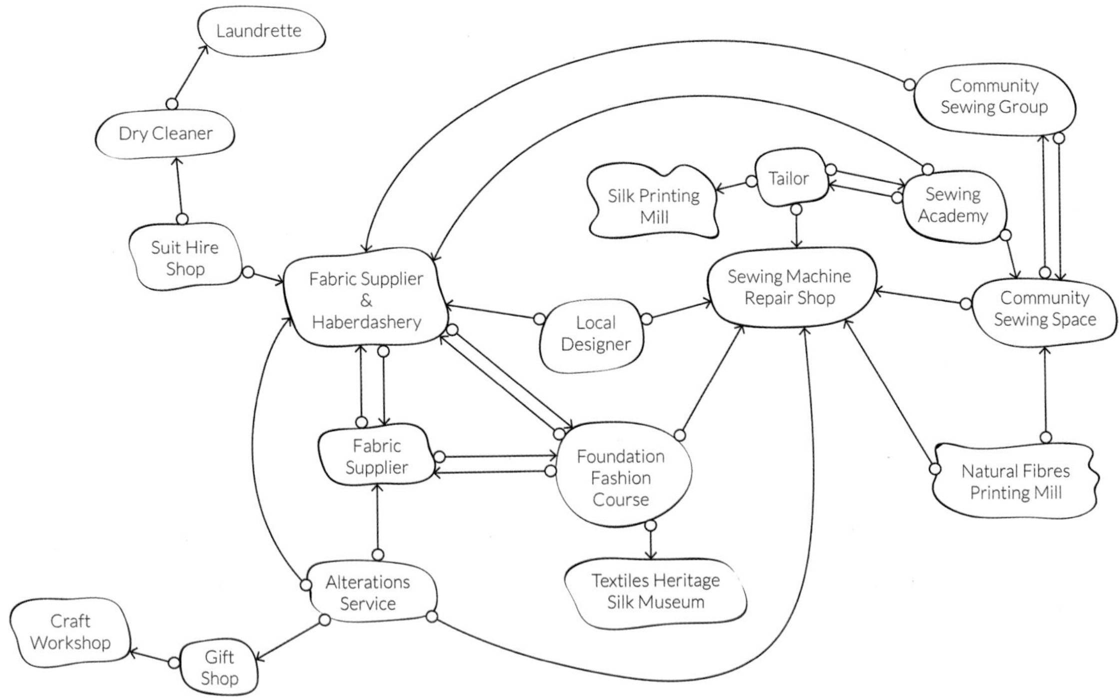

Figure 5.3 *The Fashion Ecologies project investigated the fashion landscape in Macclesfield, a town in the north of England. Part of this research involved mapping social assets associated with the creation, maintenance and use of clothing, as shown here. Kate Fletcher, who led the project, notes that these social assets typically rely on personal relationships and self-created networks – in contrast to the town's chain-store fashion retailers, which benefit from formal infrastructural support.*

reshoring is typically driven by a need to reduce lead times in order for brands to remain competitive in an ever-more frenetic industry.[23] The tone of the fictional worlds is very different, connecting much more with Fibershed's regional 'soil-to-skin' textile systems and ethos of respect for natural cycles and cultural change, discussed in Chapter 4.[24] In **World 175**, for example, 'bioregional fibres [are] grown in regenerative mixed farming systems',[25] while in the Mexico City of **World 76**, an initiative to make genderless school uniforms from locally grown undyed cotton is recognized as 'a dignifying moment for [the] Mexican population and its indigenous identity'.[26]

In some of the fictions, the interest in localized production is channelled into alternative materials: in **World 53**, 'programmable biological cultures' are used to grow clothes at home or in local 'material-makeries'.[27] Dyestuffs, too, form part of localized fashion systems. We have already encountered **World 28**, in which natural dyeing is widespread, in Chapter 4. Rachel, one of the duo exploring the world at a Stage 2 workshop, described the world's culture: 'What you eat and what colours of clothing you wear depends on what you can grow in your area … [it] creates quite different cultural identities … everyone just celebrates the local of where they're all from.'

In this description of life in World 28 I perceive a rejection of the homogenization and erosion of place that is readily perceived in contemporary society. Geographer Tim Cresswell connects this homogenization to mass communication, mass culture and mass production.[28] It is evident in fast food outlets and airports – and even in the independent cafes that, regardless of their global location, abide by a consistent hipster aesthetic.[29] Such placelessness can also be observed in the high-street shops that peddle the goods manufactured by the globalized supply chains of the fashion system. As Cresswell notes, 'These are spaces that seem detached from the local environment and tell us nothing about the particular locality in which they are located.'[30] Placelessness is countered by local distinctiveness, the quality that Sue Clifford and Angela King propose 'makes each place unique … the conspiracy of nature and culture; the accumulation of story upon history upon natural history'.[31] As they explain, local distinctiveness – whether notable or mundane – is crucial for place-based identity:

> The unusual, the special, the idiosyncratic or the rare may be important factors in giving a place a sense of itself – the fortifications, the football team, the fritillaries, the fair. But identity is not bound up only in the symbolism of features and festivals. It is the commonplace that defines – the locally abundant plants, the specific wall-building methods, the accents and dialects – the context that exerts the binding force.[32]

Several of the fictions that focus on localized production describe locally distinctive garment styles. In **World 42**, for example, a growing interest in environmental transparency and provenance leads to the rejection of mass production and the emergence of a system in which each neighbourhood produces its own 'base-line' garment type to be customized by wearers, creating an 'ever-evolving … hyper-local vernacular'.[33] In **World 250**, regional styles flourish in the absence of the internet.[34] In the Stage 2 interpretation of **World 124** discussed in Chapter 4 (see page 98), the group envisioned the wool from each urban sheep herd being used to create a locally distinctive style – 'so there might be the Glasgow jacket, or the Nottingham shirt, or whatever it is'. Both fibre and garment thus offer a sense of place – supported by the development of folk cultures surrounding the fibre and garment-making practices. Inspired by the songs that have traditionally been sung to accompany the repetitive physical task of 'waulking' (shrinking) tweed in the Outer Hebrides,[35] the group imagined the emergence of music genres influenced by the new obsession for sheep.

In the two worlds just discussed, the garment designs are newly developed; in others, locally distinctive styles build on long traditions. This was the case in the version of **World 12** created by Nada Koreish (represented in the magazine cover shown in Figure 3.9). Her vision is located in a North Africa that has not been subject to European colonization, enabling the flourishing of a culture in which traditional styles, patterns and techniques linked to particular regions are celebrated and constantly renewed. As she developed her ideas, Nada discussed the stigma regarding traditional clothing that she has observed – and experienced – in the real world. She noted that some would perceive people wearing styles rooted in the traditions of North Africa as 'backward', somehow not fully connected with contemporary life – particularly in a professional setting. This perception, while offensive and short-sighted, reflects a long history of dress being used as a tool of colonialism – and the complex and multi-layered responses that this practice has provoked, including adoption, adaptation, subversion and resistance.[36] As Carla Jones and Ann Marie Leshkowich note, 'colonial discourse and domination linked dress to specific kinds of meanings, meanings that continue to circulate in the contemporary era'.[37] Indeed, these meanings are so entrenched that imagining a world in which localized dress styles have been able to evolve and intermingle without the violence of colonialism is both challenging and radical.

In Nada's fictional vision and in various other Fashion Fictions, the desire to connect with tradition is portrayed in a positive way. It is important to acknowledge, however, that – as Alison Goodrum observes – the 'search for roots and familiarity … is itself not an entirely unproblematic contention'.[38] She notes that attempts to connect with tradition, in the fashion industry and beyond, have a tendency to utilize a version of history that is bourgeois, restrictive, regressive, sentimental and exclusionary, leading to the 'caricaturing of local cultures'.[39] Interestingly, the fictions created for the project that focus on local distinctiveness tend to take a different path: they emphasize inclusiveness, with styles evolving through cross-cultural exchange, and often focus on practice and process rather than aesthetics.

For a final example of localized clothing production, let us return for a moment to the reimagining of trade routes. **World 41** offers an alternative take on this notion by describing a worldwide ban on the importing of secondhand clothes.[40] This challenge to widespread practices of waste colonialism[41] is reminiscent of the East African Community trade bloc, which in 2016 recommended banning imports of used apparel – at that point valued at $151 million per year for the region – in order to stimulate the local textile industry.[42] For those countries that have been exporting huge quantities of discarded garments, such a shift would require a rapid reckoning with the reality of this waste stream. In the fictional World 41 clothes are cut into usable components, leading to the emergence of a vibrant spare parts trade. I have written in the past about the enticing prospect that local waste might provide its own sense of local distinctiveness.[43] I see this as a version of the concept of *terroir*: the specific environmental conditions that give a wine created in a particular place and in a particular year its characteristic taste. Could the unique characteristics of waste arising in a particular place be seen as a type of *terroir*, reflecting the practices of making and use taking place there?

In another set of worlds it is the localized *choice* of clothing, rather than its manufacture, that is placed in the foreground. The **World 183** fiction, for example, describes the distinctive stylings and idiosyncratic fashion practices of people in the English county of Yorkshire.[44] In **World 5**, meanwhile, an organized system generates aesthetic variation from place to place: a standardized garment range

Figure 5.4 *Artist Rachael Matthews works with waste textiles in her project Rag School.*[45] *This piece of weaving reflects the waste generated on one specific road in East London: heavy-duty printed bags from an upmarket Indian takeaway and discarded t-shirts, left on the pavement by users of the nearby gym.*

was introduced by the government, with designs selected by public vote on a town-by-town basis. The ranges available in different regions have consequently diverged, creating local distinctiveness.[46] Another fiction, **World 99**, focuses on a local community that acts to prevent the unauthorized sharing of their local sense of style:

In 1980s New York, libraries loaned out cameras and audio recording technologies and public tv sponsored young cool people to share what they saw on their streets. This brought the blood-sucking activities of 1990s 'coolhunters' to the attention of the whole community. Rotting fruit was thrown at them as they cruised into the neighbourhoods, staining their threads and vilifying them as the thieves they were. Corporate brands could be fined for using such tactics, along with guerrilla/stealth marketing. Small local notions of cool dress flourish.[47]

The New Yorkers of World 99 were able to drive off the 'blood-sucking' coolhunters who sought to steal the community's distinctive ways of dressing. But in the real-world fashion system, visual markers of local distinctiveness are highly susceptible to appropriation by trendspotters, designers and stylists: professionals who pick things up and feed them into the mainstream system. Some cases of appropriation focus on a specific item. In 2015, for example, fashion label KTZ was accused by Salome Awa of replicating a traditional Inuit garment worn by her great-grandfather, a shaman, without permission.[48] Awa described the reproduction of the garment's distinctive design, which had been documented in a 1922 photograph, as 'almost like (a) mockery of my great-grandfather's spiritual well-being'.[49]

In other cases, appropriation extends to multiple visual and material elements of a particular culture. Consider, for example, the global 1990s trend for adopting styles from Asian cultures, which was embraced by fashion elites and celebrities.[50] Sociologist Nirmal Puwar frames this trend as an expression of multicultural capitalism: 'capitalism based on the production and consumption of cultural diversity and the marketing of packaged versions of the "exotic"'.[51] She articulates the impact of this appropriation on South Asian women, describing 'the rage induced by the power of whiteness to play with "ethnic" items which had not so long ago been reviled'.[52] Writer Jarune Uwujaren similarly highlights issues of power and privilege: 'One of the reasons that cultural appropriation is a hard concept to grasp for so many is that Westerners are used to pressing their own culture onto others and taking what they want in return … using someone else's cultural symbols to satisfy a personal need for self-expression is an exercise in privilege'.[53] These examples indicate the care that will be needed if local distinctiveness is to play a role in real-world sustainable fashion systems.

Places for togetherness

World 124 – the world in which herds of sheep roam the streets of London – is notable not only for the local distinctiveness of its woollen garments, but also for its community action. The group exploring the world at Stage 2 described each household taking turns to care for their neighbourhood herd and coming together to make decisions. A strong community ethos was also apparent in the Stage 2 exploration of **World 28**, in which natural dyes are grown in every area and people informally share their resources. In fact, an interest in community – in the sense of a social network grounded in a particular locale, which offers a shared sense of belonging[54] – arises in many of the fictional worlds. This interest reflects a wider thirst for community, a thirst which Gerard Delanty suggests is a product of late modernity: 'a response to the crisis in solidarity and belonging that has been exacerbated by globalisation'.[55]

Do wearers enjoy any sense of community in the mainstream globalized fashion system? It could perhaps arise through shopping – an activity that has been established in countries including the UK, France and the US as a form of leisure since the mid-nineteenth century. Before this point, as Elizabeth Wilson explains, 'to enter a shop still implied a commitment to buy, stocks were limited, and of course there was nothing ready made'.[56] The innovation of the department store opened up new opportunities for middle-class women – not only to browse but also to socialize.[57] A century later, the London boutiques of the 1960s and 1970s created a new kind of social space; Mary Quant's Bazaar, for example, 'demonstrated the need for young consumers to have a place to congregate as well as shop'.[58] Yet it is a stretch to suggest that the high-street shopping experience supports the development of community connections. In the 1980s, Ray Oldenburg argued that malls were organized to maximize consumption, rather than socializing, and treated people as individual strangers, rather than fostering genuine communities.[59] Today, the shift to online shopping means that retailers are seeking to design spectacular shopping experiences[60] – though any connection generated is likely to be between customer and brand, rather than among peers. A sense of community could be more likely within alternative consumption spaces such as vintage clothes fairs or community clothes swaps.[61]

As noted in Chapter 3, shopping is largely absent from the visions created in Fashion Fictions; contributors commonly imagine people coming together through practices of making, wearing and maintenance, rather than acquisition. Many of the fictions envision people gathering in communal spaces dedicated to sewing and mending, within cultures in which clothes-making practices are widespread. In **World 30**, for example, sewing becomes an unstoppable trend among young people:

> During the 2010s in World 30, young people drove a radical shift first towards second hand clothing, then towards making/mending. The rise of Depop was followed by a burst of passion, action and creativity as the Climate Strikes swept the globe. Policy was introduced to put sewing machines in public spaces like libraries, and high street brands followed suit in an effort to stay relevant to young people.
>
> Sewers can book a sewing machine in advance or just turn up. Local enthusiasts and experts are around to support, and short classes are offered for free. Young people influence and inspire each other, creating localised trends that diverge from mainstream fashion. The surge of creativity prompts people to bring other unwanted items into their clothes-making, so that waste and recycling bins are emptier than ever before.[62]

World 17 presents a similar vision – although in this case it is young men who, following an unexpected surge in popularity of paper patterns and making in the 2010s, 'thronged to overlockers to make up fanciful, belogoed sportswear-inspired confections and to repair sought-after vintage styles'.[63]

In **World 9**, sewing skills are widespread:

Learning to sew is a teenage rite of passage in World 9. Growing out of 1960s youth culture and the punk attitude of the 1970s, sewing your own clothes became the pinnacle of cool.

Using sewing skills to express individual identity and independence is seen as something to aspire to. Learning to use a sewing machine is as common and as gender neutral as learning to drive. Weekend 'meets' where people parade their home-constructed garments and share construction/reconstruction tips are common. Annual conventions also award winners of various creative and technical categories with support to publish their DIY clothing zines.[64]

The group who worked on World 9 at a Stage 2 workshop enjoyed exploring this sewing-centric culture. They envisioned young people making bespoke items to fit their bodies and personal sense of style, catalyzing subcultural variation and localized trends. Their vision of collaborative making spaces is similar to the World 30 fiction discussed above:

> you'd have collaborative spaces on the high street, where you'd go in, and there'd be a facilitator there to help you use a sewing machine, who would teach you to get through that bit of difficult pattern cutting or whatever. And also providing the space and resources, if you don't have them in your tiny flat in the tower block. You've got places to go where you can create your garments, and so it's more democratic that way.[65]

The World 9 group saw these spaces not only as places to create clothes but also as places to socialize, to show off recently completed homemade items, to share and swap clothes, and to upcycle, repurpose and remake.

There are some community-oriented spaces for making and mending, of the type envisioned in the fictions, in the real world. Stitched Up, a not-for-profit Community Benefit Society that aims to inspire communities across Greater Manchester to take action on sustainable fashion, has run a pop-up hub in a shopping mall – 'a space for crafters, makers and tinkerers, providing an alternative to the chain stores and empty shops of your average British high street'.[66] Other community workshops are part of the worldwide makerspace movement, which first arose at the turn of the millennium. As Matti Kurzeja, Katja Thiele and Britta Klagge explain, makerspaces and fab labs 'make available tools and technologies which were originally confined to the sphere of industrial production', enabling people to work on individual and collaborative creative projects.[67] While these workshops typically focus on hard materials and digital technologies such as 3D printing and laser cutting, textile-related processes are sometimes included – or may even be the central focus. Le Textile Lab in Lyon, for example, is kitted out with equipment for sewing, knitting, weaving, embroidery, printing, pattern-cutting, tufting and textile recycling, along with a lab for the exploration of natural dyes and biomaterials.[68]

These community-oriented spaces for making can be described as 'third places'. Ray Oldenburg defines third places as places where people meet that are separate from home and work. He suggests

Figure 5.5 *In World 225, clothing workshops across Colombia provide space for creation, customization and collective learning.*[69] *In a Stage 3 enactment that brought one of these workshops to life, visitors engaged in the practice of textile printing. The use of everyday objects for the prints is commonplace in World 225, leading to a visual and material language that is distinctively Colombian.*

that such places are found in diverse societies in different forms, including cafes, bookstores, hair salons and pubs, and are essential for thriving communities.[70] Third places offer neutral ground to which nobody has strong personal ties; they have low thresholds for participation and social status is less important than in other settings.[71] They connect those within a neighbourhood from different demographic groups, laying the ground for cooperative projects to be organized and friendships to be formed. They also provide space for fun, for political debate and for intellectual exchange.[72] Indeed, research into makerspaces has identified learning and social opportunities as important motivations for participation. As Kurzeja, Thiele and Klagge explain, 'There is continuous interaction between collaboration, mutual teaching, learning by making and the finished products. Makerspaces … thus become places of informal education and demonstrate the strong link between social capital and lifelong learning.'[73]

From a sustainability perspective, making-related third places have great potential for catalyzing positive transitions. Kurzeja, Thiele and Klagge explain that these places contribute to inclusive social, cultural and technical infrastructures that support wellbeing and social cohesion. They can enable and promote practices of distributed making, repair and tinkering, contributing to a reduction in resource use and associated impacts.[74] They set precedents for resourceful practice, such as the collective use of high-quality long-lasting tools rather than the individual purchase of cheap tools.[75] More generally, they 'point to paths towards a sustainable post-growth economy'[76] – that is, as discussed in Chapter 1, an economy organized to meet fundamental human needs, rather than economic growth.

In **World 3** – one of the original five fictions that I wrote to kick off the project – I envisioned a different kind of clothes-related community space:

During World 3's second wave of feminism, housework was a key concern. British activists set up one of the movement's most enduring practical initiatives: a network of community laundries.

Forgoing the convenience of frequent small washes at home, laundry members dropped off wash-loads every week (freshening items in the interim) and shared duties on a rota system.

Figure 5.6 *While some community-oriented spaces for making and mending are permanent, others are temporary. The Collective Mending sessions, a project led by artist Catherine Reinhart, aims to 'cultivate care for cloth and community' through workshop events at which participants come together to mend a single quilt.*[77]

Washdays became vibrant social events; other benefits included the sharing of clothes-care knowledge, informal loans and the passing on of unwanted items.

While some laundries closed when washing machines became cheaper, others survived and are thriving today, with long waiting lists for membership.

I wrote this fiction because for most of my life my clothes have been washed in a machine at home; the thought of this being a social and pleasurable activity is quite alien to me. I was fascinated to later read about a historical parallel: *'la grande vessive'*, a communal wash that took place over a few days, a couple of times a year, in rural France from ancient times until the twentieth century.[78] Peter Ward describes the wash as 'a moment of feminine solidarity, a time in the annual cycle when women shared domestic chores, along with some fun and a chance to gossip'; yet it was also 'an occasion when household riches were on view, when prestige was claimed and tested, when women asserted their rank in the village social order, and when local hierarchies were affirmed or altered'.[79]

One of the participants who explored World 3 in the Stage 2 workshop, Kaavya, had rather different lived experiences to me. She grew up in India and described people in rural areas without access to electricity, washing their clothes together by hand on the river bank. Later, while living in New York, she used the laundromat – and formed a WhatsApp group with friends to coordinate the timing of a shared white wash. Kaavya, along with the other members of the Stage 2 workshop group, built on these experiences when developing the fictional proposition: they decided that the use of communal laundries would be widespread in World 3 and imagined communities gathering at these launderette hubs to wash and care for their clothes and to socialize.[80]

The Stage 2 group sought to frame clothes-washing as an enjoyable activity rather than a chore, and envisioned a culture in which people have respect for their clothes and the knowledge to care for them is widely held. This emphasis on knowledge-sharing echoes research into makerspaces; the exchange of practical knowledge in these contexts has been highlighted as particularly valuable in terms of sustainable transitions. As Martin Langlinderer, founder of an open workshop in Stuttgart, explains:

> The mutual exchange is an extremely important element because otherwise, to put it bluntly, we all degenerate to simple consumers who just believe what people tell them: it's not possible to repair that, the only option is persistent gluing, there are no replacement parts, you need to throw that away and buy a new one, the fabric can only be washed three times. As a consumer, you become increasingly dumb if you're not knowledgeable about these things and then you can't make any active, conscious decisions in terms of a post-growth economy, which is about long-lasting, resource-saving products and processes.[81]

The Stage 2 group particularly enjoyed inventing a variety of washing-related activities that would happen in the World 3 community space. They imagined people choosing to wash their clothes by

Figure 5.7 *In World 3, community laundries are thriving social hubs. A profound respect for clothing and its care has also contributed to an increase in hand washing and a range of cultural techniques, previously lost, are practised. Here, a participant at the Stage 2 workshop is stitching a name label for a personalized World 3 laundry bag.*

hand together, with songs to keep the beat passed down from generation to generation. 'Washercise' and 'ironing pilates' sessions offer the opportunity to wash and keep fit; 'washing and wellbeing' sessions invite participants to 'beat the hell out of a garment' as a form of stress relief; and couples' laundry sessions provide space to work through relationship issues and 'wash the negativity out'.

* * * * * * * * *

As with several other ideas that we have encountered already, there is a danger in romanticizing communal spaces for craft and creativity. Clare Daněk describes the open-access community making space as a '*permission space*, in which the user is afforded the opportunity to create' but is also subject to 'constraints and power dynamics'.[82] For example, ambitions of inclusivity do not always play out in practice, because – as Kurzeja, Thiele and Klagge explain – 'makerspaces are embedded in existing social power relations and produce their own exclusions'.[83] Those involved in the maker movement are typically male, white and well educated,[84] which affects the experiences of those outside this demographic; people with disabilities can find themselves excluded,[85] as can those on low incomes.[86] These issues are exacerbated by the growing capitalist appropriation of makerspaces and the consequent prioritization of commercial concerns over inclusivity.[87]

Conscious of these dangers, Kurzeja, Thiele and Klagge discuss how to make third places open and accessible, emphasizing the need for a welcoming and playful atmosphere that gives members 'a feeling of warmth and belonging'.[88] Ann Shivers-McNair, who undertook an extended ethnography of makerspaces in Seattle, presents a useful account of this approach in practice. She discusses the work of Clarissa San Diego, a professional who liaises between providers and users in the maker movement with the aim of designing thriving maker communities.[89] San Diego's practice involves gentle probing and attentive listening; then, using the understanding she has gained, prototyping connections between individuals, groups and resources. As Shivers-McNair explains, this process requires the same open-minded attitude and many of the same skills as are needed for material prototyping.[90] While demanding, this approach has great potential value: social ties – which support interpersonal connections, boost wellbeing and counteract corporate power – are crucial in an uncertain and volatile world.[91]

Ritualizing fashion

Having thought about places in which people can gather, let us now turn to events and activities that bring people together. There are numerous events in the fictional worlds: competitions, festivals, parties, mending circles, catwalk shows. The events are often described as a twist on a real-world norm. For example, for the Stage 1 version of **World 4** (the rather different Stage 2 interpretation of which I have discussed in Chapters 3 and 4) I described a culture in which 'Every Friday night ... the British streets are awash with eye-catching fashion statements'. In the real world these statements are typically created using the goods provided by fast-fashion retailers, but in World 4 they are inventively constructed from foliage harvested from community gardens. In **World 48**, talent competitions are the subject of the twist:

In World 48 garment production from raw materials became outlawed and socially despised after textile wastefulness was identified as the source of a major pandemic in 2020. Textile resourcefulness becomes the most highly valued social attribute.

Talent competitions on prime time television celebrate the most socially responsible and eye-catching dressing practices and major governmental awards with vast cash prizes are given annually for innovations. Children are trained in textile resourcefulness techniques at school and in the evenings they stage competitions in each other's homes. At night they dream of winning the Nobel Prize for Textile Resourcefulness when they grow up.[92]

In **World 173**, slimming clubs are reinvented:

> In 2015 in World 173, bored by gender-normative idealised bodies and microtrends, people in the UK stop binge watching Love Island and take matter(s) into their own hands.
>
> At Sewing World, instead of counting calories we 'notch up' techniques. BMI stands for Bodies, Materials & Inspiration. The philosophy is one of radical self-acceptance and body-positivity. Sessions start with a show-and-tell and 'Sewist of the Week' award for the best told sewing story. Budding sewists pledge their intended sewing activities for the week ahead.
>
> As people find their personal style and learn to make clothes that fit better, the fashion industry falters and athleisure wear is consigned to history. Cosmetic plastic surgeons retrain to become expert pattern cutters and alteration aficionados who tour the Weave Watchers circuit.[93]

The events described here are altered versions of everyday occurrences: rowdy nights out, talent competitions, weekly clubs. Other fictions describe clothes-related events with a heightened sense of meaning and significance, framed as rituals. One such example is shown in Figure 3.16: a **World 221** ceremony in which people adorn their body with an artefact linked to a mythical beast. Two further examples were discussed in Chapter 4: the **World 91** ritual of presenting oneself to the mushroom spiritual guides (see page 106) and the **World 45** rituals of hanging a new curtain and, a year later, cutting the curtain fabric to make a garment (see page 120). In all three cases, the fictional rituals are associated with some kind of spirituality. As Catherine Bell notes, this association is familiar:

> In modern Western society, we tend to think of ritual as a matter of special activities inherently different from daily routine action and closely linked to the sacralities of tradition and organized religion. Such connections encourage us to regard ritual as somewhat antiquated and, consequently, as somewhat at odds with modernity. Hence, ritual often seems to have more to do with other times and places than with daily life as we know it in postindustrial Europe and America.[94]

Yet, Bell goes on to explain, rituals can be entirely secular and are widespread in contemporary life. Diverse activities can be ritualized, without any religious component. Richard Schechner – who writes about ritual as a concept closely connected to performance – explains that rituals, whether spiritual or secular, can help people through periods of transition; build community and social solidarity; negotiate conflicts and hierarchies; and deal with desires that clash with societal norms.[95] Byung-Chul Han engagingly describes rituals as 'symbolic techniques of making oneself at home in the world', which provide stability and 'render time habitable'.[96]

Bell discusses six attributes that may be present, to a greater or lesser extent, in rituals of various types: the use of formalized movements and activities; a sense of connection to tradition; the precise repetition of actions; governance by rules; and a distinction between the sacred and the profane.[97] She also differentiates between different types of ritual. The act of presenting oneself to the mushroom spiritual guides in World 91, for example, could be understood as a rite of exchange and communion, in which 'people make offerings to a god or gods with the practical and straightforward expectation of receiving something in return – whether it be as concrete as a good harvest and a long life or as abstract as grace and redemption'.[98] Bell explains that such rites 'invoke very complex relations of mutual interdependence between the human and the divine' – and are also important at a societal and cultural level, shaping connections within communities and supporting a sense of identity.[99]

World 80 is another fiction in which rituals were invoked. The Stage 1 text describes a society in which water scarcity leads to a dramatic decrease in the frequency of washing clothes.[100] In this culture it is normal to wear the same outfit for a whole month, and stains and other signs of wear are readily accepted. This is a fascinating provocation, given the demanding hygiene standards of real-world society.[101] A group of four workshop participants came together to explore and prototype World 80 at Stage 2.[102] The group connected the world's rhythms of renewal to the lunar cycle and invented an organization named Lunar Synk, which 'coordinates a rolling calendar of social events focused on garment refreshing, repairing, refashioning and caring, as a means of promoting more efficient use of resources [Figure 5.8]. Its aim is to reduce the environmental and social impact of fashion consumption and laundering practices.'

Lunar Synk's events are both practical and social; they support the community in wearing the same outfit for an extended period and fulfil a need for socializing and novelty that would, in the real-world fashion system, be predominantly met through shopping. A hedonistic 'wash and swap party' marks the transition between cycles, providing an opportunity to perform the much-anticipated garment wash and exchange items to create a fresh look for the new month. Events taking place during the period of wear allow people to refresh their garments without washing, through the use of sunlight, rain or freezing; to care and repair for intensively worn garments; and, in the case of the 'free body cafe' in the final week of the cycle, to socialize without clothes – which would be likely, by that point, to have acquired some rather unsavoury aromas. World 80 citizens plan their activities around this calendar, with important celebrations scheduled at the start of the cycle.

The Stage 2 group described the World 80 events as 'a social experience, a collective ritual, almost necessity'. Using Bell's categorization, I would frame them as calendrical rites: rituals that recur at periodic intervals. Such rites are typically tied to natural cycles, whether the phases of the moon, as in this case, or the changing seasons. As Bell notes, calendrical rites lay cultural meanings on natural processes and thus 'harmonize the activities and attitudes of the human community with the seasonal rhythms of the environment and the larger cosmos'.[103]

In this Stage 2 vision of World 80, ritual served as an effective device for creating a situation in which the unthinkable – people willingly wearing a single outfit for an entire month – is widely

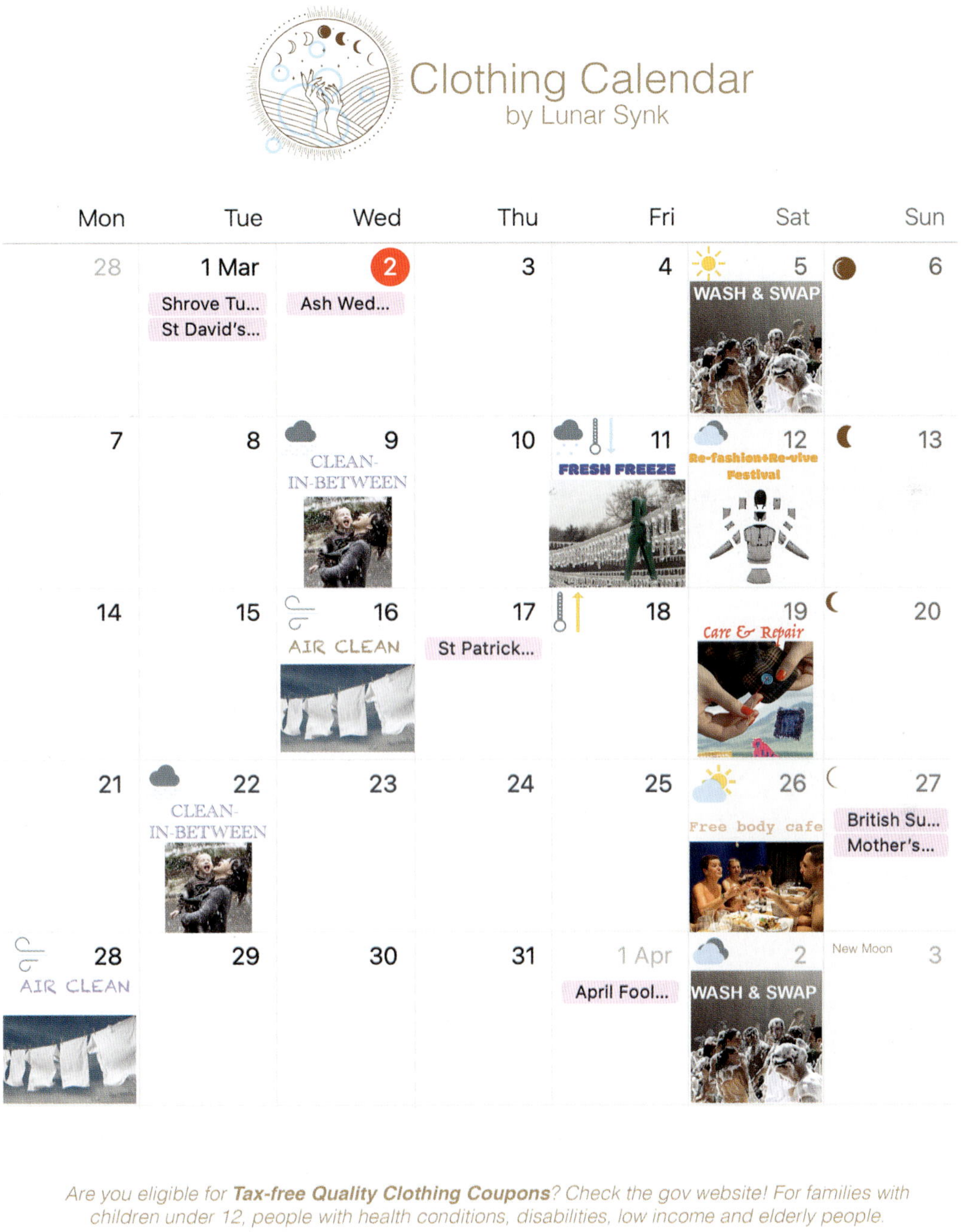

Figure 5.8 *This calendar shows events coordinated by Lunar Synk, a World 80 organization that supports the community to wear a single outfit for an entire lunar cycle.*

accepted. As Bell notes, 'Ritualization tends to posit the existence of a type of authoritative reality that is seen to dictate to the immediate situation.'[104] The inclusion of a ritual in the fiction explains why the people of World 80 are behaving in a way that seems alien to us. It makes sense to the people in the world: *it's our ritual, it's just what we do.* And it makes sense to us, thinking about the world: *it's their ritual, it's just what they do.* Much as I observed in Chapter 4 with regard to spirituality, ritual acts as a narrative tool that helps us to think the unthinkable.

Bell explains that the strength of a ritual's authoritative power can vary:

> The degree to which activities are ritualized—for instance, how much communality, how much appeal to deities and other familiar rites, how much formality or attention to rules, and how much emphasis on performance or appeal to traditional precedents—is the degree to which the participants suggest that the authoritative values and forces shaping the occasion lie beyond the immediate control or inventiveness of those involved.[105]

In the case of World 80, the ritualization appears to be fairly low-level; even so, its appeal to an authority beyond the immediate community is sufficient to create a social consensus that limits the frequency of washing clothes. Respect for the shared ritual is placed above the freedom of the individual to act as they desire. Han explains that rituals challenge the individualism of capitalist society, because rituals 'produce a distance from the self, a self-transcendence'.[106] Rituals also deepen attention through repetition, challenging the constant barrage of novelty that is intertwined with overconsumption.[107] In the mainstream fashion system, we need to step away from individualism and to find ways to slow down our practices. Might rituals, I wonder, help us to create new ways of being with our clothes?

* * * * * * * *

Rites of passage form another category of rituals discussed by Catherine Bell. These 'life-cycle' ceremonies accompany major events – such as birth, coming-of-age initiations, marriage and death – and thus 'culturally mark a person's transition from one stage of social life to another'.[108] Bell outlines the complex rites of passage that are involved in various religious traditions and notes that, in predominantly secular societies, life transitions are still marked but rites of passage are typically much less organized. Rites of passage arise from time to time in the fictions created for the project. Learning to sew is explicitly described as a rite of passage in **World 9**, discussed earlier in the chapter. The group exploring World 9 at Stage 2 created a sewing kit, awarded to each young person as part of this rite, as their prototype (Figure 2.4). **World 106**, meanwhile, describes a birth rite: the gifting of twenty kilograms of silk yarn to each citizen when they are born (Figure 5.9).

Figure 5.9 *In World 106, each citizen receives twenty kilograms of silk yarn at birth. This precious material is used later in life for a collection of garments, handmade to suit the wearer's personal taste and style. Designers employ zero-waste cutting methods to show respect to the precious fibre. As no further consumption of new materials is possible, pieces are traded from person to person.*[109]

In the early twentieth century, ethnographer and folklorist Arnold van Gennep proposed that all rites of passage – and, in fact, all forms of ritual – involve three phases: the preliminal, the liminal and the postliminal.[110] Through these phases, Bell explains, 'the person leaves behind one social group and its concomitant social identity and passes through a stage of no identity or affiliation before admission into another social group that confers a new identity'.[111] Anthropologist Victor Turner was particularly interested in the liminal phase – a 'between' time in which social and cultural norms are suspended – in rituals of all types. His interest encompassed both obligatory rituals that had long been embedded within particular societies, which he described as 'liminal', and voluntary ritualized activities that he identified within contemporary Western society, which he described as 'liminoid'.[112]

As Schechner explains, liminal and liminoid rituals 'are transportations … one enters into the experience, is "moved" or "touched" … and is then dropped off about where she or he entered'.[113] Within the liminal/liminoid space, people can think and act differently than they do in everyday life, and may be transformed, to a greater or lesser extent, by the experience. Having encountered the ideas of van Gennep and Turner, I now see Fashion Fictions workshops as a kind of liminoid ritual. In the preliminoid phase, people are guided away from everyday life; in the liminoid phase they freely explore an imagined world, sometimes to the extent that it begins to feel quite real; in the postliminoid phase they are supported to reengage with the real world, while holding on to the insights they gained through speculation and reflection.

To think about these ideas further, I will examine the enactment of **World 27**, in which – as discussed in Chapter 3 – garments are valued for their embedded stories and exchanged at seasonal events. The Stage 2 group exploring this world explicitly described these events, which they imagined taking place at equinoxes and solstices, as rituals. In order to enact this world at Stage 3, I needed to design one of these rituals. (Ritual design is an intriguing challenge; designers Arvind Venkataramani and Adam Menter have developed a toolkit to enable the conscious development of secular rituals in service of systemic change.[114]) In fact, using the understanding of rituals gained from the work of van Gennep, I would say that I actually designed two rituals: the fictional World 27 ritual and the Fashion Fictions workshop that included an experience of the fictional World 27 ritual. For the former, I created an outline to describe the event:

In World 27, textile histories are central to the way garments are valued: the greater the number of associated stories, the greater an item's desirability. Wearers are therefore motivated to keep items in circulation, rather than hoarding them, and ritual events throughout the year provide opportunities for storytelling and swapping.

In the East Midlands of England, a notable exchange follows celebration of the first harvest in August. At the event, wearers document the latest instalment of their garment's story and enshrine it in a digital repository as an enduring textile 'deed'; others then bid to be the item's next custodian.

The design of the workshop, meanwhile, involved detailed planning, with consideration for the characteristics of ritual along with various practical issues. A key element was identifying a suitable location: after a search, I settled on a wooded quarry in Derbyshire with a distinctive otherworldly feeling. (If a portal between worlds *were* to open up, I thought, it would surely be there.) On the day, the participants arrived by train and walked – as part of the preliminoid phase – along a canal and through a picturesque woodland to the workshop site. In the clearing where we assembled, I had strung washing lines between trees in preparation for a later part of the ritual and as a way of demarcating the space. The preliminoid phase continued with a welcome and briefing on the plans for the afternoon. I explained to the participants that we would be enacting a ritual from World 27, acting as parallel-world versions of ourselves; while we had the outline to guide us, we would be extending the fiction together as we went along. My role was in keeping with the *both/and* approach to enactment described in Chapter 3: I was simultaneously acting as the coordinator of the World 27 ritual *and* the facilitator of the real-world workshop.

The liminoid phase of the workshop – the enactment of the ritual itself – involved four activities. The first was a warm-up activity in pairs, which – in my World 27 voice – I explained was part of the exchange ritual. (In reality, it was adapted from an activity devised by environmental activist Joanna Macy.[115]) Each person was instructed to ask their partner a question: *Who are you?* The partner answered on behalf of the 'story-full' garment they had brought to offer for exchange; when they completed their response, the question was repeated. Once again, the speaker answered. This was repeated for five minutes, and then a second question was asked and repeated: *What happens through you?* Next, the roles were reversed, with the original questioner answering on behalf of their garment. I selected this questioning technique to give the participants – in their World 27 guises – a chance to spend some last quality time with their garment before offering it for exchange, and to dig into the stories embedded within.

Two individual activities, already outlined in Chapter 3, followed the warm-up activity. First, each participant documented their garment's story to create an enduring 'deed' (see page 62) in a format of their choice. After exchanging their deed for a fabric label bearing a unique URL, they stitched the label into their garment to enable future custodians of the garment to access the deed online (see Figure 3.8). We then gathered in a circle; each participant shared their garment's story orally and the other members of the group were invited to respond, in just three words, with a request for the garment or a proposition for the next chapter of its life. Finally, each item was ceremonially offered for exchange by being hung on the washing line.

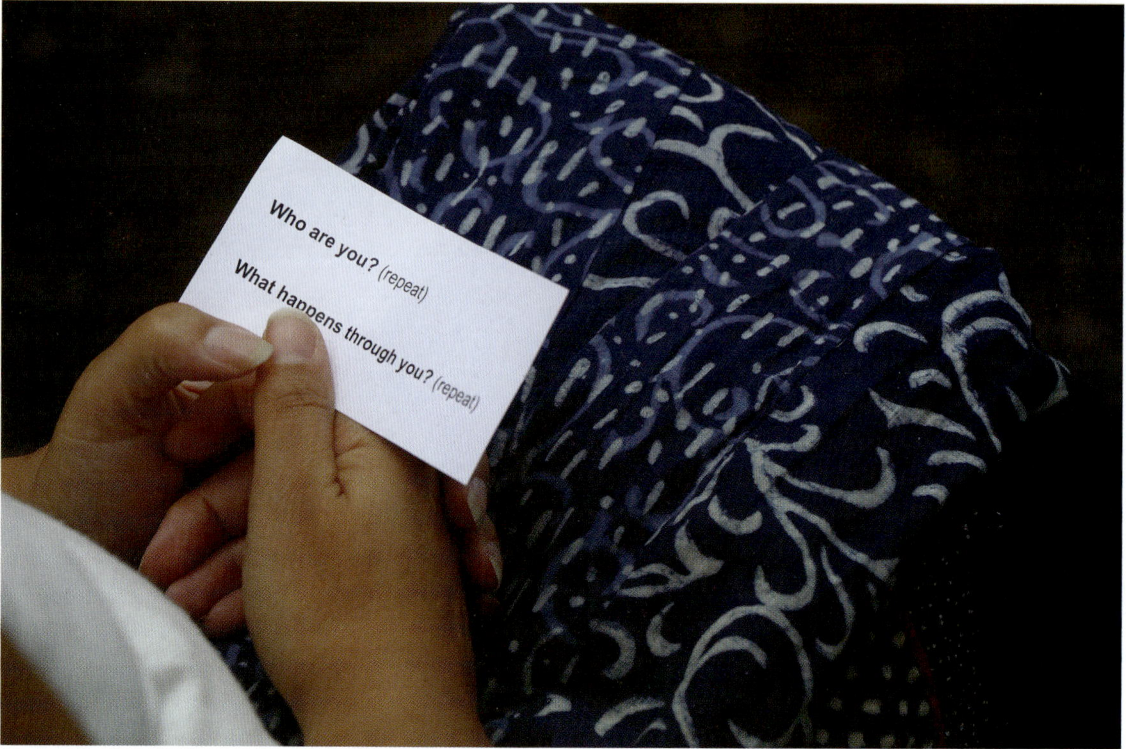

Figure 5.10 *The first part of the World 27 garment exchange ritual involved each participant answering two questions on behalf of a 'story-full' garment from their wardrobe.*

Our enactment of the World 27 exchange ended with the garments on the washing line. The ritual of the workshop, however, involved further activities, which formed the postliminoid return to the real world. Each person recorded a reflection about the real world via one of the three wonder paths outlined in Chapter 2 – *questions, ideas for action* and *precedents* – and then shared them, once again standing in a circle. In return for their reflections, each participant received a 'wonder token': a small textile feather intended to act as a reminder of the ritual experience and an encouragement to carry forwards the sense of possibility that the workshop would – I hoped – have generated. The postliminoid phase was rounded off with applause, thanks and the retracing of the route back to the train. (The whole enactment was beautifully captured in a short film, which gives a strong sense of the experience of the setting, activities and discussions.[116])

Various elements of the workshop connect to the attributes of ritual discussed earlier in this section. There were moments of discipline: two minutes to share each garment story; three words in response; three formats for the wonder thoughts. There were symbolic actions: exchanging deed for

Figure 5.11 *In the second World 27 enactment activity, each participant recorded a garment 'deed' in a format of their choice.*

garment label and wonder thought for wonder token; hanging the garment on the line and walking away. There were repeated motifs, such as the circle formation used for the sharing of stories and reflections, and the walk to and from the workshop site. Materiality played a part: the hard-copy deeds, deed records and instructions; the garment labels and act of stitching; the wonder tokens. The whole event had a pleasing sense of ritual-like collectivity and care, with the participants 'treat[ing] not only other people but also things in beautiful ways'.[117]

As with the other enactments, embodied experience was crucial. As Bell explains, 'A lecture about the power of the ancestors will not inculcate the type of assumptions about ancestral presence that the simple routine of offering incense at an altar can inculcate. Activities that are so physical, aesthetic, and established appear to play a particularly powerful role in shaping human sensibility and imagination.'[118] Acting with the body starts to make the authority invoked by a ritual feel relevant – even to those of us inventing and enacting it for just one August afternoon in the Derbyshire countryside.

Figure 5.12 *Each garment 'deed' was exchanged for a garment label printed with the URL of a unique space on a digital repository. Paper records and an inked stamp formalized this element of the ritual.*

Figure 5.13 *After stitching the labels into their garments, the participants gathered in a circle to share an oral version of their stories before hanging the items on the washing line to ceremonially offer them for exchange.*

Activity 5.1: Take action – ritual garment exchange

Use these instructions to enact a ritual exchange from **World 27**, in which textile histories are central to the way garments are valued (see page 150).[119] The activity involves each participant documenting and sharing the stories embedded in a garment from their wardrobe and symbolically offering it for exchange. It is designed for a group meeting in person and takes a few hours; it may be helpful for one person to act as a facilitator and 'keeper of stories'. If you wish to store the 'deeds' (stories) digitally, you could use a blog, digital pinboard or social media.

The instructions can be adapted as needed, for example eliminating the oral sharing of stories (Step 4) or adding an element of actual exchange. Sewing Cafe Lancaster, for example, incorporated ideas from the World 27 enactment recipe into a real-world clothes swap. The instructions could also be adapted for individual use.

1. To warm up: in pairs, take turns to ask two questions: *who are you?* and *what happens through you?* Reply on behalf of your garment. Take five minutes for each question per person, repeating the question as needed.

2. Document your garment's story in a format of your choice, e.g. audio recording, video, text, image.

Figure 5.14 *Garment stories can be recorded in a variety of formats. Here, Wendy is creating an audio recording to capture a taste of her waterproof coat's many adventures.*

3.   Submit the story for display and/or storage, as appropriate. If the story will be made available online, the participant should receive a record of its location so this can be attached to or stored with the garment (e.g. via a garment label, as in Figure 3.8).

4.   Share the garment stories orally, hanging each item on a washing line (see Figures 1.3 and 5.13). Others in the group bid to be the garment's new owner by outlining the life they will give to it, or suggest the type of owner that the garment needs, in three words.

5.   Take some time to reflect (see Activity 2.4) and return garments to their owners.

Figure 5.15 *I ran a simplified version of the World 27 enactment, involving only steps 2 and 3 from the step-by-step instructions, at a drop-in Fashion Fictions workshop. The garment stories were displayed at the event and then shared in an enactment report on the project website.*[120]

Trends and connection

Let us now shift to another aspect of togetherness: the trends that arise as people influence one another through their dress. This dynamic lies at the heart of the phenomenon of fashion. Linda Welters and Abby Lillethun define fashion as 'changing styles of dress and appearance that are adopted by a group of people at any given time and place'.[121] Joanne Entwistle, meanwhile, helpfully explains the interaction of fashion and dress: 'fashion refers to the systems for the production and circulation of prevailing aesthetics in clothing, while dress refers to the daily, embodied practices of *getting dressed*'.[122]

As noted in Chapter 1, in the dominant mainstream system, fashion shapes all clothing decisions – including our daily dressing practices – regardless of our personal feelings about the notion of fashion.[123] Various theorists, from Georg Simmel and his contemporary Thorstein Veblen onwards, have sought to establish why fashion occurs, focusing on themes such as emulation, identification and differentiation. Entwistle, however, argues that such attempts to explain the 'why' of fashion simplify a complex phenomenon that intersects with multiple social forces, such as class and gender.[124]

For a long time, fashion was understood as a solely Western phenomenon, rooted in European culture and the development of the city in modernity. Simmel, for example, contrasted fashion with dress cultures in non-Western contexts, which he considered to be stable and unchanging.[125] Yet this thinking about non-Western contexts is wrong: change can, in fact, be identified in many dress cultures, even if it is not easily apparent to outsiders.[126] Jennifer Craik thus argues that 'fashion is *not* exclusively the domain of modern culture and its pre-occupation with individualism, class, civilisation and consumerism'.[127]

In their book *Fashion History: A Global View*, Welters and Lillethun identify change, and therefore fashion, in many cultures across time and space.[128] They discuss, for example, Chinese words from almost a thousand years ago that meant 'the prevalent style fit for the time'[129] and records that show shifts in demand for cloth and beads in Indigenous North American societies in the nineteenth century.[130] They draw on the work of anthropologist Aubrey Cannon, who argues that 'Fashion, in some sense, has characterized human culture since the first adornments of the Upper Palaeolithic'.[131] Welters and Lillethun thus claim that changing dress is a universal human behaviour.[132] We might, then, say that fashion is everywhere, in all cultures. But some feel that this extension of a concept rooted in Eurocentrism is deeply problematic: Sandra Niessen, for example, questions whether the dualism inherent in the notion of fashion established by Simmel and others – the distinction between fashion and unchanging dress – can simply be waived, or whether it is 'time to tear [fashion] down from its pedestal'[133] – for example through the 'defashion' movement, mentioned in Chapter 3.

Trends – changing fashions – are often framed negatively in conversations about fashion and sustainability; indeed, I flagged the problem of homogenized global trends while discussing the mainstream fashion system in Chapter 1. Yet it would be problematic to simplistically view *all* trends as inherently negative, given the complex social functions of fashion. Happily, contributors to Fashion Fictions are typically sensitive to these issues. Conversations tend to distinguish between emergent, bottom-up trends and the top-down promotion of trends by businesses to stimulate consumption. As such, contributors' ideas gesture towards a different form of *how change* (in the sense of fashion) could *look*. In Fashion Fictions worlds we see many different kinds of trends. We see trends, but with biodegradable materials – such as trends in the foliage used to adorn the body for nights out in **World 4**, as mentioned earlier in the chapter. We see trends, but slower – as in **World 25**, which describes an uprising against wasteful, 'flimsy' clothing and the subsequent implementation of policies for the 'rigorous manufacture of durable clothing'; trends, therefore, are less frequent and people dress according to their signature style.[134] We see trends, but localized – as in **World 9**, in which (as already discussed in this chapter) learning to sew is a teenage rite of passage; the Stage 2 group building this world talked about localized trends and micro-trends spreading rapidly via social media. Trends also arose as a topic in the conversations about **World 62** – in which images of clothes cannot be distributed, as discussed in Chapter 3. The group imagined trends being hyper-local and thus diverging from place to place. As Wendy commented, 'you're only influenced by what you directly see around you in your everyday life, and the people that you see a lot'.

* * * * * * * * *

The group that developed **World 54** at Stage 2 envisaged a resourceful world in which textile production is severely limited and people dress inventively with unconventional items, including curtains and other household objects. Trends, they thought, would manifest through styling – such as the way a sash is tied – rather than consumption. I picked up on this interest in trends and wove it into the design of the Stage 3 enactment I created to explore World 54. (This enactment was also captured in an evocative short film, which offers a window into the hands-on activities and the participants' reflections.[135]) As I explained in Chapter 3, the first part of this enactment involved performances in which participants used a randomly assigned set of instruction cards – which I had created – to guide their dressing (Figure 5.16). Several of these cards asked the participant to imitate or respond to the outfit of another person in the group. The affordances of the sheets and straps, however, meant that imitation was difficult. This gave the process a generative quality, as participant Gautham reflected: 'rather than, like, imitating, you make something new'.

This sense of creation rather than copying contrasts with the established practices of mainstream industry, in which imitation is rife. It speaks more to the idea of adaptation, as discussed in Chapter 3: a process that 'involves interpretation or translation and transformation'.[136] I am intrigued by the notion of trends encountering friction: the flow of social influence being slowed and disrupted by the material qualities of clothing. Katherine shared another thought-provoking reflection following this activity. When her cards had instructed her to copy the outfits of others, she had enjoyed looking at those around her and picking up dressing tips. She commented, 'I just thought, maybe that's a really generous thing that fashion can become – it's not about your individual identity, but you do it to give entertainment to everyone else.'

The second element of the enactment involved small groups acting out five imagined scenarios from World 54. I wrote outlines for these scenarios, again incorporating ideas about trends and social influence. One outline described a person confidently striding into a nightclub in a notably unconventional outfit and onlookers questioning whether this style of dress was intentional rebellion or unintentional mistake. The group acting out this scenario decided that in their interpretation

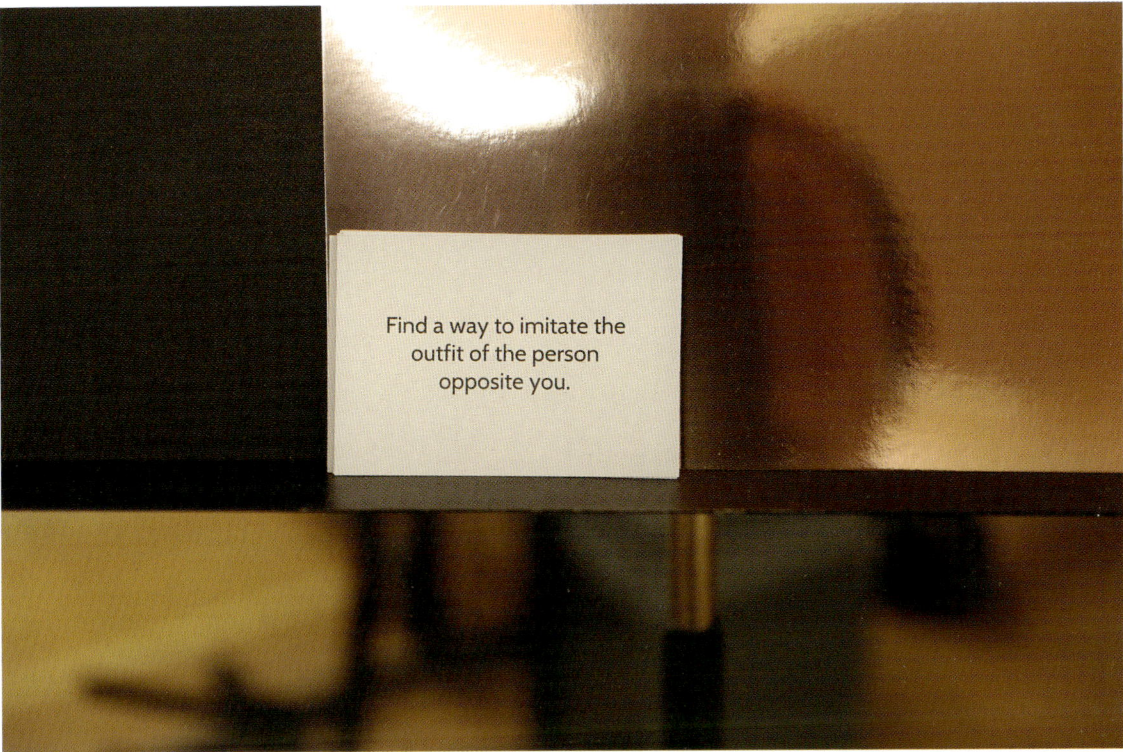

Figure 5.16 *Instruction cards at the World 54 enactment guided participants to imitate the dress of others, in order to explore how trends might play out in a fashion culture based on styling rather than consumption.*

of World 54, flamboyant styles were fashionable and aspirational. When one person chose to dress in a very simple way, the others initially questioned their style – before, under the influence of the newcomer's confidence, rushing to change their own dress to match (Figure 5.17). Elly, a member of the group, reflected that this scenario mirrors how fashion works in the real world. Challenging an established norm takes guts, but could influence others. This led to a debate about what or who initiates trends in fashion. As Sian asked, 'do you follow the trend first or the confident person that entices you into that trend?'

The participants raised further fascinating issues in their reflections. Sarah – who had acted out a scenario in which several people vie to secure a rare item at a World 54 swap meet – noticed that her group had transposed real-world behaviour into the fictional world, without considering how the society and culture of World 54 would shape that behaviour. She noted that they could, with more time and more effective scaffolding from me as facilitator, have dug into deeper questions about how interpersonal dynamics might play out in a different fashion system. Another participant, whose group had acted out a scenario in which a bride and her bridal party disagreed about the styles that should be chosen for an upcoming wedding, expressed disappointment at the framing of the task. I

Figure 5.17 *Participants at the World 54 enactment acted out a scenario in which a person confidently strides into a nightclub in a notably unconventional outfit and onlookers question the thinking behind their style of dress. Here, we see the onlookers' sudden realization that they may need to change their style of dress to remain on trend.*

had written all five scenarios in a way that assumed there would be some influence between people on what should or should not be worn. (I was careful not to say what this influence would be: I was interested to see the groups' interpretations.) The participant explained that her 'utopian' vision of World 54 would involve no expectation to dress in a certain way. This raises the fascinating question of whether social influence on dress – even if low level and inclusive – is indeed present in every society.

Further insights generated by the enactment related to the lack of mirrors in the workshop room. This was not an intentional choice but simply a characteristic of the only room of a suitable size that I could book on the required day. I tried to mitigate this issue by providing metallic cardboard sheets, which gave a reflection reminiscent of a fairground hall of mirrors. I also shamelessly took advantage of the project's fictional construct, explaining to the participants that in World 54 the production of mirrors had been limited along with that of textiles. Yet the truth is that dressing in the World 54 outfits is demanding; without the benefit of a full-length reflection it is difficult to see the position of buttons and straps, and to assess the aesthetic being created. Therefore, the lack of mirrors played an unintentionally large role in the experiences of the participants. This absence had differing impacts: one person said it gave her confidence while another found it fundamentally disorienting, even threatening her sense of self.

The lack of mirrors led to participants dressing together, helping one another create and refine their outfits. While I had encouraged this in the first part of the workshop to help the participants get acquainted with the sheets and straps, the reflective discussions suggested that this collaborative approach would be integral to the fashion experience in World 54. Katherine enjoyed this aspect of the workshop: 'I was completely stuck and I had to turn to Jay to help me, and it was really nice … It's a joy watching people helping one another.' For Kate, however, the exposure of dressing alongside others was jarring:

> I would never normally ask anyone to help me dress. And I would never normally let anyone see me getting dressed … it felt very vulnerable to even allow people to see me put in so much effort. Because I'm like, oh no, no, I've got to look like I've just stumbled out of bed like this, whatever. So … I could see how it would be a really beautiful world where there's this community of care where people dress one another and look after each other … I don't want to do that though, I want to be independent. That's really interesting.

Several of the participants felt that dressing without mirrors would lead to a shift in priority between aesthetics and comfort. Anja suggested that in World 54 she might 'become less worried about my look'. Sarah agreed: 'I think I would be less concerned with how my clothes looked and more concerned with how they felt … and how they functioned on my body'. Ruhee, reflecting on the experience of World 54 dressing, explained that the decision of which button to place in which buttonhole was based on feeling, rather than aesthetics: 'People were stopping the moment they felt alright.'

The relationship between looking and feeling, which arose in these experiences of dressing in World 54, is linked to another core concept of fashion theory: the gaze of others. When we dress we anticipate people seeing and judging us, and make dress choices according to what we want to communicate.[137] As outlined earlier in the chapter, the notion of the gaze of strangers is central to the longstanding association between fashion and the city, which arose in modernity. A concern for the gaze of others was apparent in other Stage 2 conversations and prototypes. For example, the magazine from nature-centric **World 19** (Figure 4.4) mentions 'must-have nails' alongside an image of a pair of mud-encrusted hands. When the creator, Jade, presented this prototype at the end of the Stage 2 workshop, she explained, 'That's what everyone wants to be seen with this season.'

Negotiating the gaze can be a source of anxiety; worrying about what other people think can be exhausting and, for a day-to-day task such as dressing, never-ending. A concern for the judgement of others tends to direct us to stay within established modes of self-presentation and dress-related behaviour. Yet it is exactly the norms of self-presentation and dress-related behaviour that we need to shift if we are to transform fashion culture. Lessening our concern for the gaze, as fleetingly occurred when the World 54 enactment participants prioritized feeling over looking, could have far-reaching consequences.

The group exploring **World 50** at Stage 2 also considered the issue of the gaze. In this world, as introduced in Chapter 2 and featured in Figures 3.5 and 5.2, signatures are stitched on garments to signify social connections. One group member, Ruhee, suggested that personal meanings would be privileged in World 50. She explained that the value of a garment would not be rooted in what the wearer wanted others to think of them, but rather in their identity and where they were trying to belong. The difficulty is that *belonging* is inherently social; I find it hard to envisage a mode of belonging that does not carry some sort of concern for the feelings of others in a group. Perhaps

Figure 5.18 *Even in worlds with very different social norms, dress can communicate identity. In World 97, stains are celebrated. This Stage 2 interpretation of the world, which is quite different to that shown in Figure 1.8, envisages white stain bibs being worn to catch organic stains from falling food; beading and embroidery are added to accentuate the markings. The stains communicate status, with the most colourful and intense indicating wealth and privilege. This is an engaging reversal of the real-world situation in seventeenth- and eighteenth-century Europe, where 'a hierarchy of clean clothes paralleled the social hierarchy … from the cleanest at the top to the unclean at the bottom'.*[138]

what is being suggested is actually a distinction between known and unknown others; in this vision of World 50, connections with friends and family are strong, underpinned by the materiality of each signed garment.

It is tempting to think of personal connections as being positive and supportive, although in reality the opinions of those we are connected to can exert as much, or even more, restriction in comparison with the anticipated gaze of unknown strangers. Nevertheless, more intimate connections are apparent in various Fashion Fictions contributions – and return us to the theme of community. Some worlds, for example, describe people connecting with their friends and peers through appreciation of styling skills. In **World 89**, a group of older women living in a retirement facility for former creatives develop a distinctive aesthetic and become influential on social media (Figure 5.19). Their approach to fashion, which eventually reshapes the wider culture, is 'applauded by care professionals as beneficial for elder mental health'.[139] Another fiction, **World 8**, focuses on connections forged through clothing within subcultural communities, with members commonly handing down garments to younger generations. Every subculture in World 8 has developed a unique approach to mending, upcycling and adapting garments that communicates identity and belonging.[140]

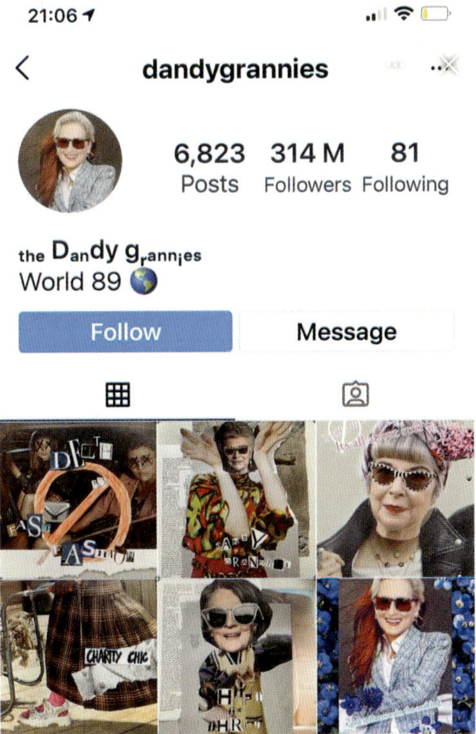

Figure 5.19 *In World 89, 'dandy grannies' are social media influencers, drawing on their lifelong experiences of fashion to promote comfort, uniqueness and thrift.*

* * * * * * * *

Let us return to the **World 91** enactment, discussed in detail in Chapter 4, to close this discussion of connection and togetherness. The culture of this world is shaped by its fungi-centric spirituality: mushrooms are widely recognized as spiritual guides, which people seek to connect with on a weekly basis. As they sought to bring this fictional world to life, several Stage 3 participants – drawing on their understanding of mycelial networks – made reference to the human networks that can be traced through garments. One week, for example, Elly wore an outfit

> made up of clothes given to me by my sister, to bring her with me on my mushroom visit, and to reflect the importance of family and symbolise the gifts we can give one another that might be outwardly visible through physical items, but at their most vital are things we can't buy, like time, and love.

Jade, meanwhile, talked about

> the invisible connections radiating from my clothes. Time, place and people. Some of my clothes have existed much longer than me, and may continue to exist after I am gone. I think about all the people and materials involved in the creation of the jacket. I visualise all the invisible connections between the people who have worn the jacket.

In Jade's comment, I sense connection and solidarity with those involved with her jacket, whether as makers or wearers – a far cry from the perceived judgemental gaze of unknown others. Solidarity is a powerful concept that can be described as a kind of 'we-thinking'[141] or a 'conscious or wilful commitment to a shared world'.[142] Arto Laitinen and Anne Birgitta Pessi explain that solidarity can be identified at different scales, from group cohesion in small communities and political solidarity that responds to instances of injustice or oppression to, at a much more fundamental level, 'the thought that all individuals are neighbors'.[143] While the social ties of traditional societies have been eroded by the changes wrought by modernity/coloniality, opportunities have arisen for a new kind of solidarity, more tolerant of individuality. Consequently, today 'we are all parts of multiple solidarities'.[144] To act in solidarity means taking others into consideration, even if that requires a sacrifice in terms of short-term pleasure or long-term benefit. Fred Dallmayr argues that while such an approach could be seen as curtailing freedom, freedom and solidarity are mutually constitutive, for we 'cannot be genuinely free as long as others are oppressed, dominated, or exploited'.[145]

Laitinen and Pessi explain that every situation involves 'competing interpretative frameworks': while there is the possibility to act in solidarity, there is also the possibility to act in a self-interested way.[146] In an individualistic society, cues can be useful in prompting us to prioritize solidarity. Activism such as the Clean Clothes Campaign, which links wearers in the global North with garment workers in the global South, provides one type of cue; since 1989, the campaign's collective action has addressed factory-level labour violations and defended the rights of garment workers to organize safely.[147] Fashion Revolution, a campaign founded in the wake of the Rana Plaza tragedy in 2013, encourages wearers to act in solidarity with who make their clothes by demanding information from fashion brands. Taking the lead from Jade, I wonder whether further prompts could be identified. Could we use close examination of our garments as a cue for solidarity? Could noting the many connections, apparent and hidden, embedded in our garments help us to think of those implicated in our fashion systems as community members, neighbours, friends? Could this solidarity extend to nonhuman species?

A tantalizing suggestion of the possibilities for fashion-system solidarity can be found in the deed – the garment story documented in the **World 27** enactment – created by Sally for her homemade cotton jumpsuit:

In thinking about the coming together of this garment there are many things to be thankful for: the earth and the sun that gave rise to the cotton, the cotton farmer, cotton pickers, spinners, weavers, dyers, printers, the sari seller, the good fortune that enabled us to meet, my mother and my grandmother who passed their skills to me, the sea and the molluscs that gave rise to the buttons even. If this garment comes to you I am hoping this list will grow.

Activity 5.2: Take action – resourceful styling

In **World 54**, a limited supply of new textiles has led to a resourceful and inventive fashion culture (see page 81). This enactment activity is designed to give a group of people an experience of World 54, but could be adapted for individual use.[148] You will need space to spread out; mirrors, if available, will be useful.

The core idea is to explore ways of dressing the body using old sheets or curtains, plus straps to secure them and random lightweight found items as adornments. For the enactment featured in this chapter, each sheet had at least one hole or ripped opening and small buttons added in a grid formation (approximately 50 cm apart). Our multi-strand straps, each around 1.2 m long, were made from buttonhole elastic and ribbon; the openings in the elastic allow the straps to be attached to the buttoned sheets with great versatility. We added fine-gauge cardigans with small buttons for further variation, and attached our found lightweight items to large hair grips so they could easily be added to the outfit.

1. Start with one sheet and one strap each and explore the possibilities of dressing with them, either individually or in pairs.

2. Create a performance: each person follows a randomly shuffled set of ten dressing instructions, without talking. (A sample set of cards is available online; print one set per two participants.[149])

3. If you wish, repeat the performance, adding in further dressing options such as adornments and cardigans. Each person uses a new set of instructions each time.

4. Working in groups of three or four people, devise and enact a performance of a World 54 scenario, lasting 2–3 minutes. Consider how the scenario would play out in the fictional fashion culture of World 54. (You can download suggested scenarios,[150] or think of your own.)

5. Reflect on the experience (see Activity 2.4).

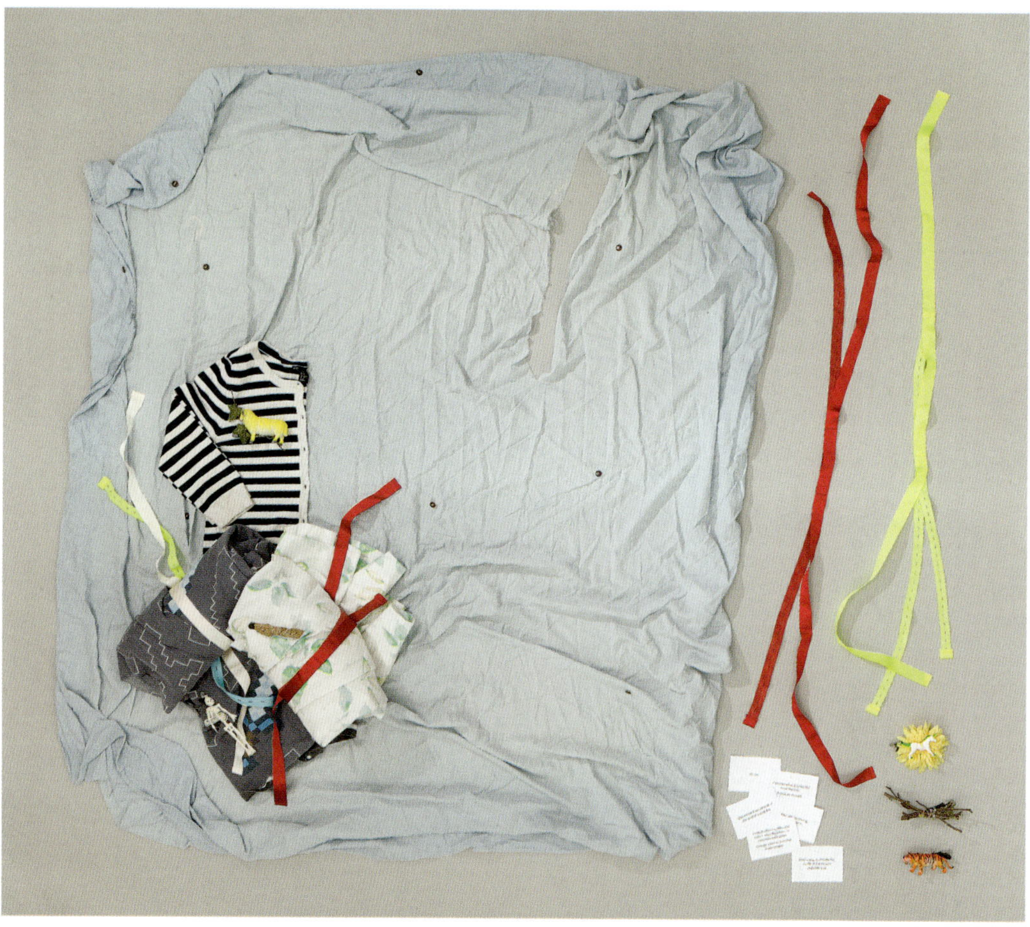

Figure 5.20 *Equipment for a World 54 enactment may include worn-out sheets with sewn-on buttons, versatile straps, fine-gauge cardigans, lightweight adornments and instruction cards.*

Figure 5.21 *A drop-in version of the World 54 enactment focused on Step 1 of these instructions. Participants were invited to explore the creative possibilities of the sheets, straps, cardigans and adornments, resulting in some striking silhouettes.*

Place and togetherness: ideas for the real world

Many rich ideas have offered themselves up for further exploration in this chapter. Here are five that spoke to me:

1. Localism

How can we dive deep into localism in fashion? What is the potential for local materials, local vernaculars, local choice, local waste, local songs and dances that connect us to our clothes? How can we celebrate flows and linkages between particular places and celebrate diverse local voices?

2. Third places

How can we create 'third places' for clothes-related activities, whether permanent or temporary, that are radically inclusive and actively break down established power relations and associated expectations of who makes, mends and styles clothes? How can we design these third places to be playful and conspirative? How can we prototype connections between people, technologies and resources to allow new communities of care to emerge?

3. Ritual

What rituals could we design to support post-growth fashion systems? How might these rituals transform us and reshape our real-world practices?

4. Feeling over looking

How can we collectively value the embodied experience of wearing over the aesthetics of our fashion choices? How can we lessen the intensity of the gaze of others? Could developing a sense of fashion as community in varied settings weaken the established relationship between fashion culture and the intense gaze of the city?

5. Solidarity

How can we act in solidarity with others involved in our fashion systems? How can we support one another, even if geographically distant? What cues can we put in place to prompt us to think in terms of solidarity, rather than selfishness?

* * * * * * * *

The chapter has also shown that there are dangers inherent in the work of bringing people together:

Romanticization

As with various compelling ideas discussed in earlier chapters, there is a risk that we could romanticize the notion of community. Communities are not inherently positive; they can be regressive, exclusionary and fraught with tension. We must be alert to these risks when seeking to build fashion-related communities.

Appropriation

Fashion has a long history of appropriating markers of local distinctiveness. Trendspotters, designers, stylists, consultants and everyday wearers are all capable of intentionally or unintentionally adopting 'exotic' or 'traditional' aesthetic styles in the pursuit of self-expression or commercial success, in a way that causes harm to the originating culture and its communities.

Locally distinctive *practices* might be more resistant to appropriation by commercial elements of the fashion system, yet we should remain alert to appropriation in this sphere. A hunger for meaning could lead us to adopt rituals from cultures other than our own, without appropriate knowledge.

DITTO-KIT
£$€
CLOTHES
AND SHOES
BUY BUY BUY
BANK
GOVERNMENT ISSUE
64

6

Organization and adaptation

Organizing fashion

How do you organize your clothes? For a long time I had an utterly dysfunctional approach: the clothes I rarely touched were hung neatly in the wardrobe, while those I actually wore were piled, layer upon layer, on a chair. The pile would grow, occasionally being mined for desired items, until it finally toppled over and revealed forgotten treasures that had been crushed in its depths. Some years ago I resolved to come up with a better solution and installed some shop fittings, with a series of hooks and hangers where I can easily hang or drape each item as I take it off. This keeps the clothes visible and lets them air in between washing – and radically reduces the risk of mislaying anything. (I was delighted when I discovered that the story of my system had inspired **World 71**, in which legislation is introduced to integrate space for clothes airing within new buildings in order to reduce unnecessary laundry.[1])

This chapter considers how fashion systems can be organized and how people navigate and respond to these systems. As Martin Parker explains, '"Organization" simply refers to patterns of people and things that humans arrange in order to get things done, the outcome of the patterning of people, technology and finance.'[2] I will look at the patterning of fashion at different scales, drawing on both real-world examples and ideas that have arisen across diverse Fashion Fictions visions. We will be skipping between worlds more quickly than in previous chapters – but, as throughout the book, I will explain the context of each world as it is introduced. I will signpost earlier mentions of each world but you should not need to refer back unless you want to explore other dimensions of the fictional vision; you can find all of the pages on which a particular world is mentioned in the World index at the start of the book.

Figure 6.1 *Frustrated with real-world fashion organizations that promote endless consumption, fictional visions such as World 64 explore restriction and resourcefulness.*

Describing the organization of the mainstream contemporary fashion system is a rather intimidating task. The system is based around a dynamic globalized industry with countless stakeholders; this industry is shaped by ever-shifting consumer demand, international trade deals and the imperative of growth common to all capitalist industries. From the layperson's perspective, the most visible organizations in this system are retail businesses, including high-street fast-fashion companies, their online-only competitors and luxury brands. The market is dominated by powerful multinationals, many of which own multiple brands.[3] While 'vertically integrated' companies have their own manufacturing facilities, many retailers and brands work with a less visible set of organizations: manufacturing businesses. Beyond the manufacturers lie further organizations, which produce the materials used in garment production: cloth, yarn, thread, dye, labels, zips, buttons. Further up the chain are the organizations that produce and trade fibre and other raw materials. All of these production-related organizations, which vary vastly in size, are connected via dispersed and flexible supply chains that are typically formed, order by order, according to supplier capacity and customer expectation.[4] Sitting alongside are organizations that stimulate desire for garments via branding, marketing, communication and promotion, and – at the other end of the product lifecycle – those that deal with discarded clothing. Then there are the institutions such as trade bodies, certification authorities, trade unions, non-governmental organizations, charities and think tanks that interact with other stakeholders, each according to their own purpose and agenda. In summary: the array of entities involved in the production, promotion, sale and disposal of clothing is dizzying.

* * * * * * * *

The organization of the contemporary mainstream fashion system is historically specific, having arisen in its current form only in recent decades. There are countless other ways in which fashion systems could be arranged; as Parker notes, 'human beings have organized themselves in a vast variety of patterns … [that] vary across space and time'.[5] If we were to look back at the origins of the European fashion system that developed into today's globalized industry, we could highlight examples of these different patterns. We might point out the organized system of annual change that was codified in the 1660s and 1670s for silks woven in Lyon – applying, of course, only to the elite[6] – or the conventions of the haute couture system that shaped the industry for a century from the 1860s, based around the release of two collections per year and an 'orderly flow' from design house to high street.[7] We could equally point to the organizations that produced readymade clothes before fast fashion first emerged in the 1980s; this earlier system used a Fordist manufacturing model based on the mass production of standardized and slow-changing styles.[8]

If we were to look beyond the elite and the mainstream in this historical sweep, we would find countless more patterns, such as – to pick just one example that I find particularly intriguing – the combination of professional and amateur activity in the manufacture of workers' smocks in areas of rural England in the nineteenth century.[9] If we were to extend our view beyond Europe or look further back in time we would encounter still more. Many of the visions created for the Fashion Fictions project suggest their own alternative configurations that, in very different ways, push beyond the current mainstream system. This is heartening, given that the aim of Fashion Fictions is to open up space for people to dream how fashion might be otherwise and to challenge the widespread sense that the established mainstream system can only be tweaked, rather than fundamentally reimagined.

Many of these fictions reimagine the organization of production: how clothes are made. In Chapter 5 we encountered a number of worlds that envisage localized production, such as the locally distinctive vernacular styles created in each neighbourhood of **World 42**. In **World 57** a trend for tailor-made clothes spreads from town to town,[10] while in **World 52** bespoke making takes a different form, with digital technologies enabling makers to serve international clients.[11] (Although making clothes to measure is unusual in many places today, there are parts of the world where this practice is still common, reminding us of the variety of practices that survive within and alongside the globalized fashion system.) Some contributors to Fashion Fictions imagine production being managed in a more coordinated way. **World 81**, for example, describes a government-enforced 'connection economy' in which consumers and local companies collaborate to establish 'the design needs of garments and textiles for each country to ensure a reduction of waste, material and inventory'.[12]

This outline reminds me of a proposal for the organization of the clothing trade developed by Jeanne Deroin, a self-educated dressmaker and committed feminist, in France in the mid-nineteenth century. The capitalist economy was in a period of dramatic transformation at that time, with the clothing trades shifting from custom making to the production of readymade clothing.[13] Deroin proposed a federation of workers' associations that would create a balance between production and consumption, researching consumer needs and production methods and adjusting the number of workers in each trade to avoid unemployment.[14] She envisaged goods and services being exchanged directly between the workers, with their relative value managed by the associations to ensure fairness. As Deroin put it: 'The hairdressers will do the hair of the shoemakers who will supply their footwear.'[15]

The connection between consumers and producers in World 81 also brings to mind a present-day story of solidarity and organization, this time from Italy. In 2021 the owners of the GKN car parts factory in Florence announced its closure, with the loss of hundreds of jobs. A collective of workers occupied the plant and launched a campaign to challenge the closure. As part of this campaign the striking workers formed an unlikely alliance with climate justice activists, drafting a plan to repurpose the plant to manufacture equipment needed for sustainable transitions, such as cargo bikes and solar panels, rather than parts for private cars.[16] I am inspired by this example of workers and activists collaborating to align the needs of workers with those of the wider society. It makes me wonder what proposals a comparable alliance between garment workers and sustainable fashion activists could generate.

In some fictional worlds the making shifts from the professional to the amateur sphere. Again, I highlighted some of these worlds in Chapter 5, including **World 30**, in which sewing becomes an unstoppable trend among young people, and **World 173**, in which sewing clubs are more common than slimming clubs. **World 172**, meanwhile, describes an influential community of 'radical anarchist sewists' who 'appropriated and repurposed defunct department stores, devoting floorspace to pattern & tool libraries, machine "garages", skill & material exchanges, cutting rooms, fitting rooms, cafes, crèches and bartering halls where diverse communities of amateur designers/makers swap elaborately patch-worked, pieced, embellished and repurposed garments for other goods and services'.[17] While this might appear to be a fanciful proposition, I am reminded of Sparks, a real-world 'creative sustainability hub' set up in a former department store in Bristol, incorporating installations, events, artists' studios and rehearsal and performance spaces alongside shops selling secondhand and upcycled goods.[18]

An interesting variation on the theme of do-it-yourself making can be found in fictions that describe the integration of wearer activities to larger-scale industry. In **World 65**, for example, customers must spend time working in agricultural fibre production for each item they purchase,[19] while in **World 82** all citizens must learn to disassemble waste garments into their component materials to maximize recycling.[20] A similar sense of partnership between larger and smaller organizations can be identified in **World 53**, the world briefly mentioned in Chapter 5 in which biological garments are grown at home or in local material-makeries. The fiction explains that this practice 'is supported by an internationally connected network of culture guilds that store, develop and share programmable biological cultures and materials. They partner in symbiosis with citizen guilds and individuals to guide the development of new cultures.'

The **World 14** fiction sees value in citizens gaining access to factories:

A global economic collapse in World 14 led to collapse in high street fashion giants followed by the luxury behemoths. A government finally realised that the UK has a wealth in fashion graduates and skilled makers – who are often blocked from making micro business work because of accessing production.

A subsidised system is worked out so garment workers have a living wage and factory down periods are covered, allowing people to access the factories and have clothing made in small batches – this invigorates local economies, democratises style as people are freed to choose what suits them rather than it being an instructed top down 'choice' and regional fashions become a thing![21]

I explored this fiction in an intensive Stage 2 workshop with two collaborators.[22] Together, we built a vision of a factory that has been run as a cooperative of workers and users for over twenty years and provides accessible skilled garment production to local designers and individuals (Figure 6.2). The cooperative's commitment to regenerative practices has led to various initiatives, including the

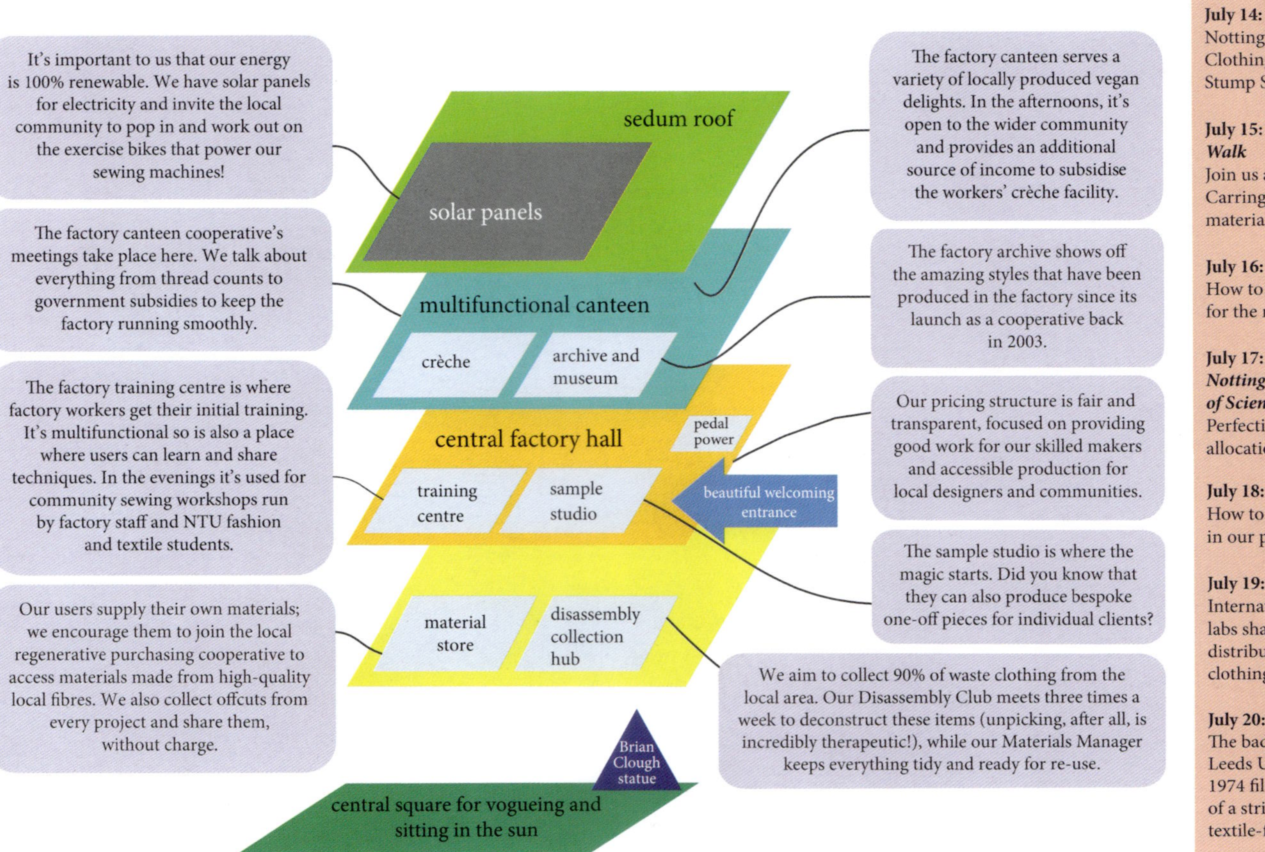

Figure 6.2 *In World 14, clothing production is open to all. This cooperative factory – presented here via an informative webpage aimed at new members – is a vibrant neighbourhood hub of making activity and fashion excellence.*

gathering of local textile waste for reuse, the development of skills through informal events and formal education, energy self-sufficiency, and networking with similar organizations in other towns and cities.

* * * * * * * *

Learning is another domain of organization that arises frequently in the fictions. In many cases, an interest in learning overlaps with the visions of DIY making and local production already discussed. While the fictions often describe informal types of learning, some worlds focus on formal settings, and especially the incorporation of sewing or textiles skills into the core of school education. This is certainly the case in **World 9**, in which – as discussed in Chapter 5 – learning to sew is a teenage rite of passage. The group exploring the world at Stage 2 discussed textiles being a compulsory subject to the age of sixteen, followed by specialist studies such as boot-making or

Figure 6.3 *Fashion activities can be organized digitally, as well as physically. In World 145, digital clothes must be worn on social media;[23] this platform, Pool, offers an interface through which users can buy, sell and exchange digital garments using a virtual currency.*

buttonholes. In **World 83**, sewing and textiles is a core subject taught at all schools in Denmark,[24] while in **World 23**, 50 per cent of the time traditionally allocated to maths in primary schools is replaced by crafts.[25]

What about the organization of clothing maintenance activities such as washing and mending? When I wrote the **World 3** fiction – a Stage 2 interpretation of which I have discussed in earlier chapters – I was keen to stretch my ideas about how washing might be organized by describing a network of community laundries, founded by second-wave feminists in the 1980s. Other fictions show contributors' interest in *professional* support for maintenance, especially mending. In Chapter 5 I briefly mentioned the **World 36** fiction, in which mending studios are widespread – as widespread, in fact, as tattoo parlours. A similar notion is described in the original fiction for **World 12**, in which 'repair salons' are found on every high street – ubiquitous, mainstream and diverse, to suit many tastes and needs.[26] This vision, while far-fetched in the context of consumer society today, does have real-world precedents. In the Soviet Union of the 1960s and 1970s, for example, there was a huge network of repair services, with thousands of repair shops in Moscow and Leningrad dealing with clothing and shoes as well as domestic appliances and furniture.[27]

A final dimension of clothing organization that I will consider is exchange: swaps, libraries and shared wardrobes. At clothes swaps, wearers become suppliers: they contribute their unwanted garments to a communal collection and earn the right to select garments from that collection for themselves.[28] Having grown in popularity in recent years, clothes swaps are now found in diverse locations, with many organizational variations. The principle has also transferred online, with app Nuw enabling wearers to 'Join the Thrift Swapping Revolution'.[29] Where swaps appear in the fictions, they push beyond the present in different ways. **World 143**, for example, describes a twice-yearly *global* clothes swap – quite the organizational feat.[30] The Stage 2 development of nature-focused **World 19** included a vision in which fashion and other household practices were entwined through the integration of seed-sharing and garment-sharing practices.

In Chapter 3 we encountered the Clothing Library of **World 120**, a rich and varied clothing collection with integrated customization and repair support and a system for connecting borrowers via notes that document their wearing experiences. **World 26** also focuses on libraries, this time for school uniforms:

In World 26 in 1999 the Department for Education introduced School Uniform Libraries in every school and a ban on the sale of school uniform by private companies. Uniforms were standardised across schools, and the libraries run by a network of social enterprises that form a co-operative big enough to work directly with manufacturers ensuring ethical and sustainable manufacture and a comprehensive recycling system.[31]

The fiction goes on to explain that the normalization of pre-used clothing changes attitudes to secondhand items in World 26, with a long-term impact on clothing behaviours.

Another fiction, **World 176**, describes a Scottish island community's shared wardrobe, which has a more informal feel in comparison with a library. The text explains that the practice of sharing clothes has an impact on the community's culture; inclusivity in terms of gender and age is fostered, as 'the semiotic communications present in garments are recreated and subverted'.[32] Rather wonderfully, the practice spreads to other locations via the export of the island's whiskey. A similar setup is described in **World 55**, in which 'shared community wardrobes can be found in each city and village: one city, one wardrobe'. Although it was originally triggered by a clothing shortage in the 1950s, today the system has created a culture in which 'fashion becomes part of the greater good of the society. Because of the diversity of garments in size, colour and style everyone can play around with this and there are no boundaries anymore. Fashion, in this collective wardrobe, is a party'.[33]

Figure 6.4 *This Stage 2 interpretation of World 120 presents a clothing library that spans an entire mall. The storefronts are used to organize the inventory and house tools, documentation and publications along with galleries and event spaces.*

Clothing libraries are being established in the real world, often with a particular focus such as clothes for babies and children, outfits for special occasions or interviews, or vintage and designer items. Websites promoting such initiatives give a sense of the way in which they are organized: how many items can be borrowed and for how long; the cost of borrowing and deposit required, if any; arrangements for accessing the library to borrow and return items. A group seeking to establish a new library might productively learn from others who are further along the path – or, perhaps, from similar initiatives in other fields. I enjoyed reading, for example, about a community bike-sharing scheme in Bratislava, White Bikes, through which hundreds of registered users can borrow bikes distributed across the city using an open-source digital platform.[34] The scheme is free to use, but has rules to minimize abuse: users lose credit points if they keep a bike for longer than an hour or do not lock it safely, but can replace these points by cleaning bikes or relocating them to where they are needed. Through this system, the initiative is self-sustaining. Could a similar system work for coats or frocks rather than bikes, I wonder?

NOTTINGHAM COMMUNITY WARDROBE

Mission Circle Agenda
Monthly meeting
14 July 2023, 17.00–20.00

Attending Circle members, representing:
- Local community
- Employees
- Volunteers
- Education partner
- Government funding partner
- Future generations
- Local nature (forests, rivers)
- Global supply chains

1. Broad reflection on our purposes
   - Go over our purpose: We exist to guarantee all people
     in Nottingham are clothed in a way that provides

Figure 6.5 *In World 55, shared community wardrobes are widespread. This intentionally mundane Stage 2 prototype – a meeting agenda – provides a glimpse into the working practices of one of these wardrobes. The wardrobe is organized using sociocracy, a 'peer governance system based on consent'.[35] As the agenda indicates, the attendees include people representing local nature and global supply chains alongside employees, volunteers and other partners.*

Organizing otherwise

In the previous section I discussed the organization of fashion in terms of activity: making, learning, swapping, sharing. Another approach would be to foreground the economic context for these activities: whether they take place in the public sector, the private sector or the third sector – that is, 'a space for social, economic and political activities that offer an alternative to both state command and free-market economies'.[36] Perhaps surprisingly, there is plenty to say about the public sector: Fashion Fictions participants come up with all kinds of visions in which the state takes a lead. We readily imagine laws, policies and schemes that encourage, prohibit or manage certain behaviours – such as **World 159**, in which clothing designers and suppliers must be licensed.[37] Taxes and subsidies can play a role in supporting these policies. For example, the Stage 2 workshop group exploring **World 9** – the world in which learning to sew is as familiar and widespread as learning to drive – imagined that a shop selling readymade clothes would be taxed at a higher rate than a communal making hub. Likewise, readymade garments would be taxed, whereas raw materials would not; in fact, subsidies would promote the use of locally produced cloth. A state could also instigate official investigations to inform future policy – such as the 'commission on fashion's role in ecocide' that is underway in nature-focused **World 16**.

Real-world governments intervene in clothing and textile industries in various ways, for example using subsidies to promote restructuring and rationalization and through agreements that aim to stimulate international trade or protect their domestic industries.[38] Today, policies are increasingly focused on the environmental and social impacts of the industry. The Garment Worker Protection Act, which came into force in California in 2022, aimed to end wage theft and improve working conditions in garment manufacturing by outlawing the piece-rate system of payment and, through legal liability, incentivizing brands to tackle workplace violations.[39] In 2024 French legislators passed a bill to impose a surcharge on fast-fashion products and ban fast-fashion advertising, building on a scheme set up the previous year in which citizens can claim up to €25 towards the cost of mending clothes or shoes.[40] These examples are part of a wider shift towards greater regulation of the textile and fashion industries.

Stepping back from a focus on fashion, we can consider the role of the state in social-ecological transformations more widely. Ulrich Brand and his co-authors note that this role is compromised, for national governments are deeply dependent on economic growth and the taxes generated through capitalist activity. This dependence 'pushes state agency toward securing unsustainable structures, processes, and power relations even with respect to policies that, at first sight, intend to deal with the ecological crisis'.[41] They suggest that the state could play a more positive role by strengthening regional and city authorities and facilitating democratic deliberation regarding the measures needed to pursue sustainability.

There are some fictions that focus on action at the municipal, rather than national, level. In **World 109**, for example, the Group Representation Constituencies in Singapore are given the responsibility to establish repair salons in their respective areas,[42] while in **World 59** a city council declares a climate emergency. This declaration prompts a coalition of citizens, institutions and businesses to work together to understand the social and environmental impacts of textile waste and transform their local practices.[43] Those keen to pursue action at a municipal level in the real world could take inspiration from localized policies in Berlin that support fashion designers with benefits such as subsidized space,[44] and from initiatives such as the Amsterdam Doughnut Coalition. This network of public, private and third-sector organizations uses Kate Raworth's post-growth 'doughnut economics' principles – which seek to meet human needs within planetary boundaries – to work towards 'a city where both people and nature can thrive, locally and globally'.[45]

* * * * * * * *

In the real-world fashion system, the private sector dominates: there are many big companies, owned by shareholders and driven by growth. The form of organization used within these companies is management, a hierarchical system that mediates between owners and workers. Kiri Langmead, Chris Land and Daniel King describe management, which dominates the teaching in business schools around the world, as a 'constitutively irresponsible' form of organizing due to its prioritization of shareholders' interests above all other considerations – including the environmental and human costs of pollution and carbon emissions, which do not show up on companies' balance sheets.[46] In the fictions there is little explicit discussion of private-sector businesses, especially retail businesses. This absence is, I think, understandable: contributors are conscious of the urgent need to reduce fashion consumption in the global North and are taking the opportunity to imagine spaces and activities beyond shops and shopping. It may also be that contributors do not see capitalist industry as a leader for change. But Talia, a Stage 2 workshop participant who had spent time browsing the collection of worlds, offered a thought-provoking perspective on the absence of commerce in the fictions. She noted, 'I think it's really strange that we wish away the market … in these worlds that have been invented for this project, no-one goes shopping … [but] we've had markets for millennia, long before capitalism.'

Indeed, commerce and capitalism are not the same thing. There are many possible trading enterprises other than privately owned companies driven by growth, just as there are many possible forms of organizing other than management. Martin Parker explains that organizations can be endlessly variable, according to an array of factors:

This might involve size, structure, division of labour and specialization, use of material or virtual technologies, tenure of position, tenure of employment, decision-making structure, physical location of members, what can be expected for and from the worker …, employee ownership and raising of finance, nature of rules (informal or formal), assumptions about growth, assumptions about core business, distribution of profits or losses, accountability, relation to customers or clients, forms of co-ordination, degree of centralization or redundancy, extent of flexibility and so on.[47]

He goes on to describe a second set of distinguishing factors, this time relating to exchange:

who sells, who buys, who competes, what can be bought, sold, or exchanged, when and where, for how much or how little, under what rules, using what medium of exchange, with what information, derived from where, available to who and audited by who, with what assumptions about property rights, and to what end.

By varying these multiple factors we could generate, in a kaleidoscope-like fashion, an endless array of combinations. Some combinations would fall within what we typically think of as 'the economy': capitalist businesses, staffed by waged labour, producing goods or services for a market. Yet as J. K. Gibson-Graham (two feminist geographers who write under a shared pen name) explain, there are many other economic practices that both support and challenge the mainstream economy, including practices of nonconsumption and nonmarket consumption such as gifting, loaning, sharing and bartering.[48] Many of the organizational combinations generated by our kaleidoscope would involve such practices – which 'have other principles of functioning and value practices that are alternative to the hegemonic profit-oriented ones'.[49] For an example of one possible alternative, let us consider worker cooperatives. These organizations, which trade in goods and services and are found in most sectors of the economy, can be defined as 'groups of workers who democratically control and collectively own the businesses they work in'.[50] In contrast to workers in privately owned companies, employees share responsibility; they collectively organize both the goals of the organization and the means by which they pursue these goals. A further difference is described by Langmead, Land and King: 'As many cooperatives are held in-trust, so co-operators cannot simply sell out their shares for personal profit, this model also removes the motivation to accumulate found in capitalist businesses.'[51]

Langmead, Land and King locate worker cooperatives within a broader form of organizing, which is quite different to the management of conventional business: commoning. I think of commoning as a practice of negotiated sharing; this sharing takes place within a system known as a commons. Massimo De Angelis and David Harvie describe commons as 'social systems in which resources are shared by a community of users/producers, who also define the modes of use and production, distribution and circulation of these resources through democratic and horizontal forms of governance'.[52] There are three key elements in any commons: the resource, which might be material or immaterial; the commoners, who have both rights and responsibilities in relation to the resource; and the activity of commoning, which involves maintaining and managing the resource by collectively negotiating a set of protocols and norms. Commons might be formally established and subject to carefully articulated rules; they might equally be informal, mobile and temporary, improvised through the act of commoning. Regardless, as David Bollier explains, commons are characterized by 'bottom-up participation, personal responsibility, transparency and self-policing accountability'.[53] Leila Dawney suggests that commoning is therefore 'about inhabiting a different set of relations: a set of relations that are incongruous with the individualism, atomisation and privatisation that mark the contemporary condition and leave us feeling unsupported, isolated and precarious'.[54]

I was first introduced to the concept of the commons in high-school history lessons: I learned about the Enclosure Acts of the seventeenth, eighteenth and nineteenth centuries that transferred the ownership of common land in England into private hands.[55] While land is probably the most familiar form of resource that can be held in common, alongside other physical things such as buildings, fish stocks or even the air, immaterial resources such as knowledge and information can equally be shared through commoning. Examples of thriving commons can be found all over the world. The White Bikes scheme in Bratislava, mentioned earlier in the chapter, is just one of several case studies in a guide to creating and maintaining commons, *The Urban Commons Cookbook*;[56] dozens of further examples, across many domains of everyday life, can be found in another publication, *The Commoner's Catalog for Changemaking*.[57]

The idea of the commons is rapidly spreading within the fashion context. A report by Zoe Gilbertson for South West England Fibreshed, for example, explores the potential for commons-based organizations, such as cooperatives, to support the development of a regenerative regional textile system.[58] The Shared Stewardship initiative of the Netherlands-based Linen Project, meanwhile, has brought commoning principles to life by forming a community that can 'intimately experience the material, agricultural, and social processes involved in collectively cultivating textiles, objects and garments from seed … [to] enact a new economic, social and cultural paradigm'.[59] The groundswell of interest in commons is further catalyzed by a new online platform for commoning initiatives, Our Common Market, coordinated by activist organization Fashion Act Now.[60]

Long after my school history lessons, a basic understanding of the commons stayed with me – along with an enduring rage at the injustice and violence of enclosure. Both influenced the notion of the 'fashion commons' that formed the foundation of my PhD research and the book that research grew into, *Folk Fashion: Understanding Homemade Clothes*. At that time I was thinking about the fashion commons in a conceptual way, proposing that we see 'all of the garments in existence – new, old, fashionable and unfashionable … [and] every way of dressing throughout history' as a valuable common resource that should be shared by all.[61] This collective resource, I argued, has been enclosed through the industrialization and professionalization of clothing production; amateur making provides us with an accessible yet powerful means of challenging this enclosure.

Fashion Fictions prompted me to return to the idea of the fashion commons, this time working in a more practical way. I invented **World 43**, in which the sale of all blue textiles, whether new or used, has been banned for environmental reasons. With the supply of new items cut off, systems of exchange have developed in which blue items are traded and repaired at commoning hubs.[62] I had the opportunity to create one of these hubs as an interactive installation, *A Temporary Outpost of the Blue Fashion Commons*, for a touring exhibition entitled *We Are Commoners* (Figures 6.6 and 6.7).[63] Exhibition visitors were invited to try out life in this alternative fashion system by exchanging and mending blue garments at the real-world hub. My aim was to give people an embodied and hands-on experience of a different economic model in order to provoke discussion and reflection. As Bastien Kerspern notes, 'Economics is part of our daily life, but it is regarded by many as an abstract concept. The human scale is about making new economic perspectives tangible, relatable and ready to be debated beyond a community of experts.'[64]

Figure 6.6 A Temporary Outpost of the Blue Fashion Commons, *an installation that formed part of a national touring exhibition in the UK, invited exhibition visitors to exchange and mend blue clothes as part of a slow enactment of World 43.*

Figure 6.7 *This sign articulates the protocols and norms of the World 43 commoning hub. The rules were designed to cater for a shifting community of commoners while ensuring that the resource did not become depleted over time.*

* * * * * * * * *

In Chapter 1 I explained that capitalism – an economic system in which wealth is invested to generate more wealth – is so entrenched and dominant that we find it difficult to imagine alternatives. Fashion Fictions has proved to be a productive platform for participants to notice, reflect on and challenge this dominance. Johnny, for example, commented on how the Stage 2 workshop he attended had led him to reflect on the system he has grown up within:

> I'm sure lots of people my age kind of feel the same thing … you should be constantly consuming, you know, it's a bit lame to be always wearing the same pair of shoes. … It made me realise that I've had this way of thinking and maybe question, like, where has this come from. … We're all from birth, I guess, especially my generation, brainwashed to be good little consumers, constantly feeding the capitalist system.

Ideas that critique the fundamentals of capitalism certainly arise in the fictions. The Stage 2 group exploring the fungi-centric **World 91** discussed in Chapter 4, for example, suggested that the world would have seen 'a massive shift on things like capitalism, financialization, universal basic income and welfare and benefits, the nature of work'. These ideas are reminiscent of activity in the degrowth movement that examines the role of policies such as 'caps, green taxes, worktime reduction, or a basic and a maximum income' in fostering prosperity within planetary boundaries.[65] **World 49** goes as far as to describe the abolition of waged labour and the creation of 'a ludic society where people provide for one another through play and experimentation'.[66] Even in fictions that describe less extreme diversions from the status quo, the theme of work/life balance is a common feature; in various worlds it is common to take time away from paid work for domestic making and mending, other creative endeavours and community activities.

The Stage 1 fictions, then, present an array of ideas for alternative ways of organizing fashion and the wider economy. And there are many alternatives already up and running in the real world, such as retail cooperatives, local exchange trading systems, B-corps, trusts, co-producers, collectives,

Figure 6.8 *World 107 has an unconventional system of exchange: garments and their components are used as a form of money. The value of each component derives from various factors including cultural influence, craftsmanship and quality. This system can be traced back to the Silk Road trade routes which connected China and Europe for over 1,500 years until medieval times.*[67]

Figure 6.9 *Some fictions do not just reimagine how fashion works: they reimagine the wider economic system. Stage 2 workshop participant Benji described how societies in World 4 had shifted from capitalism to a new system, 'thrivenism'. The two systems are described in the memoir that Benji created as their Stage 2 prototype (see also Figure 3.11).*

sociocracies, family businesses, trade unions and social enterprises.[68] Yet many people, even those convinced of the shortcomings of capitalism, find it difficult to get a handle on what alternative systems could look and feel like. At the end of a Stage 2 workshop, as the participants were reflecting on the experiences of imagining fictional worlds, one person noted the absence of shared reference points for alternatives to capitalism. The conversation had, she observed, tended to lurch either to communism or some sort of 'tribal' society – rather than the many possibilities that can already be found coexisting alongside and within the capitalist system, in our history books and in the speculative realms of the possible.

The Stage 2 discussions revealed further blind spots, including inequality. Many conversations mentioned, or hinted at, divisions based on class and wealth in the fictional worlds. These differences sometimes arose in the context of concern: concern for how those who were economically disadvantaged might navigate a particular imagined world, or for how rich people might game the system. A few groups did take a different approach, such as the group exploring the resourceful **World 54**, in which – as discussed in Chapters 3 and 5 – textile production is severely limited: they made a conscious choice to imagine a world *without* class inequality. But looking back, I was surprised that more groups did not question the presence of inequality in their fictional worlds – given that they had been invited to imagine enticing systems, with every aspect of society and culture on the table.

It was not always clear whether the groups had not thought to question whether inequality would arise in a positive society, or whether they felt that stratification is inevitable in *any* society. I would argue that inequality is not, in fact, inevitable. In *The Dawn of Everything: A New History of Humanity*, David Graeber and David Wengrow challenge the widespread view that as societies develop and become 'civilized', they automatically become less equal; as evidence, the authors highlight numerous examples of large-scale societies that have existed without ruling elites and hierarchical systems. This tendency to accept inequality without question appears to be an example of present reality shaping our imaginative visions. As Fredric Jameson describes, 'our imaginations are hostages to our own mode of production (and perhaps to whatever remnants of past ones it has preserved)'.[69]

Restriction and rebellion

When we pattern people and things – when we organize ourselves – we shape behaviour: we enable certain activities and practices and restrict others. In some visions generated for Fashion Fictions, there is *less* restriction; societal expectations are lessened or lifted. In Chapter 5 I mentioned the genderless school uniforms of **World 76**; a related approach can be identified in **World 166**, in which all students wear uniforms traditionally gendered as female one year and male the next, fostering a culture of inclusivity. Over time, the association between particular garments and a particular gender is dissolved.[70] In **World 88**, a similarly inclusive culture can be traced back to the influence of Elizabeth I wearing 'an adapted version of her father's armour' and a Royal Proclamation declaring that 'clothing would not designate gender – merely rank'.[71] Various Stage 2 conversations explored the lessening of other social expectations. The group exploring **World 3** (discussed in detail in Chapter 5), in which people come together to do their shared laundry, thought that this practice would lead to less taboo about menstruation. Similarly, the group exploring **World 80**, in which people wear the same outfit for a month, thought that bodily smells would be accepted – perhaps even to the point that smelling 'good' would be stigmatized.

In many of the fictions, however, contributors imagine more, rather than less, restriction. Earlier in this chapter I discussed the role of the state in shaping a fashion system by setting up schemes, subsidies and taxes that influence and limit certain activities, sometimes decreed by law. There are many real-world examples of such laws. In 1700, for example, a British Act of Parliament banned the import of all Asian textiles other than unfinished and plain cottons, in an attempt to protect the silk and wool industries.[72] (This measure led to the growth of the British cotton industry, which came to destroy India's centuries-old industry in a devastating example of colonial power.[73]) In the USA at the turn of the twentieth century, meanwhile, laws were passed to restrict the use of birds' feathers in hats, after hunters decimated entire colonies of herons and egrets.[74]

Restrictive laws abound in the fictions. In **World 62**, the distribution of images portraying clothes is outlawed; in **World 48**, it is a ban on the production of garments from raw materials that leads to a culture of resourcefulness. A law is a convenient fictional device to explain a rapid shift in fashion culture – and indeed a device that I mention within the Stage 1 guidance as a possible way of explaining why a parallel world developed differently to our own. Like spirituality, discussed in Chapter 4, and ritual, discussed in Chapter 5, a law is an effective means of explaining why people in a fictional world behave in a way that would seem utterly unthinkable in our own context. Yet the frequency of legal measures in the fictions and discussions gives me a sense that there could be a genuine appetite for stronger governance in the fashion system.

Figure 6.10 *The Stage 2 group exploring World 3, who envisioned a thriving network of community laundries, felt that red socks – which carry the danger of inadvertently contaminating a white wash – would be restricted. This government-issued poster invites citizens to report transgressions.*

Voluntary agreements by industry stakeholders are another means of restricting activity. Textiles 2030, for example, is a UK-based voluntary initiative that requires signatories to commit to targets including a 50 per cent reduction in the overall carbon footprint of new textile products and a 30 per cent reduction in the overall water footprint of new textile products.[75] Other initiatives include certification and labelling schemes that promise to improve sustainability standards across the industry. Yet such schemes are not binding and may serve to confuse, rather than improve, issues of sustainability. As a report from the Changing Markets Foundation argues, 'the existence of these schemes and the inherent lack of accountability within them are a key part of the greenwashing machinery of the modern fashion industry'.[76] In **World 47**, a fiction that I co-authored, an activist campaign by a radical group of fashion students forces a more impactful industrial agreement, with business owners agreeing to limit clothing production. The students also implement a fifteen-year apprenticeship scheme for fashion designers, involving on-the-ground training in every facet of the fashion system. This initiative develops into an ethical code for designers – another type of rule that governs behaviour: 'With designers now guided, like doctors, by the principle of "do no harm", great ethical deliberation precedes every design act'.[77]

Formal laws and industry agreements are not the only means by which activities are shaped and influenced. In many fictions, restrictions are enacted through informal social norms: 'socially constructed guidelines that suggest appropriate behavior in certain social situations'.[78] In Chapter 4 I mentioned the prohibition of artificial fertilizers in **World 28**, where natural dyeing is widespread. The group exploring the world at Stage 2 explained that because understanding of nature is widespread in World 28, laws are not needed to manage behaviour: 'because we, in this world, are already convinced that that's the right way to do it. Because that's going to affect our food as well, and everything's interconnected.'

Formal rules and informal norms combine to shape behaviour in the fictional worlds and span many different kinds of activity. As I mentioned in Chapter 5, some worlds imagine restrictions on international trade; others imagine restrictions on clothing production, whether halting the manufacture of new textiles entirely or limiting their use in some way. In **World 140**, for example, clothes that cannot be recycled are banned;[79] in **World 84**, sweatshop production is illegal.[80] In the Stage 2 exploration of nature-centric **World 19**, discussed in Chapter 4, it was suggested that plastic fibres would be eliminated and all synthetic garments removed from circulation. Another type of restriction relates to convenience. In **World 71**, for example, the 'mismanagement of utilities on a mass scale by the British government' causes power cuts and water shortages. The authorities prioritize energy and water for essential activities, 'leaving individuals to create resourceful approaches to "non-essential" activities such as laundry' – which eventually develop into the architectural schemes to facilitate clothes airing that I described at the start of the chapter.

Restrictions could also limit the size of the wardrobe. An example of this approach can be found in **World 37**, in which a working group of experts and wearers came up with a global mandate: that 'every person on the planet – including celebrities, leaders, everyone – could only have a capsule wardrobe', comprising:

5 pieces of underwear (bottom), 5 pairs of socks, 5 short-sleeve or sleeveless shirts (can mix them), 5 long-sleeve shirts, 5 sweaters, 5 bottoms (skirts and/or pants), 5 pairs of shoes, 3 jackets/blazers, 2 coats, 2 scarves, 2 hats, and 2 pairs of gloves. An additional 2 piece underwear (top) allowance applies for those who want to cover their top region (ie: a bra, binder, camisole).[81]

Alternatively, the rate of clothing consumption could be limited. In **World 58**, each family is allocated a monthly carbon budget to cover all daily necessities, including clothing.[82] In **World 106**, each person is given twenty kilograms of fibre at birth, to provide their clothes for life (see Figure 5.9), while in **World 241** people are allowed to acquire just 100 items of clothing in their lifetime.[83] In **World 45**, as discussed in Chapter 4, superstition means that textiles must be used for a year as curtains before they can be cut into clothing. This superstition acts as a form of restriction, slowing

Figure 6.11 *In World 200, a five-piece mandatory wardrobe is issued by the government: a t-shirt, shirt, trousers, long skirt and jacket. All genders are given the same wardrobe, which is refreshed every three years.*[84]

consumption. Social restriction is also at play in **World 180**, in which 'there is no concept of "more"'.[85] This intriguing proposition reminds me of the concept of languaging, discussed in Chapter 3, which describes the dynamic interplay between what is sayable and what is doable in any particular culture.

Various fictions explore the restriction of choice via systems based on the issuing of standardized garments, eliminating the excess production and consumption associated with choice and changing fashions. Sometimes these are regulation uniform garments, echoing ideas such as the Tuta, a functional one-piece garment designed by Italian Futurist artist Thayaht in 1919–20.[86] In **World 64**, for example, uniform garments are issued to all citizens; these items are creatively customized through the addition of small accessories such as fragments of pre-regulation garments, found objects or materials found in nature.[87] In other fictions, standardized ranges offer a degree of choice. The designs to be included in the standardized garment ranges of **World 5** – mentioned in Chapter 5 – are selected by public vote, meaning that the styles available vary from place to place. Occasionally, standardization is motivated by a purpose other than the reduction of consumption. In **World 139**, for example, clothing options are limited as a strategy for world peace after the Second World War, to minimize perceived differences between different peoples of the world.[88]

* * * * * * * * *

From the earliest Fashion Fictions workshops I discovered that discussion of restriction, whether enforced via formal laws or informal norms, often leads to debate about whether people would push back against that restriction through protest or non-compliance. Non-compliance exists on a spectrum, from 'behaviors that are considered acceptable … although they technically might violate a norm' through to rebellion, or – in sociological terms – deviance.[89] These possibilities were a regular feature of conversations in the Stage 2 workshops. The group exploring **World 124** (discussed in Chapters 4 and 5), in which sheep graze on city streets, wondered about protests against the system – from, perhaps, 'the allergic movement' or even the 'flax liberation front' – which might be expressed as peaceful demonstrations or violence. The group exploring **World 62** (discussed in Chapter 3), in which the distribution of images of clothes is banned, even demonstrated deviance themselves. The cover of the fashion magazine that they created as their prototype not only used rich descriptive words to describe a particular textile, but – bending the World 62 rules – arranged the words in patterns to give a sense of its visual impact.

Intriguingly, the notion of black markets – 'illegal economies that exist parallel to formal, legal markets'[90] – arises frequently in the fictions. The World 62 group mentioned a 'black market in images' as a particularly deviant route of rebellious behaviour; the concept also appeared in the very first fiction that I wrote, in which the buying and selling of clothing has long been illegal. In **World 1**, I explained, 'Those who are unwilling or unable to make for themselves must rely on bartering, gifts (including the ultimate jackpot – an entire inherited wardrobe) or the inevitable black market.'[91] Insights into how such activity might play out could perhaps be gleaned through examination of the illicit consumption practices that arose alongside the planned economy of the Soviet Union to address the mismatch between supply and demand of clothing – including engaging a 'domestic personal sewer', buying from an unregistered maker or sourcing goods from illegal traders, or 'speculators'.[92] As Larissa Zakharova explains, 'The dream of Soviet economists of egalitarian consumption was very far from real Soviet consumer practices.'[93]

Another world explored at the Stage 2 workshops, **World 72**, helps us to look at the theme of rebellion in more detail. The first part of the original fiction deals with restriction: 'In World 72, in the noughties, cotton farmers and clothing workers revolt and demand living wages and ecological safeguarding. Rationed clothes and sustainable utility garments are compulsory.'[94] The group of participants who chose to explore World 72 at a Stage 2 workshop found that this was a tricky world to see in a positive light, with clear potential for a dystopian element in the idea of rationing and compulsory garment choices.[95] The group found themselves imagining an unflattering and unloved boiler suit as the standard-issue garment, while group member Maz expressed incredulity at the notion of trusting 'the government, the state, especially the British post-imperial state, to have that much control over how resources are organized'. These instincts influenced the group's thoughts about the wider political situation in a country that would introduce such a policy. Kara, another member of the group, suggested at one point, 'it's pure control, military … I kept imagining *The Hunger Games*'. Fellow group member Annebella wondered, 'is it just the clothes that are controlled or is everything repressed?' These interpretations were interesting, given that the original fiction does not indicate that the choice of sustainable garments in World 72 is overly limited, nor suggest a repressive regime; it would seem that the participants were drawing on their knowledge of past and present real-world societies in which clothing options are limited and pulling those assumptions into the fictional world.

Through further discussion, the group did manage to conjure up a more positive version of fashion culture in World 72. Rather than a boiler suit, they imagined that the garment range might be 'a few tops, a jumper, a pair of trousers, a pair of shoes and a coat … it's all in the same colour; it's all in the same fabric.' I am reminded of the brief that was given to clothing designers in the real-world Soviet Union in the 1950s and 1960s, to create ranges of neutral, classic clothes. The economists briefing the designers explained that the clothes should not be fashionable:

the task of providing all the population with the most fashionable clothes cannot be imposed on industry because the communist society has as its aim the satisfaction not of all the needs, but only of reasonable needs. The premature withdrawal of huge material values from the field of consumption due to the specificities of changes in fashion is out of the sphere of the reasonable.[96]

Back in World 72, the group imagined that some people would find that this system was adequate to meet their needs. In fact, those with a puritanical streak might enthusiastically embrace the restricted options. But many, they thought, would not. Indeed, the original Stage 1 fiction highlights the shortcomings of the World 72 system, stating: 'A need for individualism and flamboyance remains.'

The Stage 2 group dug into this need for self-expression through dress. In her initial notes about the world, Annebella suggested that the desire for self-expression would be amplified by restriction: 'With daily clothes prescribed to be simple, well-fitting, easy-clean, comfortable, flattering, durable … All the opposites emerge as forbidden fruit – delightfully ill-fitting, fragile/ephemeral, complex, minuscule (sizing) and outsize, unrelated to body shape and bodily movement.' The group thought that people would find ways to express themselves via styling and customization – but, as Maz noted, 'for people who are very aesthetically minded, and the kind of people who are perhaps drawn to rebellion, you know, adding a patchwork appliqué to a hemline wouldn't be enough'.

The World 72 rebels turn for satisfaction to the clothing that remains from the pre-rationing era. These garments cannot be worn in public, being shunned as wasteful and decadent; thus, the Stage 1 fiction states, the items become fetishized by a hedonistic subculture:

> A speakeasy club scene emerges in the post-industrial fringes of many cities. A ticket generator assigns you a wild assemblage and allows freedom of expression for a night. Costumiers are in demand to restore and rework black market, vintage and historical clothing. Periodically, these establishments are raided by the authorities and a denuded clientele are seen fleeing into the night.

The Stage 2 group threw themselves into imagining this 'incredibly diverse, thriving nightlife culture', noting that 'the one-night-only quality encourages impracticality and impermanence'. They imagined speakeasy clubs springing up in the former clothing factories, mills and department stores that had been left vacant in the rationing era (Figures 6.12 and 6.13), and envisaged multiple micro-cultures within the wider scene. Annebella suggested, 'you might have particular sub-groups, like … you would have people who are obsessed with knitwear, or people who are obsessed with tweed'. The group envisaged the subculture being led by young people, who had known only the current system and thus were 'romanticizing, yearning for this world that they were denied'.

Some in World 72's underground party culture have developed their hedonism into a full-blown human rights campaign, pressuring the government to, as Annebella put it, 'recognize that clothing has this essential expressive function … it's this sort of irrepressible urge'. What form would this campaign take, I wonder: would it be petitions, marches, advocacy? Or would more rebellious strategies come into play? Civil disobedience, for example, involves breaking the law as a means of nonviolent protest. Kimberley Brownlee explains that such disobedience 'must include a deliberate breach of law taken on the basis of steadfast personal commitment in order to communicate our condemnation of a law or policy to a relevantly placed audience. That audience is usually our society

Figure 6.12 *This Instagram post by a leading World 72 speakeasy, Cotton Club, promotes a forthcoming event in Nottingham.*

or the government.'[97] Gandhi famously developed a practice of civil disobedience or *Satyagraha* in the first half of the twentieth century, campaigning for civil rights in South Africa and challenging colonial rule in India.[98] More recently, Extinction Rebellion has adopted strategies based on principles of civil disobedience, arguing that 'When government and the law fail to provide any assurance of adequate protection of and security for its people's well-being and the nation's future … It becomes not only our right but our sacred duty to rebel.'[99]

The cause of the rebels in World 72 is rather complex, because they meet what they see as a human need for self-expression by celebrating the relics of an environmentally unsustainable culture. As Maz noted, 'we've accidentally created the problem where people have now come to associate a very, kind of, wasteful hedonism with freedom, with self-expression. It's, like, how you balance it that makes World 72 … a tough ethical nut to crack.' A participant from another group, Alis, summarized this ethical conundrum: 'if we were all asked, you know, you can create a totally fair society where … basically

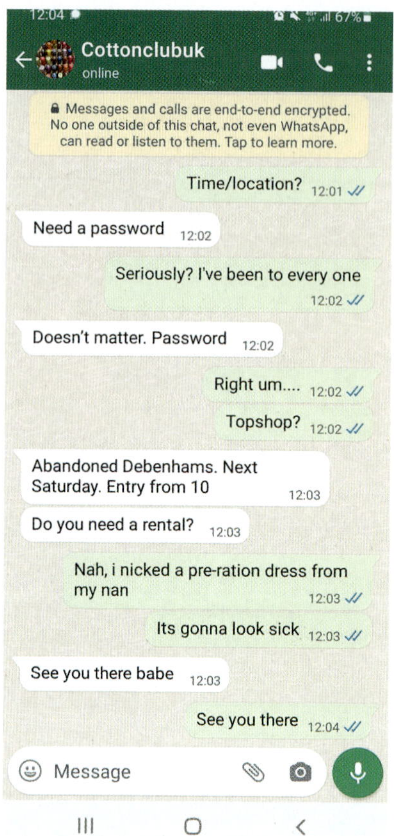

Figure 6.13　*In this World 72 WhatsApp chat a prospective partygoer is discovering the location of the illegal Cotton Club party – an abandoned department store – and confirming that they have managed to arrange their own outfit for the event.*

all the horrible things that are related to the fashion industry have gone, but there's no, like, self-expression through clothing … what would you choose?'

Limits, resourcefulness and adaptation

It is probably fair to say that restriction holds limited appeal within mainstream Western culture. At a recent event organized by the British fashion industry to catalyze action for sustainability, there was a clear desire for regulation that would 'level the playing field' by ensuring minimum standards on workers' rights and environmental impacts. Yet the issue of volume – the number of garments being produced by this industry every year – was not addressed. The notion that we might agree, or even legislate, to limit the number of garments being produced as a strategy for sustainability was, in this context, unthinkable. This resistance is shaped by the four dominant metaphors that Harold Glasser sees guiding development across much of the world: 'anthropocentrism, individualism, exploitation of humans and nature, and unfettered economic and technological growth'.[100] As Christopher Wright and his co-authors note, 'Western liberal democracies (and most developing economies) have embraced the capitalist imaginary of unlimited expansion of production and consumption'.[101] It is no surprise that Kate Fletcher and Mathilda Tham identify 'less' – one of the six landscapes around which *Earth Logic Fashion Action Research Plan* is structured – as the most provocative idea within their report.

Yet there are, of course, limits that we need to countenance at a societal level. Consider, for example, the planetary boundaries identified by scientists at the Stockholm Resilience Centre. These quantitative boundaries – several of which have already been breached – relate to nine processes that regulate the earth system's stability and resilience and represent a 'safe operating space' within which humanity could thrive in the future.[102] Online tools that enable us to calculate individual or national environmental footprints also present limits, expressed as the number of earths needed to sustain a particular lifestyle.[103] Those seeking to bring our consumption levels into balance with the planet's limited biocapacity identify further limits: they find ways to calculate the levels of activity that are possible and then explain the reductions in resource use that will be needed. I have shared several such studies, which help us to countenance the scale of change that is needed, in the previous chapters of this book.

Yet, Giorgos Kallis argues, we must be wary of the way we think about natural limits. We often think about such limits as being objective, imposed by 'Mother Nature'. Yet any limit is actually socially constructed. It is people, rather than nature, for example, 'who decide how much temperature rise we can afford to risk given what we know about the consequences of doing so and what we think we can or cannot achieve'.[104] The sense that limits are externally imposed brings multiple problems, Kallis suggests: it creates the impression that sustainability is a technical, rather than a political challenge, and suggests that only experts, rather than all citizens, can identify what we should do in response. It disguises the fact that we are not all equally responsible for the climate crisis and ecological devastation. Furthermore, it fails to address the extractive mindset that has caused the devastation in the first place: 'The wants fueling a system that destroys the environment remain unquestioned'.[105]

Kallis argues that instead of blaming the planet for limits on our activity, we should instead embrace 'the establishment of self-imposed and deliberately chosen limits'.[106] These limits can be expressed as societal boundaries: 'collectively defined thresholds, that societies establish as self-limitations and conditions for a "good life for all"'.[107] Crucially, thresholds could be not just about resource use or carbon emissions, but also 'poverty, inequality, ecological destruction, injustices, subordination, exploitation, consumption, defense of the commons, and so forth'.[108] In this mindset, then, 'we insist to think of the planet as potentially abundant – as long as we limit ourselves collectively and make space for others to share the resources it has to offer in a responsible way among current living and future generations'.[109]

Self-imposed boundaries can be found in many cultures and spiritual teachings. In fact, Ulrich Brand and his co-authors explain, 'historically, societies always established limits in different forms' – including the governance of resources as commons, as described earlier in the chapter.[110] In her book *Craft of Use*, Kate Fletcher draws on the work of economic historian Avner Offer to discuss 'commitment strategies' that enable societies to balance the needs of present and future, such as values of prudence and self-control or socially enforced agreements. As Fletcher explains, 'Strategies of commitment aid us to sacrifice something now for the sake of something better later; they help us forgo the immediate demands of isolated individuals in order to benefit long-term, shared societal objectives'.[111] Self-imposed limits also often play a part in utopian visions. Lisa Garforth discusses utopian ideas based on the principle of sufficiency – 'modest, careful ways of life that value proximity to nature and conserving resources' – in influential texts by Aldous Huxley, William Morris, Peter Kropotkin, Henry David Thoreau and even in Thomas More's original *Utopia*.[112]

Proposing sufficiency in a culture that rejects limits will inevitably provoke opposition. As Kallis notes, 'Once the genie of limitless expansion is out of the bottle, it is not easy to put it back in.'[113] The situation is complicated further by the double standards already at work in many societies: 'a growing number of us are being told that there is not enough for everyone and that we should learn to live within limits while the fat cats do not'.[114] Yet, Kallis argues, we should not be discouraged from pursuing societal boundaries underpinned by principles of equity and justice: 'it is necessary, I insist, to find a way to defend collective limits, without accepting unjust ones'.[115]

The tension between autonomy and restriction presents a further challenge. Within a mindset of modernity, self-limitation is seen as an affront to 'the idea of an independent, individual self that is not determined by external norms and therefore free'.[116] But as Martin Parker notes, although autonomy and collectivity may appear to be in tension, in fact they reinforce one another:

How can we be both true to ourselves, and at the same time orient ourselves to the collective? How can we value freedom, but then give it up to the group? The answer is that these aren't contradictions. … The individual freedom to be who we want to be rests on our freedoms from hunger, dislocation, violence and so on, which can only be pursued collectively. We can only exercise our autonomy within some sort of collective agreement which provides us with a shelter against events.[117]

Parker's words echo an argument presented in the Chapter 5 discussion of solidarity. As Brand and his co-authors state: 'freedom as autonomy *begins* with the self-imposition of limits to make space for others to simply be'.[118]

* * * * * * * *

Any agreement to limit resource use has to be negotiated at the human scale. Reductions in consumption will necessarily involve people adapting their expectations, doing more with less and making the most of what they have: in short, being resourceful. Resourceful practices can be identified in countless cultural settings, past and present – particularly in settings where material goods are scarce. And there are plenty of examples of resourceful adaptation in the fictions. In Chapter 4 I mentioned several worlds in which textiles are produced from food waste; unsurprisingly, there are also many fictions in which textile waste is celebrated. In **World 207**, for example, people wear textural sculptures made from textile scraps.[119] Earlier in this chapter, I mentioned worlds with widespread professional mending services; in many other fictions, mending is deeply embedded within domestic practice – such as **World 15**, in which people wear a single outfit for life and their items evolve through intensive and continual repair.[120] In fact, my analysis of the first 120 Stage 1 fictions showed repair to be the most frequently mentioned topic overall.[121]

Figure 6.14 *Resourcefulness is not only a topic of interest within Fashion Fictions worlds; it is also readily apparent within the activities themselves. At Stage 2 workshops, participants work with the materials at hand, adapting to their affordances in order to create their visual or material prototypes.*

Figure 6.15 *In World 41, usable elements of damaged garments circulate in a vibrant spare parts market. Here, the group exploring the world at a Stage 2 workshop are combining parts that originated in three separate garments, along with additional trims.*

The **World 41** fiction is particularly interesting in terms of resourcefulness:

In World 41 from 2015, countries worldwide ceased importing secondhand clothes due to diminishing quality and a desire to reinvigorate local textile cultures and economies. Consequently UK charities start cutting damaged garments into component parts for reuse.

While unusable bits are still ragged, the usable elements enter a vibrant and growing spare parts market. Shop staff with making and design skills advise customers on selecting and combining components from a colour-blocked array of garment parts. This has led to an enhanced understanding of clothes, proliferation of making skills and more bespoke and imaginative attitudes to clothes that evolve over time.[122]

The Stage 2 group exploring this world enjoyed running with the idea of garment elements being traded as spare parts.[123] They imagined people hunting high and low for another pair of sleeves to match their favourite jumper, a replacement leg for a pair of trousers, a substitute zip for a

Figure 6.16 *These World 41 advertisements give us a sense of how the spare parts market in World 41 is organized, and the innovations – such as the ingenious 'Join-o-matic' – that have arisen to support the resourceful reuse of garment elements.*

much-loved coat. At one end of the market would be the equivalent of the car scrapyard, with huge piles of garment parts sorted by colour and weight. At the other would be luxurious spare parts outlets, specialist traders with the networks to source a desired item, and skilled experts who could combine disparate elements to create a garment that appeared newly made. One member of the group reflected on the specialist knowledge that would be needed in World 41: 'You might have a mohair cardigan with an acrylic body and a leather sleeve. And how do you wash this and care for this? This new hyper-specialized textile knowledge comes into play … we all learn how to take care of clothes on this whole new level.'

A final return to **World 54**, which I discussed in Chapters 3 and 5, provides an opportunity to think further about adaptation and resourcefulness. As a reminder, the Stage 2 group exploring this world envisaged a society in which textile production is limited and people dress inventively with unconventional items, including household textiles and other everyday objects. For their prototype the group created a photograph from a fashion magazine that, they imagined, would inspire creativity rather than promote consumption (Figure 6.17). Group member Kate explained that the model is wearing a curtain – perhaps taken down for the purpose, and then rehung – because World 54 citizens 'dress up in all sorts of things that they find in the home, or … things that they find. For variety and to be creative, they have to … be resourceful as to how they can dress.'

I used the Stage 3 enactment of World 54 to focus on the experience of dressing in a resourceful fashion system. For one afternoon nineteen participants stepped into the fictional culture together, exploring the possibilities of a collection of sheets and curtains, cardigans, versatile straps and quirky

Figure 6.17 *This photograph from a World 54 fashion magazine is intended to inspire readers to work creatively with items that they may find around the house, such as a curtain.*

adornments (Figure 6.18). Together, the group discovered that this form of dressing is a creative and involved process that requires experimentation; one person reported tweaking a 'horrendous mess' into 'something quite flattering' by merely tweaking a couple of buttons. Some found these possibilities stimulating and exciting, relating the process of dressing to experiences of sculpture, draping, or the trial and error of making clothes. But others found the options overwhelming. Several people commented on how time-consuming the job of creating every outfit from scratch would be, and the problem this would present on a daily basis – as well as the frustration that would arise when having to deconstruct a successful outfit, with no guarantee that it could be recreated the next day. The group also reflected on the skills and attributes needed for dressing in World 54, including imagination, patience and the ability to visualize, as well as physical dexterity.

Some members of the group reflected on whether they felt 'like themselves' in their World 54 outfits – whether they could express who they were through this unfamiliar way of dressing. A few people said they felt like 'a different version' of themselves, while others could not sense themselves in the outfits at all. In contrast, one person said they felt like 'a new me' – or *more* able to express themselves than usual. The discussions also highlighted the capacity of this way of dressing to encompass wider gender expression. Another strand of conversation concerned the aspects of real-world clothes that

Figure 6.18 *The Stage 3 enactment of World 54 provided an embodied experience of resourceful dressing, highlighting both benefits and limitations of an unfamiliar dress culture.*

the participants would miss, if they were to find themselves in World 54 permanently: tailoring, underwear and stretch garments. The issue of warmth arose frequently; no matter how much we talk about fashion as enabling expression and connection, the fact remains that our clothes address much more basic human needs.

Overall, then, the group was able to identify many joys that they felt would arise from the resourcefulness of World 54 and gave a sense of a different, potentially more inclusive, fashion culture that would emerge – while also highlighting the difficulties that would come with a more resourceful approach to dressing. The enactment certainly prompted reflections on the rigidity of the real-world mainstream fashion system, its lack of inclusivity and its promotion of consumption as the sole route for creativity in dress.

Taking a step back, World 54 – along with the other worlds that focus on resourcefulness – pinpoints the urgent need for us to come to terms with working with existing 'stuff', rather than always expecting the blank slate of virgin production. This shift presents a significant challenge in a mainstream culture that values originality, innovation, newness; in fact, it requires us to embrace humbleness, as discussed in Chapter 4. A similar shift is needed in terms of lifestyles. If we were to work within societal boundaries for the use of energy, for example, we might find that we need to adapt our everyday practices. Thomas Princen, in his book *Treading Softly: Paths to Ecological Order*, offers an example of this kind of adaptation in his own family's laundry practices: 'We wash and dry according to the weather. Sometimes we go without. Sometimes we celebrate several sunny days and our ability to clear out a backlog of dirty clothes.'[124] He suggests that a similar approach could be needed for *all* energy-using activities in a world dependent on solar and wind energy, which are inherently intermittent. Again, this involves a shift: from the expectation that we can do anything at any time, which we have become used to in the rich countries of the world, to a more humble position that is willing to adapt to the conditions at hand.

To live with less, we have to be resourceful; to be resourceful, we have to be willing to work with what is already in the world, to adapt to its materiality and the possibilities and limitations that it carries. As Fletcher and Tham note, 'only by staying with the trouble of less can the scale of change deemed necessary be achieved'.[125]

* * * * * * * *

To conclude the chapter I will to zoom out to look at adaptation on a larger scale: the shifts we will need to make in order to adapt to a changing climate. Even if we manage to mitigate our impacts on planetary systems and the planet slowly stops warming, significant adaptation will be needed. As the MIT Climate Portal explains, 'we will already have created a hotter world, changed the Earth's weather patterns, and "locked in" some future changes – like sea level rise, which may continue for hundreds of years after the Earth's temperature stabilizes'.[126] Adaptation measures might include installing infrastructure to deal with increased flooding, restoring wetlands to buffer hurricanes or growing crops to suit a changed climate.[127] When contemplating adaptation, those of us in the global North would do well to learn from the communities and societies that have, for centuries, been navigating the intense social-ecological changes brought about by colonialism. As Kyle P. Whyte notes, 'the hardships many nonIndigenous people dread most of the climate crisis are ones that Indigenous peoples have endured already due to different forms of colonialism: ecosystem collapse, species loss, economic crash, drastic relocation, and cultural disintegration'.[128]

Despite the impacts of climate change already becoming apparent, adaptation has been largely overlooked in terms of investment and coordinated action. Furthermore, attitudes and approaches differ around the world. Daniel Nyberg, Christopher Wright and Vanessa Bowden note that discussion of adaptation in rich countries tends to focus on property and the economic impacts of extreme weather, based on 'the notion that environmental devastation can be managed'.[129] At the same time, these rich countries are failing to follow through on promises to provide funding to less economically developed countries, in which the impacts of a changing climate are being felt far more acutely.[130] Consider, for example, the devastating and increasingly intense flooding in Bangladesh or the impending loss of low-lying Pacific islands due to rising sea levels. As Nyberg, Wright and Bowden explain,

> adapting to climate change in poorer regions involves more vulnerability, greater acquiescence to Western notions of development and a need to negotiate simply for the right to survive … At each and every turn, climate adaptation in communities is pitched as a concern subservient to economic growth. It is depicted as a problem that can be contained within space. It is portrayed as an issue that only the maintenance (in richer nations) or speeding up (in poorer regions) of existing practices can solve.[131]

Some commentators, when studying the impacts of climate change forecast by scientists, predict widespread societal collapse. The world's richest respond by preparing refuges and bunkers and fantasizing about colonizing Mars.[132] Others propose an approach of 'deep adaptation' based on resilience, relinquishment, restoration and reconciliation.[133] I am drawn to thinkers who, while acknowledging the scale of the climate and ecological crisis, talk in a more tentative, open-ended, uncertain way about the changes ahead. Dougald Hine, for example, gives a sense of the adaptation that could be needed:

> I get a glimpse of how we might soften the fall for each other as the growth economy falls apart. It looks like a patchwork of undertakings that don't make sense according to the dominant economic logic around which modern societies have been organised. Because of that dominance, such

undertakings have to struggle for a place in the world as it works just now; yet as the feminist economist duo J.K. Gibson-Graham point out, even in industrial societies, there is already far more of this about than we are told. It looks like ways of meeting each other's needs that operate close to the ground, creating capacity that finds its strength in people coming together to make things happen for reasons other than because we have been paid or told to do so.[134]

The picture being painted here is not of a coordinated and carefully managed process of degrowth, but rather a bottom-up, fragmented, plural, evolving patchwork. In Hine's roughly sketched vision I find myself drawn back to another meaning of adaptation, discussed earlier in the book: the adaptation of stories to generate multiple co-existing interpretations. It strikes me that we could apply this idea to the ways in which we live with our clothes. We need not try to come up with the perfect fashion system – a task that would, after all, be doomed to fail. Instead we can interpret, improvise, explore as we find 'the paths which lead to the unknown world ahead of us'.[135] We can create endless adaptations of our fashion systems to fit the contexts in which we find ourselves, just as we create endless adaptations of our fictions.

Organization and adaptation: ideas for the real world

What new ideas could we explore in relation to organization and adaptation? The following five themes are full of possibility:

1. Collaboration

How could activists and wearers collaborate with garment workers to pursue sustainable and socially just change? What new initiatives might grow from such collaborations?

2. Organizational kaleidoscope

What are the possibilities for organizing fashion, beyond the usual setup of capitalist businesses jostling for market share? How could alternative values be embedded in our fashion organizations? How could the principles of commoning – negotiated sharing – be enacted in the fashion context?

3. Thrivenism

A Stage 2 exploration of World 4 presented the enticing idea of 'thrivenism' as an alternative to capitalism. In this economic and political system, society is structured to enable all species to thrive. What would thrivenism look and feel like? How could we build a fashion system rooted in thrivenism?

4. Societal boundaries

Our societies need self-imposed limits in order to support a good life for all; these limits must be underpinned by principles of equity and justice. How could we express these limits? How could we embed them within our everyday lives and shout about their benefits?

5. Adaptation skills

What skills and knowledge do we need to act resourcefully? How can we work with what has already been produced? What knowhow should we nurture in order to be able to adapt not only our clothes but also our lifestyles and our fashion systems to changing conditions?

* * * * * * * *

As ever, these inspiring ideas carry with them cautionary tales. Here are three issues to consider when working for change:

Gig economy

Many peer-to-peer sharing platforms which initially seemed like opportunities for commoning have instead been converted into harmful and exploitative manifestations of the gig economy. Commoning principles need to be embedded into the core of an organization to avoid such appropriation.[136]

Gaps in awareness

Capitalism is so dominant that when we try to discuss alternatives, many of us have a tendency to clutch at the few other systems we are aware of – whether Soviet-era communism or a stereotype of 'tribal' societies. We might then carry forward assumptions about those systems to the alternatives being discussed. We need to consciously hold space for unknown possibilities as we explore alternatives together.

Resourcefulness without restriction

The circular economy, in principle, nurtures resourcefulness by keeping materials in use. Yet, as Dagna Rams explains, 'circular economic schemes win popularity with corporations and governments because … they redefine sustainability to privilege economic interests'.[137] Be wary of initiatives that promise circularity without consideration of the volume of material in circulation, the resources consumed in the process, or the behaviours and attitudes that are promoted.

7

Pulling the possibilities

Speculation, wonder and change

The writing of Diana Wynne Jones took root in my brain when I was a child. As I explained in Chapter 1, Jones's fantasy novels have shaped the approach that I take to speculation in general, and to Fashion Fictions in particular. When I realized the importance of her work to the project, I returned to the Chrestomanci series – the books that influenced my notion of 'parallel presents' – and was delighted to discover that Jones had added further titles in the years since I had wandered the aisles of the children's library. In one of these books, the eponymous hero of *The Lives of Christopher Chant* finds himself working in a strange mansion with a boy named Conrad.[1] A powerful resident of the mansion is causing widespread disruption by secretly 'pulling the possibilities': manipulating the probabilities that shape the boundaries between multiple parallel worlds. This is a dangerous practice, driven by greed and with potentially catastrophic consequences. Yet the visible impact of each individual instance of 'pulling' is comically mundane. An omelette cooking in a frying pan changes to fried eggs; titles of books on a shelf are subtly altered; the colours of the mansion staff's uniforms suddenly shift.

I find the premise of scrambling the mundane details of the world rather enticing. It is, after all, through mundane details and everyday practices that our fashion systems are built. Imagine the fibres in a garment suddenly changing from polyester to hemp. Imagine all the tumble dryers in the land simultaneously vanishing, replaced by intricate networks of shared washing lines. Imagine the tattoo parlour at the end of the road turning into a mending parlour, with sample patch designs hung in the window to catch the attention of passers-by.

Participants in Fashion Fictions workshops are adept at generating such ideas for tweaking reality. Working within the project's three-stage structure and the guidance that asks them to imagine enticing alternatives, they have envisioned hundreds of worlds. In these worlds, diverse elements of the fashion

Figure 7.1 *Pegging our questions, precedents and ideas for action on the washing line for all to see.*

system are otherwise: from the garments themselves to places, events and organizations and even the wider economy and geopolitical context. At their most effective, Fashion Fictions activities create liminoid spaces in which new ideas spring forth and the fictional visions come to feel, for a time, rather real. The process is engaging, thought-provoking and often great fun. Yet at times during the first couple of years of the project I questioned whether there might be a danger in this exploration of fictional worlds. Might the process of speculation, I wondered, merely provide an escapist distraction from the challenges of the real world? Might it act as a release valve that serves to maintain, rather than disrupt, the status quo?[2]

As I gained more experience of facilitating the process of speculation, I gained confidence in its benefits. Julia Bentz and her co-authors highlight the 'experiential forms of questioning' involved in creative, embodied participatory arts practices that probe issues of sustainability.[3] They explain that people often gain a fresh perspective when their thinking is slowed through doing, providing the chance to connect complex issues with their own lives. Brian Eno likewise emphasizes the value of creative practices for imagining otherwise:

> what is possible in art becomes thinkable in life. We become our new selves first in simulacrum, through style and fashion and art, our deliberate immersions in virtual worlds. Through them we sense what it would be like to be another kind of person with other kinds of values. We rehearse new feelings and sensitivities. We imagine other ways of thinking about our world and its future. We use art to model new worlds so that we can see how we might feel about them.[4]

Indeed, as I explained in Chapter 2, I have observed that when people take part in the project's activities they often experience a sense of wonder: they see the real world as if through fresh eyes. Vlad Glăveanu explains that 'The value of wonder in society … is to unsettle the status quo and unleash the power of the imagination.'[5] He suggests that wonder can make us more critically engaged as citizens and prompt us to come together as communities to reimagine the possibilities for social life. Stage 2 workshop participants commented on this new perspective. Leah noted, 'it's kind of making a story real … it makes you then reflect back on where we are now'. Alis recognized that the workshop prompted even those familiar with sustainable fashion debates 'to broaden our minds and think more radically', while Katherine reflected that the workshop discussion had prompted her to notice and challenge her own biases and assumptions. Overall, imagining alternative worlds and dwelling there for a while did, as I had hoped, impact participants' thinking about real-world systems. As Jon Alexander points out in *Citizens*, 'In order to step into a new story, we first need to learn to see the air we breathe, this story that shapes our world and behaviour, for what it is.'[6]

I found ways to capture people's thinking when in this state of wonder, hoping that these documented thoughts would help to build a bridge between speculation and real-world change. I

Figure 7.2 *The* capturing wonder *activity can be used to reflect on any Fashion Fictions activity, whether in* *person or online. This* idea for action *has been written by Ann, thinking at a policy level.*

now invite participants in the post-liminoid stage of a Fashion Fictions workshop to record three types of thinking: *questions* about the real-world fashion system; personal, collective or societal *ideas for action*; and *precedents*, whether historical or contemporary, that we could productively learn from or translate (see Activity 2.4 for instructions).

The responses I have gathered are deeply inspiring. A sample is included in Box 7.1, with a more extensive compendium assembled in a gallery on the Wonder page of the Fashion Fictions website.[7] The lines of enquiry that I have identified through writing this book – the 'ideas for the real world' presented at the end of Chapters 3, 4, 5 and 6 – have been generated by the wonder that *I* have experienced, through facilitating the activities and reflecting deeply on the conversations and creations that have taken place there. In both cases the ideas, questions and examples could be used to inspire new real-world initiatives – or to spark further speculative investigations.

Box 7.1: Wonder gallery

This sample of questions, precedents and ideas for action has been gathered from participants in various Fashion Fictions activities in diverse contexts.

Questions

- Why is novelty prized over nostalgia, and retail over remembrance?

- Why do we exploit women and children for endless clothes?

- Why is there an expectation that garments should be cheap?

- Why can't I find what makes me comfortable?

- How is shopping more fun than exchange?

- Would a different fashion system make us better people?

- Why do I buy clothes I'm not sure I'll wear?

- Why aren't bartering systems considered to be as sophisticated or valid as monetary systems?

- Would a society less obsessed with cleanliness be healthier?

- Why aren't all garments compostable?

- How might we use clothes/fashion as a means to alter behaviour?

- Can you get the self-expression you need through other means?

- Why is wasteful hedonism associated with freedom?

Precedents

- Share clothes with friends and family

- Reinstate home economics classes so that people can learn to mend their clothes

- Use natural powers to meet our needs (air, sun for drying)

- Hand-arounds – like hand-me-downs for adults

- Ask friends what is in their closet before buying a new garment for an event

- French seams

- Wash overlayers less

- In my grandmother's world, everyone knew how to use a sewing machine

- Replaceable underarm gussets and dress shields

- Historically, no textile would be thrown away

- Second World War, UK: Utility Clothing Scheme

- Peer-to-peer connections in the early days of eBay

- Building community through mending

Ideas for action

- Nurture critical thinking

- Share these worlds with my friends to get them thinking

- Improve my embroidery skills

- Treat fast fashion clothing items like cigarettes, with a disclaimer (e.g. 'smoking kills')

- Tax virgin materials, not labour

- Cherish our textiles

- Increase my fibre knowledge

- Show friends and family how many amazing vintage shops there are

- Change the aesthetic we deem desirable

- Look at my wardrobe through fresh eyes

- Shift priorities away from 'the economy'

- Find joy and creativity in dressing

- Return to the mending practices I grew up with

- Raise consciousness of the connection between materials, energy and earth

* * * * * * * * *

It is clear, then, that the process of speculation generates an array of ideas for the real world. I have observed that it can also stimulate an appetite for and belief in the value of real-world action. But what happens next? How can we activate these thoughts to pursue genuine change? Transformation is, after all, urgently needed. The dominant globalized fashion system is contributing to the devastation of the earth and causing harm to many of the millions of people working in its supply chains around the world. The same can be said of the economic system that the fashion system sits within; as Martin Parker and his co-authors explain, 'Irreversible environmental degradation, increasing economic inequality, and a stunting of human growth and diversity are all well-recognized results of the capitalist imperative to endless accumulation for its own sake.'[8] In fact, it can be argued that we need to move not only beyond capitalism, but beyond modernity itself. Vanessa Machado de Oliveira describes the 'hospicing' of modernity/coloniality, a process that 'recognizes the eventual inevitable end of modernity's fundamentally unethical and unsustainable institutions, but sees the necessity of enabling a "good" death through which important lessons are learned'.[9]

In place of the status quo, we need plural fashion systems that respect ecological limits and meet our human needs – as both wearers and producers. In quantitative terms, this means reducing the use of resources by as much as 95 per cent.[10] In qualitative terms, we need to fundamentally reshape the norms and cultures of fashion. This means challenging the economic systems and colonial structures within which the industry sits, transforming our day-to-day dress practices and shifting the imaginaries that shape our experiences of the world. To hark back to the high-street fashion retailer's tagline discussed in Chapter 1, we need to rethink *how change* – in the sense of *both* fashion *and* transition towards sustainability – *looks*.

When training ourselves to contemplate radical change, it is useful to look to the past. History provides abundant evidence of dramatic technological, social and cultural shifts – whether the development of hygienic sanitation systems in the Netherlands in the late-nineteenth century[11] or the breakthrough of rock 'n' roll in the middle decades of the twentieth century.[12] As Elizabeth Shove and Nicola Spurling point out, 'what is normal today has not always been so and, as such, there is no reason to suppose that currently familiar arrangements will stay the same for very long'.[13] Indeed, the origins of the fast-fashion era can be traced back only forty years or so.[14] Ursula K. Le Guin takes a longer and larger-scale view to argue that seemingly permanent systems are actually historically situated: 'We live in capitalism. Its power seems inescapable. So did the divine right of kings. Any human power can be resisted and changed by human beings.'[15] Le Guin's words should inspire us to reject claims that the current system is inevitable or natural, and that there is no alternative.[16]

So, we need radical change, and can see, in retrospect, that such change can happen. But *how* does change happen? One idea, widespread in popular culture, is that 'attitudes drive behaviour, which produces change':[17] that is, social change is driven by rational choices made by many individuals. A contrasting view sees individuals as entirely lacking agency, with change 'an outcome of external forces, technological innovation or social structure, somehow bearing down on the detail of daily life'.[18] Writing in the 1980s, sociologist Anthony Giddens rejected these polarized views and offered an influential alternative theory, which understands human activity and social structures as influencing one another in recursive loops. Elizabeth Shove, Mika Pantzar and Matt Watson helpfully summarize Giddens' position: 'activities are shaped and enabled by structures of rules and meanings, and these structures are, at the same time, reproduced in the flow of human action'.[19] Giddens sees this dynamic interplay taking place through 'social practices ordered across space and time': everyday activities – such as dressing – that are guided and influenced by wider social structures.[20] Andrew Sayer thus describes practices as being 'socially and materially embedded, so that individuals are constrained, enabled, motivated and pressured into acting in ways that are consistent with them'.[21]

Change, then, can only happen through evolution in both everyday practices *and* the wider systems in which those practices are embedded. If we want to influence such change, we need to identify systemic sticking points and consider how they might be addressed, while acknowledging the complexity of our socio-material systems. This complexity is evident in research that seeks to understand how societies might pursue sustainable transitions: the research reveals that fundamental change occurs across different scales and different phases, spans multiple dimensions of society, from technology and economy to ecology and belief, and is characterized by co-evolution and co-learning.[22] As Michele-Lee Moore and Manjana Milkoreit suggest, 'What matters for any sustainable and just transformation will be how a change restructures, reconnects, and remakes the meanings of relationships between people, and between people and the ecosystems in which they are embedded.'[23]

In his book *Envisioning Real Utopias*, Erik Olin Wright talks about change being driven by a combination of unintended effects of an established system and intentional interventions that try to seed alternatives.[24] While we might think about interventions as constructive new propositions – and indeed I will return to this idea later in the chapter – it is valuable to note that interventions could focus on *un*making, as much as making. Giuseppe Feola, for example, argues that degrowth will require us to unmake the current socio-economic order at the same time as building the alternative systems and imaginaries that will take its place. Unmaking is thus described as 'a diverse range of interconnected and multilevel (individual, social, socioecological) processes that are deliberately activated in order to "make space" (temporally, spatially, materially, and/or symbolically) for radical alternatives that are incompatible with dominant modern capitalist configurations'.[25] This 'making space' involves liberation from 'the religion of growth', which he describes as a kind of decolonization.[26] Harold Glasser talks in a similar way about what is needed to move from the metaphors of a system rooted in modernity to a life-affirming alternative paradigm. He explains that we need to learn about the roots of the status quo and understand why many taken-for-granted assumptions are no longer – or never were – appropriate before we can envision alternatives and work to transform the present.[27]

This notion of unmaking and learning connects with the idea of third-order change, or 'seeing things differently',[28] discussed in Chapter 1, and the related concept of transformative learning. Amish Morrell and Mary Ann O'Connor explain that 'Transformative learning involves experiencing a deep, structural shift in the basic premises of thought, feelings, and actions. It is a shift of consciousness that dramatically and permanently alters our way of being in the world.'[29] This shift of consciousness can be incredibly powerful. As Walida Imarisha explains, 'The decolonization of the imagination is the most dangerous and subversive form there is: for it is where all other forms of decolonization are born. Once the imagination is unshackled, liberation is limitless.'[30]

* * * * * * * * *

The way we think about change matters. If we approach change using the rational mindset of modernity/coloniality, as can be identified in the incremental initiatives led by the mainstream fashion industry and in techno-optimist efforts more broadly, it seems inevitable that we will only intensify the predicament in which we find ourselves. If our well-meaning efforts do not address the thinking that underlies the system we seek to change, there is a real danger that we will reproduce the problems we seek to address and only reinforce the unsustainable status quo. Instead, as I have argued in the preceding chapters, we need to dwell in uncertainty, negotiation, adaptation, plurality – but this can be difficult in a rational world.

One way to rebel against the rationality of modernity is to actively embrace a lack of 'usefulness'. In *Bad Environmentalism*, Nicole Seymour discusses creative works that 'not only … fail to follow the available scripts for appropriate environmental feeling but … fail to feel in ways that are clearly

Figure 7.3 *Questions, precedents and ideas for action, influencing real-world change.*

directed or obviously "useful".[31] I have been guided by this idea in shaping the Fashion Fictions project: I have steered away from any suggestion that our collective imagination activities should be immediately useful, that they should be seen as instruments that can solve our problems in a single stroke. Yet I also feel the need to identify some kind of pathway to change, to shape and give purpose to the process for myself and others.

Perhaps I want to have my cake and eat it: I want to 'pull the possibilities' to effect change, but rebel if I am pushed to map out a clear path along which that change might unfold. A brief return to Diana Wynne Jones' writing has helped me to see how I might strike the right balance. Debbie Gascoyne highlights how Jones' protagonists frequently use an indirect type of magic to overcome difficult situations, rather than tackle the problem head on. As an example, Gascoyne cites a powerful and abusive group that Christopher must negotiate with in *The Lives of Christopher Chant*. As she explains, 'A direct approach would be met with absolute resistance, so when Christopher wants to use magic against them, he discovers that "you seemed to have to work in a way that was tipped sideways from the way you did it on any other world, with a bend and a ripple to the magic".[32]

Lingering experiences: possibility and stories

In Fashion Fictions, our work for change takes the form of three interconnected ripples: *possibility*, *stories* and *prefiguration*. The first two ripples are both, in different ways, shaped by the lingering effects of project activities on those who participate in and encounter them. In the third ripple, we adopt an alternative approach to the Fashion Fictions process. This approach seeks to seed real-world action by setting up parallel-world organizations and practices and exploring them through repeated, extended or open-ended enactments.

I will start with *possibility:* that is, the sense of possibility that the project seeks to nurture. Possibility is deeply bound up with imagination. As Tania Zittoun, Hana Hawlina and Alex Gillespie explain, through imagination we explore the possible and the impossible – and this exploration 'is the germination of future possibility'.[33] After all, the boundaries between impossible, possible and actual are not fixed; history is full of situations in which initially impossible ideas have been imagined and shared and in the process become possible – and sometimes even brought to actuality.

Boundary shifts can be brought about through what Zittoun, Hawlina and Gillespie describe as 'tensions between the semiotic domain and the material or concrete domain'.[34] Such tensions can arise in two ways: first, by imagining something happening that then facilitates the concrete realization of that thing, and second, through an embodied or material experience that leads to an imagined possibility. Fashion Fictions offers the potential for both processes to unfold, through sharing stories that expand the scope for related practical action, and through organizing practical experiences that prompt us to imagine new and unfamiliar possibilities.

The project's varied speculative activities, then, provide a platform by which we can individually and collectively push and pull at the boundaries between impossible, possible and actual. Zittoun, Hawlina and Gillespie describe 'the loop of imagination': a path that moves from the here-and-now to the speculative and back.[35] Through this return, imagination makes a new contribution to the world – whether a novel discovery, an innovative idea or a compelling new story. This contribution might remain as a private personal experience or spread into collective culture. Either way, it can then act as a resource that feeds further imagined possibilities.

Wonder, which creates an awareness of alternative perspectives on the world around us, is also key to a sense of possibility.[36] As Vlad Glăveanu explains, 'The space created by holding two or more perspectives or action orientations on the same object' – which could include institutions, events or even abstract concepts such as the fashion system – 'opens up a zone of possibility concerning what can be thought about and done in relation to that object'.[37] The space can create a feeling that many more ideas are viable than we would otherwise have thought, and even that the world is fizzing with possibility and openness. Furthermore, by gaining an awareness of multiple perspectives, we become 'freer, more flexible and more open-minded' and, therefore, more able to resist the inevitability of dominant systems or positions.[38]

Time after time, I have observed Fashion Fictions participants shift their stance, from a resigned *that's never going to happen* to a defiant, hands-on-hips *why isn't this already happening?* When the activities are at their most potent, those taking part develop an increased sense that radical change is possible, in the fashion system and beyond. This is vital; as I discussed in Chapter 1, we need to think that radical change is possible in order for there to be a chance of radical change taking place. This ripple, therefore, lays the foundations for ideas to be discussed, developed and potentially taken forwards – rather than immediately dismissed.

Another way to think about a sense of possibility is as an embodied capacity, developed through action. Theatre of the Oppressed, discussed in Chapter 3, gives participants the bodily experience of rebellion, such as organizing a strike or standing up to an abusive employer; performances are seen as 'a training ground for action'[39] or even 'a rehearsal of revolution'.[40] The founder of Theatre of the Oppressed, Augusto Boal, proposed that this rehearsal would empower participants to apply the actions in their real lives.[41] Although we do not address direct oppression in Fashion Fictions, our speculative acts are built on a similar ambition: that the experience of alternatives will feed a desire and capacity for real-world action. An embodied experience lies at the heart of the Stage 3 enactments but can also arise at Stage 2 prototyping workshops, when participants undertake making activities that would occur in the parallel world or find themselves speaking as a parallel-world persona, giving voice to unfamiliar thoughts and statements.

A very different example of embodied action can be found in Scott Magelssen's account of an immersive event that simulated an illegal crossing of the border between Mexico and the US. Drawing on his own experience of taking part in this physically demanding participatory reenactment, Magelssen describes how the participants experienced, albeit in a knowingly staged way, the embodied experience of rebelling, of breaking the law. He explains, 'it is the mis behavior that makes the experience memorable; and that, as such, exists in our memories as continual potentiality'.[42] Although writing about the very different context of rituals, Byung-Chul Han makes a similar observation. He describes rituals as bodily performances in which the values of a community are 'written into the body, that is, physically internalized. Thus, rituals create a bodily knowledge and memory, an embodied identity, a bodily connection.'[43] If I rehearse an action with my body in a Fashion Fictions activity, I might be pretending – but my body has still experienced that action. It is at once false and real and will lie in my bones as an embodied memory, ripe for future restoration.

* * * * * * * * *

Let us now move on to the second ripple: the *stories* that we generate in Fashion Fictions. These stories take different forms: the 100-word Stage 1 fictions, the prototypes, the enactment reports and films, the case studies of people who have organized activities, descriptions of the precedents that the

Figure 7.4 *In World 224, clothes and ornaments are co-created with other species.*[44] *This enactment brought the world to life by inviting participants to adopt and try on one of these living garments.*

Figure 7.5　*Polaroid photographs captured the embodied experience of enacting World 224.*

activities bring to light, the personal stories that those who have taken part might share with family and friends. In Chapter 3, I discussed the importance of stories, narratives and imaginaries in shaping our societies and driving the potential for change. As Chris Riedy explains, 'It is becoming increasingly clear that a conscious transformation towards a sustainable world will require not only technological, financial and institutional innovations but also the emergence of new stories and narratives about the nature of human society and our relationship with the Earth.'[45]

Ella Saltmarshe highlights the importance of systems thinking for tackling the climate and ecological crisis and the role of story in seeing – and acting – systemically.[46] She identifies three metaphors for story that can be used to change systems. The first is 'story as light'; the idea that stories can illuminate pathways to change.[47] In Chapter 1, I described a widespread sense that the status quo will merely stretch into the future, with a few technological enhancements here and there but with no change to the underlying paradigm. This sense is partly due to a lack of positive visions of alternative systems, within and beyond the fashion context. As Matthew Schneider-Mayerson and Brent Ryan Bellamy note, '"Another world is possible" is a worthy maxim, but without further elaboration it stands like a narrow bridge to a destination shrouded in mist. Would you want to journey there?'[48] Alex Steffen emphasizes the impact of this absence: 'It's literally true that we can't build what we can't imagine. … The fact that we haven't compellingly imagined a thriving, dynamic, sustainable world is a major reason we don't already live in one.'[49]

Once we have these visions, they can help to build a sense of possibility in those who encounter them. Although they are fictional and even if only roughly sketched out, the ideas push us to recognize that the world could be otherwise and thus dislodge our minds from following familiar paths. We can also work with the stories themselves in different ways. For example, as Brian Eno notes, fictional visions can give us something to work towards:

Stories matter. They can trap us, but they can also inspire us … As soon as we sense the possibility of a more desirable world, we begin behaving differently, as though that world is starting to come into existence, as though, in our minds at least, we're already there. The new story becomes an invisible force which pulls us forward. By this process it starts to come true. Imagining the future makes it more possible.[50]

I find the thought of a story pulling us forward into a new system deeply inspiring. Eno's comments remind me of Toni Cade Bambara's proposal that the job of a cultural worker 'is to make revolution irresistible'.[51] Indeed, the way we feel about alternative visions matters; we need to be positively engaged, at an emotional level, to feel motivated to act in the present.[52]

Another characteristic of stories is that they give us a new experience, somewhat like the embodied action that I discussed in relation to possibility. Rolf A. Zwaan, drawing on research in cognitive neuroscience and cognitive psychology, explains that 'Comprehending a story amounts to a vicarious experience of the described situation. The verbal input activates traces from experience that are used in a mental simulation of the described events.'[53] Experiences, even if solely cognitive, would seem to have an impact on us. I sense some truth in the words of a character in *The Lathe of Heaven*, a novel by Ursula K. Le Guin, who states: 'you don't speak of dreams as "unreal." They exist; they are events; they leave a mark behind them.'[54]

The stories generated in Fashion Fictions extend our collective vocabulary relating to fashion and sustainability: they throw fresh ideas into the mix, creating a more varied pool of shared reference points to discuss, remix, amend, be attracted to or repulsed by. Some might even dovetail together, suggesting synergies for further exploration.[55] Although the stories are not intended as instantly actionable blueprints for a future society, they contain many ideas that could be explored and taken forward. As the participants in one Stage 2 workshop observed, none of the fictions would work well as a universal solution, but elements of all the worlds could coexist in a rich and diverse fashion ecosystem. Certainly, the ideas in the stories will not appeal to all, but by sharing them we can think these ideas through together: we can consider the benefits and costs of different strategies before having to deal with the real-world consequences.[56] Importantly, the ideas can also be opened up to critique. Whatever the outcome of these discussions, the stories remain as a 'reservoir of ideas' for further exploration, 'protected from the challenges posed by various forms of rationality'.[57]

The second metaphor for story shared by Saltmarshe is 'story as glue'. She describes story as 'a tool for building community through empathy and coherence', by generating narratives that connect disparate people.[58] I have observed this happen in Fashion Fictions activities and particularly in Stage 3 enactments, where strangers have connected through the task of bringing a story to life, whether the **World 27** garment exchange ritual in the woods discussed in Chapters 3 and 5 or the six-week enactment that explored the fungi-centric **World 91** discussed in Chapter 4.

Saltmarshe's third metaphor is 'story as web': using stories as mirrors 'to help us understand existing narratives and their impact', and as tools 'to reauthor the web of narratives we live in'.[59] Here, we can shift our focus from individual stories to the narratives and social imaginaries that underpin them. As I discussed in Chapter 3, these narratives and imaginaries shape our understanding of the world and the way we behave within it; they tell us what is normal, what is aspirational, what is stigmatized. The imaginaries that dominate in modernity have led to the contemporary crises of climate change and global inequality, for they fail 'to respect planetary boundaries or human dignity'.[60] We need to disrupt these imaginaries and contribute to the construction of compelling, 'life-affirming' alternatives.[61]

The entrenchment of dominant imaginaries means that this transformation will be far from easy, as Jon Alexander explains:

> even having recognised the Citizen in ourselves and others as individuals, the gravitational pull of business-as-usual in entrenched institutions can still drag us back to the old ways of doing

things. When it comes to taking action or facing challenges, we need mental models, structures and processes to help us. If the only apparent and accessible ones have arisen from the Consumer Story, we keep using them. As we do so, our grip on the Citizen Story inevitably loosens and soon releases.[62]

The idea of challenging a deeply established narrative is rather intimidating. But Manjana Milkoreit provides a useful explanation of how change might happen, by describing the dynamic interaction between individual imaginations and the collective imaginary. Milkoreit explains that an individual belonging to a group develops mental representations relating to the attitudes and beliefs of that group. Through social and communication processes such as chatting with friends, posting on social media, reading newspapers and attending protests, each individual contributes to discussions about ideas and values. Via these discussions, the group forms a consensus on what is desirable and undesirable in their shared understanding of the world. Over time, Milkoreit continues,

> these social processes can result in the convergence of mental representations of multiple individuals. Such convergence – the development of similar networks of mental representations across many minds – facilitates the emergence of shared or collective beliefs. Once a certain threshold has been reached, i.e., enough members of the group are perceived to hold a certain belief or value, it takes on the status of a shared belief or value.[63]

Creative works such as climate fiction novels – or, perhaps, the various types of stories created in Fashion Fictions – play a role in these processes when they become shared reference points to be debated and discussed. Milkoreit suggests that in this context, a story 'becomes an anchor point for conversations, questions of possibility, morality, risk tolerance, scientific uncertainty and so forth'.[64] As such, stories can influence political processes – bearing in mind that 'Politics is not only a matter of legislative debates and presidential speeches; it is a part of everyday life.'[65]

The notion that Fashion Fictions stories might circulate and influence collective thinking in this way is exciting, but it is far from guaranteed that any individual story will find an audience. Valuable guidance is offered by organizations that work with narrative for social change. Narrative Initiative, for example, identifies four steps that can be used to guide this work: first, identify a narrative that needs to be displaced and create a new alternative narrative; second, deploy the new narrative, locating audiences and finding ways to express the narrative to make it meaningful to them; third, design effective interventions to place the narrative more centrally within public attention; and fourth, observe what is happening, to identify what is working and where the strategy needs to be changed.[66]

Encouragingly, we can all play a part in narrative change, by talking to others about our speculative ideas and those that we encounter, whether in this book or elsewhere. How might *you* help these ideas to spread?

Making change: prefiguration

The first two ripples within the Fashion Fictions project's work for change – building *possibility* and generating new *stories* – are potentially powerful, but rather diffuse. If you, like me, are impatient for more concrete action, then you may find some satisfaction in the third ripple: *prefiguration*. This ripple explores what Walidah Imarisha describes as 'the hard work of sculpting reality from our dreams'[67] and is based on localized, real-world, grassroots action. It recognizes that, as Alastair Fuad-Luke, Anja-Lisa Hirscher and Katharina Moebus state, 'everyone and everything has agency, that is, the capacity to change what happens next'.[68] For some, this agency might be expressed through collective projects with a degree of visibility; for others it might take the form of personal, understated – even mundane – practices. All have value.

The most straightforward way in which the speculative activities might generate change in the world is through participants implementing ideas for action that have been generated in the final stages of a Fashion Fictions activity or that have emerged at some later point. Feedback from past participants has revealed a wide variety of such initiatives, from the development of darning skills and more considered use of clothes in the wardrobe to the creation of inventive new personal and collective projects. Follow-on activities could also be inspired by the historical and contemporary precedents that are identified in the process of speculation: as discussed in Chapter 1, there are countless alternatives to the mainstream system that we could notice, learn from and translate. There is likewise much to learn from individuals, communities and initiatives around the world who are already resisting growth-driven agendas in their everyday practices and forms of organizing.

As much as I love the notion of ideas generated or identified through the process of speculation taking root in the real world, I worry about the ambition of these ideas being compromised in the process: that as we try to conjure our visions into being, they might be stifled or appropriated by the capitalist mainstream. After all, capitalism is adept at pulling marginal practices to the centre, neutralizing critique. Furthermore, the Consumer Story is so widespread that it has an almost irresistible pull. It might be hard to keep the commitment, the radicalism, the creativity going in the face of the resigned rationality that drove me to develop Fashion Fictions in the first place: *that's just not going to happen. It's not realistic.* The ideas might become smaller, more reasonable, less transgressive, less transformative.

I sat with these concerns for some time, turning the predicament over and wondering about strategies that would help us to explore ideas within the real world without losing their radical edge. I found inspiration in prefigurative politics. The word 'prefiguration' is composed of two elements from Latin: *prae*, meaning before, and *figurare*, meaning to represent. Put together, the word therefore 'means, literally, anticipating or representing something that will happen in the future'.[69] Lara Monticelli explains that prefigurative politics is about embodying a society envisioned for the future in the present, in terms of 'social relations, decision-making, culture, belief systems and direct experience' – without having to wait for a revolutionary event to turn dominant systems upside down.[70]

The concept of prefigurative politics can be traced back to the 1970s but was popularized by anthropologist David Graeber after the emergence of anti-globalization protests and left-wing populist movements in the early twenty-first century. Jilly Traganou helpfully distinguishes prefiguration from other acts of political disagreement that are based on either communication – 'speaking truth to power' – or violence. As she explains, prefigurative politics involves 'a different form of resistance: dissenting through making'.[71] Importantly, prefigurative politics is concerned not only with the alternative organizations that are set up, but also with the ways in which they are organized. The Occupy Wall Street encampments that were established in Zuccotti Park in New York in 2011 provide an example of prefigurative politics in action; as Tobias Revell, Justin Pickard and Georgina Voss explain, the Occupy activists 'blended protest and speculation as a form of social critique'.[72] They set up public kitchens, libraries and other facilities 'that were meant to embody and actualize the movement's ideology and to materially sustain the mobilization over time'.[73]

Activists and organizers working in a prefigurative way consciously diverge from the mainstream system, while still sitting within that system; they 'exist within and despite capitalism, inextricably intertwined with it'.[74] As Kiri Langmead, Chris Land and Daniel King state, a prefigurative mindset recognizes that 'to act responsibly is possible here and now. It does not require waiting for the abolition of private property in some utopian future world.'[75] Organizations set up in this spirit may be somewhat compromised, yet still help to demonstrate new possibilities. Langmead, Land and King note, for example, that workers' cooperatives are not 'a perfectly formed alternative to management, but … can be understood as pre-figuring an alternative form of autonomy and responsibility'.[76] Prefigurative initiatives sit in the cracks of the dominant system, eroding it from within.[77]

Growing A.R.C. (Activate, Reciprocate, and Cultivate), a community-oriented nonprofit founded by designer Nadia Bunyan, is an inspiring example of a prefigurative initiative in the fashion context. The project explores biodiversity, sustainability and community organizing, guided by a 'farm-to-fashion' vision (Figure 7.6). I first discovered Nadia's work when she spoke at an online assembly organized by Our Common Market, the online platform that promotes and connects diverse community-driven alternatives to the dominant fashion system.[78] Nadia spoke engagingly about the challenges of working toward an ecological transition in an extractive system, and the value of prefigurative action:

How are you making this change, when you're in a frame that fights you every step of the way? … I needed to create my own space within this frame, and whoever wanted to be in that space with me was welcome … We have the power within our communities, within our spaces, to create something that is different, and separate, and what we imagine it to be. We can dream into reality what we want our new systems to be, we can have that prefiguration for something new. And we don't have to participate, in a certain way, with that bigger paradigm. We can create the paradigm shift within.

Figure 7.6 *Growing A.R.C. (Activate, Reciprocate, and Cultivate) is a Montreal-based initiative that explores relationships between fashion, nature and agriculture. Their 'playdates' invite the public to grow plants and experiment with textile processes and, along the way, to forge new connections with other species.*[79]

A prefigurative approach is clearly working for Growing A.R.C. and for other initiatives that seek to bring alternative possibilities to life, such as London Urban Textile Commons' Sweatshop intervention (Figure 7.7). I am sure that some Fashion Fictions contributors will be inspired to activate their ideas in a similar way. But I suspect that for some people, myself included, a little extra support would be welcome – and propose that fiction could offer this support. For me, fiction offers a shelter, a shield, a buffer against dismissive rationality. If we frame an initiative using fiction, we need not explain to people why the initiative should exist. The story itself somehow carries a degree of authority, but can also serve as a sleight of hand: *don't bother about us, we're just playing.*

My idea is that we can use the Fashion Fictions structure to shape prefigurative action, seeing such action as an open-ended version of a Stage 3 enactment. After all, enactments and prefigurations have much in common, including the underpinning motivation of 'cutting holes in our reality'[80] and the commitment to practical, embodied, hands-on action. The main difference is that I see Fashion Fictions enactments as temporary, one-off opportunities to step into another world, whereas

Figure 7.7 *The Sweatshop intervention, created by artists Alice Holloway and Joel Gray for the London Urban Textile Commons, demystifies and opens up the process of garment-making. Passers-by are invited to have a simple sweatshirt pattern made to their measurements and then pedal a bike to power the overlocker that is used to construct the sweatshirt.*

prefiguration offers the possibility of dwelling in a fiction for longer and creating deeper, wider, more enduring real-world change.

Thus, I propose that we might sometimes want to play Fashion Fictions in a new way: in *prefigurative* mode, rather than the default *speculative* mode that I introduced in Chapters 1 and 2. The modes are similar, but with subtle differences. In prefigurative mode, we use Stages 1 and 2 of Fashion Fictions to describe and explore a prefigurative initiative *within* a parallel world, and then bring this initiative to life in the real world through repeated, extended or open-ended enactments. One key difference is in the plausibility of ideas: I suggest that in prefigurative mode our ideas should explore the terrain just beyond the boundary of the plausible, rather than pushing deeply into the impossible. This is a mode for people who have taken part in Fashion Fictions and are hungry to engage with parallel worlds further – or those who want to work for change via an organization or practice, and welcome the shelter and inspiration offered by the frame of fiction.

* * * * * * * *

Guidance for playing Fashion Fictions in prefigurative mode is provided in Activity 7.2; to help illustrate the possibilities I will share my first attempt at working in this way, which involved the invention of a parallel-world version of my institution, Nottingham School of Art & Design. The origins of the real-world School lie in a nineteenth-century government plan to support British manufacture;[81] these close ties with the commercial fashion and textile industry continue to the present day. In order to support the exploration of alternative forms of organization in the fashion system, I organized a workshop that invited participants to imagine an alternative history of the School, rooted not in government-endorsed support for the textile industry but rather in Nottingham's history of radical thought and action.[82] In creating this alternative history we aimed to build a story of an institution that has long been shaped by social and environmental justice and, like the real-world School, continues to thrive today.

In the first part of the workshop we worked with a timeline of the real-world School and developed a rough parallel timeline showing key moments in the radical history of Nottingham. We then creatively combined elements from these timelines to generate a new narrative that blended fact and fiction. We started with the two ends of the timeline, creating a new vision for the origins of the School – now reimagined as a grassroots worker-led organization – and a vision for the present-day alternative School. We enjoyed imagining what would have happened at the School in the intervening years, from hosting a significant debate on the relationship between craft, design and industry in the early 1900s, radical rewilding in the 1960s and student occupations in the 1970s to the recent introduction of the 'degree sharing festival' that celebrates collaboration between the School and the city. Together, we came up with the **World 209** Stage 1 fiction:

In World 209, the Nottingham Independent Arts School is a thriving institution focused on people, planet and possibility. It offers space: space to think and space to make and share skills. The school is deeply integrated with the local community and guided by a focus on care and cross-disciplinarity.

Its origins lie in 1845, when local people came together to build a revolutionary institution, Nottingham Artizans Institute of Craft, which was open to all. Throughout its history it has maintained this inclusive ethos and adapted to changing times, welcoming discussion, debate and disruption in the pursuit of social and environmental justice and creativity for the people of Nottingham.

At a subsequent workshop we built on and extended the fiction, editing and remixing materials from the archive of the real-world School via hands-on exploration to create a series of speculative documents that illustrate the history of the invented School (Figure 7.8).

Figure 7.8 *I created this prototype at the second of two workshops that generated a vision of a parallel-world version of Nottingham School of Art & Design, an institution with its roots in Nottingham's radical past. The name of the original institution changed from the first workshop to the second, from 'Artizans' Institute' to 'Operatives' Institute'. While both terms are taken from real-world nineteenth-century organizations in Nottingham (specifically, workers' libraries), my research following the first workshop revealed that the latter term denoted the organizations led by craft workers rather than the middle class.[83] Inspired by the multiple adaptations of a single world generated in earlier project activities, I was happy to allow these conflicting versions of the world to coexist.*

The World 209 prefigurative initiative – the parallel-world version of Nottingham School of Art & Design – was first brought to life in a two-month-long project involving 120 students in my department of Fashion, Textiles and Knitwear Design, within a module that aims to explore principles of sustainability and community and develop the students' skills in experimentation, uncertainty and collaboration. The students were invited to step into the World 209 version of the School for the duration of the project, with a particular focus on nature connection, which we felt would be valued in the fictional School, and the skill-sharing aspects of the original fiction.

The creative brief asked the students to develop instructions for creative craft processes – whether conventional, such as a specific embroidery stitch or the correct way to wash silk, or something more

Figure 7.9 *As an introduction to the World 209 version of the School of Art & Design, in which connection with nature is highly valued, we invited students to meet a tree in the neighbouring arboretum.*

Figure 7.10 *To further embody life in the World 209 School, the students were tasked with creating instructions to share a creative skill. The instructions took various forms, including – as in this case – visual step-by-step guidance.*

unconventional – and test them with communities both within and beyond the institution. As the students generated their instructions, the idea of World 209 took on a degree of reality. Through testing the resources they created with various groups, they gained new perspectives on their real-world design practices and the wider fashion system. The prefigurative initiative of the World 209 School is now dormant, ready to be reactivated in future iterations of the student project, or in other activities in which an alternative vision could help us to think through – and experience – different ways of taking action for sustainability at a local level.

An alternative approach to playing in prefigurative mode could be to invent a new organization, rather than reimagine an existing real-world organization. For example: since I collaborated to generate **World 47**, in which fashion designers are guided by an ethical code, I have been tempted to create an institution to devise and promote such a code. If I were to take this idea forward, I might create a new Stage 1 fiction, focusing on the organization rather than the wider world (crediting the original fiction that inspired it), and then a Stage 2 prototype to investigate the organization in more detail. Giving a name to the organization would create a sense of identity and authority. I would then find a way to enact it – perhaps organizing an online assembly at which attendees could work together to devise the code, followed by regular meetings of the fictional organization to formulate and implement plans for its dissemination and promotion.[84]

A third possibility for prefigurative action within Fashion Fictions is the invention of alternative practices. Again, guidance for this approach is provided in Activity 7.2; I suggest using a structuring device to shape an imagined practice, such as a ritual, law or social norm. I find ritual particularly intriguing as a way of structuring prefigurative practices, whether daily activities or events to mark particular occasions. As I discussed in Chapter 5, rituals imbue practices with meaning and purpose. Arvind Venkataramani and Adam Menter suggest that rituals 'create space for people to play with and create new identities and selves, and provide a container for a lived experience of those selves'; they thus identify rituals as a kind of 'lost technology' that could help us to pursue and navigate systemic change.[85]

Figure 7.11 *I designed a ritual for a Stage 3 'wardrobe challenge' in early 2023. I took inspiration from the Stage 2 exploration of World 45, in which people have a spiritual connection with their textiles, and developed a vision for a simple and accessible daily ritual. The challenge, titled Material Mindfulness, invited people to look closely at their clothes every day for fifteen days, responding to a one-word prompt, and to share a photograph and accompanying comment online.[86] The challenge generated over a thousand posts on Instagram, helping the novel ritual practice to spread and become real for a time.*

Figure 7.12 *Those interested in inventing a ritual could take inspiration from Dusking, a new tradition invented by artist Lucy Wright as the counterpart to the Morris dancing that takes place to mark the arrival of summer.[87] On 31 October, those honouring the new tradition dress up to '"dance the sun down" while honouring the equal gifts of rest, reflection and replenishment associated with the darker months of the year'.[88] Lucy shared the invitation to take part in the first Dusking in 2023, and was amazed by the array of creative responses that were shared online.[89]*

* * * * * * * * *

What happens when we play Fashion Fictions in prefigurative mode and start dwelling in our fictions for longer? I have a sense that the *both/and* phenomenon discussed in Chapter 3 deepens: we are *both* operating in the fictional-world system *and* the real-world system; it is *both* a subjunctive space *and* a real space. The two overlap, potentially to the extent that the distinction between the parallel-world fiction and the real world collapses. As our activities come to life, it is my hope that we might generate what Heila Lotz-Sisitka and her co-authors describe as 'germ cell' activities, which can 'foster and lead to substantive social change at multiple levels'.[90] My dream would be for a prefigurative initiative to take root and establish its own reality. A high-profile example of this kind of success is shared by Jon Alexander. He describes an activist initiative in Taiwan that initially created shadow versions of state websites, reworked to enable citizen participation in public decision-making – which became so influential that, just a few years later, the activists were invited to shape actual government policy.[91]

An initiative does not need to operate at such a high level to be meaningful. Whether individual or collective, mundane or spectacular, an idea flourishing from the scaffold of a fiction and growing into something real should be celebrated.

Activity 7.2: Playing in prefigurative mode

Rather than envisioning an entire world, an *organization* or *practice* should instead be the focus when using a prefigurative approach to Fashion Fictions. Guidance for each approach is provided below.

Imagining a parallel-world version of a real-world organization

One effective way of working in prefigurative mode is to imagine a parallel-world version of a real-world organization. This organization might be a business, a trade union, a network, a club, an advisory body, a charity, a government ministry. It should be an organization that you have some connection with, to make the outcome meaningful.

Stage 1

- Write a 100-word fiction using the instructions provided in Activity 2.1, but with a focus on the organization rather than the wider culture or system.

- In Step 1 of the instructions you will be looking for an idea for how things could happen differently in the parallel-world version of the organization. This idea might be inspired by a frustration with the real-world situation; an element of a speculative-mode fiction or idea from the wonder gallery;[92] or, perhaps, an 'idea for the real world' offered in this book.

- You might want to imagine a different form for your organization; the ideas in Chapter 6 (see page 181) can be used for inspiration. Aim for 'forms of organizing which respect personal autonomy, but within a framework of co-operation, and are attentive to the sorts of futures which they will produce'.[93]

Stage 2

- Adapt the instructions in Activity 2.2 to focus on your reimagined organization.

- Remember to explore the terrain just beyond the boundary of the plausible: aim for a vision that feels exciting and challenging, but not so outlandish that it will feel impossible to bring to life.

- Produce a visual or material prototype that makes the alternative version of your organization feel more real. Something quite mundane could be effective, such as an agenda for a meeting of the organization (see Figure 6.5 for inspiration). Alternatively, you could create a timeline showing the organization's history, blending real-world and fictional events. Using genuine archival documents within the timeline can be helpful in grounding the organization in the local context.

Stage 3

- You should be looking to set up a deeper, slower enactment in comparison with the one-off enactments of speculative mode. You will dwell in the fiction for longer, so your connection with the fiction becomes a more enduring exploration – whether open-ended, extended (spanning months or years, for example) or repeating (taking place, for example, in the first week of every month).

- Use the instructions provided in Activity 2.3 but adapt them to your context. Give particular thought to Step 3: generating ideas for possible ways that you could bring the fiction to life.

Inventing an organization

Another approach is to call a new organization into existence, rather than reimagining something that already exists – though the process is broadly similar to that described above. To dream up the new organization you might take some of the ideas from Chapter 6 and see what they would look like in the fashion space. Or you could pick up an idea for an organization from an existing Stage 1 or Stage 2 fiction and build on it to create a new vision.

Imagining a parallel-world practice

You might choose to focus not on an organization but rather a practice. As I discussed earlier in this chapter, practices – shared patterns of activity – can be seen as the building blocks of everyday life. You might reimagine an existing practice or invent a new practice.

- Use the guidance in Activities 2.1, 2.2 and 2.3 to work through the three stages of Fashion Fictions, with the practice as your focus.

- Be particularly alert to the plausibility of the vision you are creating: aim to generate an outline of a practice that pushes beyond the familiar, but can be performed on a regular basis in the real world. A proposal that is too far-fetched or demanding is less likely to be taken up over the long term.

- At Stage 3, decide how you will bring your prefigurative practice to life. You could use your vision to guide your daily dress choices indefinitely, to shape a six-month experiment in caring for your clothes differently, or to inform a different way of working that you enact every Wednesday. It could be a solo endeavour, or you could invite others in to join you.

Consider using a structuring device to shape your imagined practice, such as a ritual (as discussed in Chapter 5) or law, rule or social norm (Chapter 6). These devices offer a rationale for acting in an unfamiliar way.

Looping back

Even prefiguration is not the end of the story. Every action, from writing a short outline of a fictional world to bringing a fiction to life through an embodied enactment or a prefigurative proposition, has the potential to inform and inspire further cycles of imaginative speculation. The actual and the possible are thus connected through endless dynamic loops of inspiration, manifestation and influence.[94]

To retrace these loops, we could start with the liminoid spaces that Fashion Fictions, when working most effectively, can create: 'settings in which new models, symbols, paradigms, etc., arise'.[95] Playfulness is key to our liminoid activities; the project is guided by the conviction that we can learn through the double-edged, ambiguous qualities of play. Imagination is likewise central – and vital for change. As John Wood notes, 'If we lose the art of dreaming for ourselves we will eventually become unable to change anything. For this reason, envisioning and exchanging dreams of better possible futures should be seen as a civic duty that is far more important than voting or paying taxes.'[96] Within our liminoid spaces we draw on the resources of the real world. We rework and mould the potential of that which exists around us, whether physical materials, tools, images, words, patterns of behaviour or ideas. Through recombination and creative imagination, we create fresh potential from the familiar.

The primary impact of these envisioning activities is internal: it creates, for some participants at least, a powerful sense of wonder. Wonder involves seeing the real world in a new light, unmaking our assumptions about systems, forces and processes that seem fixed and unquestionable. It expands our sense of possibility: our perceptions of what change can happen, how things might be otherwise, what options are available for exploration. As Loes Damhof and Jitske Gulmans note, 'In order to see more diverse possibilities in the world around us, one needs to widen the lens of perception, and imagining multiple futures attribute to that. When we *imagine* more, when we *explore* multiple futures, we *perceive* more in the present.'[97]

When we share our speculations and prefigurations, we put new things into the world. We offer fictions that people can engage with, images and objects that they can see, touch and relate to, performances, practices and organizations that they can observe or join in with. These visions show us how things could be different – often not as resolved proposals to be taken forward wholesale, but rather as intriguing compositions of ideas, riddled with inconsistencies and complexities alongside inspiration, humour and occasional moments of genius. Their stories can spread, influence others, nurture different ways of thinking, spark new initiatives, motivate people to act. They can prompt new loops of speculation and exploration. Some elements of our visions can even start to make change directly in the world, putting down roots and seeping from fiction to reality.

Through these iterative loops we pull the possibilities: we work in solidarity to pull alternative systems into reality, into our wardrobes and into our embodied experiences of the world.

Figure 7.13 *Stories spread. In April 2021, a fashion historian came to an online Stage 1 Fashion Fictions workshop and wrote a 100-word fiction – World 91 – about a world in which mushrooms are hailed as spiritual guides. At the end of that year, her words caught the attention of a group of participants at a Stage 2 prototyping workshop in Nottingham. Their conversations inspired me to write a text to guide a Stage 3 enactment and invite others to step in and explore it in early 2022. Their experiences inspired a comic that was created later the same year, an online wardrobe challenge and an enactment in the Andes mountains in 2023 and, in 2024, an editorial feature – including this image – that was produced by creatives in Berlin and published in sustainable fashion magazine* The Lissome. *Where will our tales of alternative fashion worlds travel next?*

Notes

Chapter 1

1   Alice Payne, *Designing Fashion's Future: Present Practice and Tactics for Sustainable Change* (London: Bloomsbury, 2021), 26.

2   Elizabeth Wilson, *Adorned in Dreams: Fashion and Modernity*, revised and updated edition (London: I.B.Tauris, 2003), 3.

3   Amy Twigger Holroyd, *Folk Fashion: Understanding Homemade Clothes* (London: I.B. Tauris, 2017).

4   Ibid., 169. Payne's original source is Erica de Greef, 'Long Read: Fashion, Sustainability and Decoloniality', *Twyg* (7 December 2019). Available at https://twyg.co.za/long-read-fashion-sustainability-and-decoloniality/ [accessed 17 February 2022].

5   Kirsi Niinimäki, Greg Peters, Helena Dahlbo, Patsy Perry, Timo Rissanen and Alison Gwilt, 'The Environmental Price of Fast Fashion', *Nature Reviews Earth and Environment* 1 (2020), 189–200. https://doi.org/10.1038/s43017-020-0039-9.

6   Jason Hickel, *Less is More: How Degrowth will Save the World* (London: Windmill Books, 2020), 20.

7   Ellen MacArthur Foundation, *A New Textiles Economy: Redesigning Fashion's Future* (2017), 18. Available at https://www.ellenmacarthurfoundation.org/assets/downloads/publications/A-New-Textiles-Economy_Full-Report_Updated_1-12-17.pdf [accessed 25 July 2021].

8   WRAP, *Textiles 2030 Annual Progress Report 2022–23* (2023), 2. Available at https://wrap.org.uk/sites/default/files/2023-11/textiles-2030-annual-progress-report-2022-23.pdf [accessed 29 January 2024].

9   Jason Hickel, Daniel W. O'Neill, Andrew L. Fanning and Huzaifa Zoomkawala, 'National Responsibility for Ecological Breakdown: A Fair-Shares Assessment of Resource Use, 1970–2017', *The Lancet Planetary Health*, 6:4 (2022), E342–E349. https://doi.org/10.1016/S2542-5196(22)00044-4.

10 Lewis Akenji, Magnus Bengtsson, Viivi Toivio and Michael Lettenmeier, *1.5-Degree Lifestyles: Towards A Fair Consumption Space for All: Summary for Policy Makers* (Berlin: Hot or Cool Institute, 2021), 5.

11 Luca Coscieme, Lewis Akenji, Elli Latva-Hakuni, Katia Vladimirova, Kirsi Niinimäki, Claudia Henninger, Cosette Joyner-Martinez, Kristian Nielsen, Samira Iran and Erminia D 'Itria, *Unfit, Unfair, Unfashionable: Resizing Fashion for a Fair Consumption Space* (Berlin: Hot or Cool Institute, 2022), 12.

12 IPCC, *Summary for Policymakers*, in *Climate Change 2022: Impacts, Adaptation and Vulnerability*, Contribution of Working Group II to the Sixth Assessment Report of the Intergovernmental Panel on Climate Change (Cambridge: Cambridge University Press, 2022).

13 Giorgos Kallis, *Limits: Why Malthus was Wrong and Why Environmentalists Should Care* (Stanford: Stanford University Press, 2019), 55.

14 Martin Parker, George Cheney, Valerie Fournier and Chris Land, 'Introduction', in *The Routledge Companion to Alternative Organisation*, edited by Martin Parker, George Cheney, Valérie Fournier and Chris Land (Abingdon: Routledge, 2018), 8.

15 Ibid., 13.

16 Hickel, *Less is More*, 33.

17 Ibid., 40.

18 Arturo Escobar, 'Welcome to Possibility Studies', *Possibility Studies and Society* 1:1–2 (2023), 56–7. https://doi.org/10.1177/27538699231171450.

19 Richard B. Norgaard, *Development Betrayed: The End of Progress and a Coevolutionary Revisioning of the Future* (London: Routledge, 1994), 1.

20 Rutger Bregman, *Utopia for Realists And How We Can Get There* (London, Bloomsbury 2017), 6–8.

21 Escobar, 'Welcome to Possibility Studies', 57.

22 Vanessa Machado de Oliveira, *Hospicing Modernity: Facing Humanity's Wrongs and the Implications for Social Activism* (Berkeley, CA: North Atlantic Books, 2021), 18.

23 Federico Demaria, François Schneider, Filka Sekulova and Joan Martínez-Alier, 'What is Degrowth? From an Activist Slogan to a Social Movement', *Environmental Values* 22:2 (2013), 191–215. https://doi.org/10.3197/0963 27113X13581561725194.

24 François Schneider, Giorgos Kallis and Joan Martínez-Alier, 'Crisis or Opportunity? Economic Degrowth for Social Equity and Ecological Sustainability', *Journal of Cleaner Production* 18 (2010), 512. https://doi.org/10.1016/j.jclepro.2010.01.014.

25 Matthias Schmelzer, Andrea Vetter and Aaron Vansintjan, *The Future is Degrowth: A Guide to a World Beyond Capitalism* (London: Verso, 2022), 3.

26 Thomas Wanner, 'The New "Passive Revolution" of the Green Economy and Growth Discourse: Maintaining the "Sustainable Development" of Neoliberal Capitalism', *New Political Economy* 20:1 (2015), 36. https://doi.org/10.1 080/13563467.2013.866081.

27 James D. Ward, Paul C. Sutton, Adrian D. Werner, Robert Costanza, Steve T. Mohr and Craig T. Simmons, 'Is Decoupling GDP Growth from Environmental Impact Possible?' *PLoS ONE* 11:10 (2016), e0164733. https://doi.org/10.1371/journal.pone.0164733.

28 Harold Glasser, 'Toward Robust Foundations for Sustainable Well-Being Societies: Learning to Change by Changing How We Learn', in *Sustainability, Human Well-Being, and the Future of Education*, edited by Justin W. Cook (Cham: Palgrave Macmillan, 2019), 34.

29 Schmelzer, Vetter and Vansintjan, *The Future is Degrowth*, 4.

30 Hickel, *Less is More*, 21.

31 Stephen Sterling, 'Transformative Learning and Sustainability: Sketching the Conceptual Ground', *Learning and Teaching in Higher Education*, 5 (2010–11), 22.

32 Ibid., 23 (emphasis added).

33   Machado de Oliveira, *Hospicing Modernity,* 37.

34   Hickel, *Less is More*, 29.

35   Kate Fletcher and Mathilda Tham, *Earth Logic Fashion Action Research Plan* (London: The J J Charitable Trust, 2019).

36   Ibid., 15.

37   M. Angela Jansen, 'Fashion and the Phantasmagoria of Modernity: An Introduction to Decolonial Fashion Discourse', *Fashion Theory* 24:6 (2020), 817. https://doi.org/10.1080/1362704X.2020.1802098.

38   Lucy Siegle, 'Foreword', in *Earth Logic Fashion Action Research Plan*, Kate Fletcher and Mathilda Tham (London: The J J Charitable Trust, 2019), 5.

39   John R. Ehrenfeld, *Sustainability by Design: A Subversive Strategy for Transforming Our Consumer Culture* (New Haven: Yale University Press, 2008), 49.

40   Leila Dawney, Samuel Kirwan and Julian Brigstocke, 'The Promise of the Commons', in *Space, Power and the Commons: The Struggle for Alternative Futures*, edited by Samuel Kirwan, Leila Dawney and Julian Brigstocke (Abingdon: Routledge, 2016), 20.

41   Christopher Wright, Daniel Nyberg, Christian De Cock and Gail Whiteman, 'Future Imaginings: Organizing in Response to Climate Change', *Organisation* 20:5 (2013), 653. https://doi.org/10.1177/1350508413489821.

42   Mark Fisher, *Capitalist Realism: Is There No Alternative?* (Ropley: O Books, 2009), 2.

43   Escobar, 'Welcome to Possibility Studies', 57.

44   Erik Olin Wright, *Envisioning Real Utopias* (London: Verso, 2010), 23.

45   Tania Zittoun, Hana Hawlina and Alex Gillespie, 'Imagination', in *The Palgrave Encyclopedia of the Possible*, edited by Vlad P. Glăveanu (Cham: Palgrave Macmillan, 2021), 1. https://doi.org/10.1007/978-3-319-98390-5_68-1.

46   Ibid., 2.

47   Ibid., 3.

48   Lisa Garforth, *Green Utopias: Environmental Hope Before and After Nature* (Cambridge: Polity, 2017), 3.

49   Ibid., 9.

50   Geoff Mulgan, *The Imaginary Crisis (and How We Might Quicken Social and Public Imagination)* (2020), 3. Available at https://demoshelsinki.fi/wp-content/uploads/2020/04/the-imaginary-crisis-web.pdf [accessed 3 February 2023].

51   Ibid., 7–8.

52   Zygmunt Bauman, *Liquid Modernity* (Cambridge: Polity, 2012), 7–8.

53   Garforth, *Green Utopias*, 14.

54   John Wood, *Design for Micro-Utopias: Making the Unthinkable Possible* (Abingdon: Routledge, 2017), 12.

55   Mulgan, *The Imaginary Crisis*, 9.

56   Rob Hopkins, 'Why Is Now the Moment for Social Imagination?', Joseph Rowntree Foundation, 16 May 2022. Available at https://www.jrf.org.uk/blog/why-now-moment-social-imagination [accessed 6 February 2023].

57 Institute of Radical Imagination, 'Mission & Values', Available at https://instituteofradicalimagination.org/mission-and-values/ [accessed 6 February 2023].

58 Talila A. Lewis, 'The Birth of Resistance: Courageous Dreams, Powerful Nobodies & Revolutionary Madness', in *Resistance & Hope: Essays by Disabled People*, edited by Alice Wong (Disability Visibility Project, 2018), 56.

59 Garforth, *Green Utopias*, 10.

60 Mulgan, *The Imaginary Crisis*, 10.

61 Naomi Alderman, 'Dystopian Dreams: How Feminist Science Fiction Predicted the Future', *The Guardian*, 25 March 2017. Available at https://www.theguardian.com/books/2017/mar/25/dystopian-dreams-how-feminist-science-fiction-predicted-the-future [accessed 24 August 2024].

62 Mulgan, *The Imaginary Crisis*, 10, 13.

63 Ibid., 13.

64 Ursula K. Le Guin, *The Wave in the Mind: Talks and Essays on the Writer, the Reader, and the Imagination* (Boston: Shambhala, 2004), 218.

65 Joseph Lindley and Paul Coulton, 'Back to the Future: 10 Years of Design Fiction', in *Proceedings of the 2015 British HCI Conference* (New York: ACM, 2015), 210–11. https://doi.org/10.1145/2783446.2783592.

66 Anthony Dunne and Fiona Raby, *Speculative Everything: Design, Fiction, and Social Dreaming* (Cambridge, MA: The MIT Press, 2013).

67 Near Future Laboratory. https://nearfuturelaboratory.com.

68 Tony Fry, *Writing Design Fiction: Relocating a City in Crisis* (London: Bloomsbury, 2023).

69 Thomas Markussen, Eva Knutz and Tau Lenskjold, 'Design Fiction as a Research Practice in the Social Field', *Temes de Disseny* 36 (2020): 16–39. https://doi.org/10.46467/TdD36.2020.16-39.

70 Eva Knutz, Thomas Markussen and Poul Rind Christensen, 'The Role of Fiction in Experiments within Design, Art & Architecture – Towards a New Typology of Design Fiction' *Artifact* 3:2 (2014): 8.2. https://doi.org/10.14434/artifact.v3i2.4045.

71 Markussen, Knutz and Lenskjold, 'Design Fiction as a Research Practice in the Social Field', 17.

72 Brad Haylock, 'What is Critical Design?', in *UnDesign: Critical Practices at the Intersection of Art and Design*, edited by Gretchen Coombs, Andrew McNamara and Gavin Sade (Abingdon: Routledge, 2019), 16.

73 Dunne and Raby, *Speculative Everything*, 60–1.

74 Tobias Revell, Justin Pickard and Georgina Voss, 'Valuing Utopia in Speculative and Critical Design', in *Economic Science Fictions*, edited by William Davies (London: Goldsmiths Press, 2018), 285.

75 Ross Haenfler, *Straight Edge: Hardcore Punk, Clean Living Youth, and Social Change* (New Brunswick: Rutgers University Press, 2006).

76 Otto von Busch, 'Fashion suX: A Story of Anger as (Un)Sustainable Energy', *Utopian Studies* 28:3 (2017): 505. https://doi.org/10.5325/utopianstudies.28.3.0505.

77 Emma Fukuwatari Huffman, Mending with Mycelium, 11 July 2022. https://efhuffman.com/mending-with-mycelium/. Emma later contributed to a Fashion Fictions enactment that brought the fungi-centric World 91 to life, making a series of videos as her parallel-world alter ego: https://fashionfictions.org/2023/04/08/world-91-enactment-ii-meet-the-mushrooms-report/.

78   Fry, *Writing Design Fiction*, 10.

79   Ivica Mitrović, James Auger, Julian Hanna and Ingi Helgason (eds), *Beyond Speculative Design: Past – Present – Future* (Split: SpeculativeEdu/Arts Academy, University of Split, 2021), 13. Available at https://speculativeedu. eu/beyond-speculative-design-past-present-future/ [accessed 4 August 2024].

80   Pedro J. S. Vieira de Oliveira and Luiza Prado de O. Martins, 'Designer/Shapeshifter: A De-colonial Redirection for Speculative and Critical Design', in *Tricky Design: The Ethics of Things,* edited by Tom Fisher and Lorraine Gamman (London: Bloomsbury, 2018), 109.

81   Stuart Candy, 'Gaming Futures Literacy: The Thing From the Future', in *Transforming the Future: Anticipation in the 21st Century*, edited by Riel Miller (Abingdon: Routledge, 2018), 233–46.

82   Ann Light, 'Collaborative Speculation: Anticipation, Inclusion and Designing Counterfactual Futures for Appropriation', *Futures* 134 (2021). https://doi.org/10.1016/j.futures.2021.102855.

83   Back From the Future (2020): https://munichfutures.com.

84   Alpine Community Economies Lab, Publication: Alps 2060 – a community futuring tool. https://www. alpinecommunityeconomies.org/2021/07/01/publication-alps-2060-a-community-futuring-tool/.

85   Thomas Binder, 'The Things We Do: Encountering the Possible', in *Design Anthropological Futures*, edited by Rachel Charlotte Smith, Kasper Tang Vangkilde, Mette Gislev Kjærsgaard, Ton Otto, Joachim Halse and Thomas Binder (London: Bloomsbury, 2016), 267.

86   Maja Kuzmanovic and Nik Gaffney, 'Enacting Futures in Postnormal Times', *Futures* 86 (February 2017), 107–17. https://doi.org/10.1016/j.futures.2016.05.007.

87   Kakee Scott, Conny Bakker and Jaco Quist, 'Designing Change by Living Change', *Design Studies* 33:3 (2012), 279–97. https://doi.org/10.1016/j.destud.2011.08.002.

88   Mulgan, *The Imaginary Crisis*, 9.

89   Ruha Benjamin, *Imagination: A Manifesto* (New York: W.W. Norton & Company, 2024), x.

90   Garforth, *Green Utopias*, 10–11.

91   Rike Neuhoff, Luca Simeone and Lea Holst Laursen, 'Forms of Participatory Futuring for Urban Sustainability: A Systematic Review', *Futures* 154 (2023): 103268. https://doi.org/10.1016/j.futures.2023.103268.

92   Pedro Gil Farias, Roy Bendor and Bregje F. van Eekelen, 'Social Dreaming Together: A Critical Exploration of Participatory Speculative Design', in *Participatory Design Conference 2022: Volume 2*, 19 August–1 September 2022, Newcastle upon Tyne. https://doi.org/10.1145/3537797.3537826.

93   Renata Tyszczuk, 'Collective Scenarios: Speculative Improvisations for the Anthropocene', *Futures* 134 (2021): 102854. https://doi.org/10.1016/j.futures.2021.102854.

94   James Duggan, Joseph Lindley and Sarah McNicol, 'Near Future School: World Building Beyond a Neoliberal Present with Participatory Design Fictions', *Futures* 94 (2017): 15–23. https://doi.org/10.1016/j. futures.2017.04.001.

95   Clarice Carvalho Garcia, 'Fashion Futuring: A Methodology for Enacting Values-Driven Transitions towards Sustainability', PhD thesis, RMIT (2023).

96   Clarice Carvalho Garcia, 'Fashion Futuring: Intertwining Speculative Design, Foresight and Material Culture Towards Sustainable Futures', *Futures* 153 (2023): 103242. https://doi.org/10.1016/j.futures.2023.103242.

97   Sustainable Fashion Consumption Network, FASHION FUTURES 2040. https://sustainablefashionconsumption.org/projects-2/fashion-futures-2040/.

98   Laurie Smith and Kathy Peach, *Our Futures: By the People, for the People*, Nesta, 11 November 2019: https://www.nesta.org.uk/report/our-futures-people-people/.

99   Hanna Thomas Uose, *The Collective Imagination Practices Toolkit* (Joseph Rowntree Foundation, 2024): https://www.collectiveimagination.tools.

100   Fashion Fictions. Guidance for individuals: https://fashionfictions.org/participate; guidance for organizers: https://fashionfictions.org/organise; resources for activities with children: https://fashionfictions.org/children; resources translated into different languages: https://fashionfictions.org/translations.

101   adrienne maree brown, 'Outro' in *Octavia's Brood: Science Fiction Stories from Social Justice Movements,* edited by Walidah Imarisha and adrienne maree brown (Oakland: AK Press, 2015), 281.

102   Zittoun, Hawlina and Gillespie, 'Imagination', 3.

103   Fashion Fictions: https://fashionfictions.org.

104   Farias, Bendor and van Eekelen, 'Social Dreaming Together'.

105   Nicole Seymour, *Bad Environmentalism: Irony and Irreverence in the Ecological Age* (Minneapolis: University of Minnesota Press, 2018), 24.

106   Michele-Lee Moore and Manjana Milkoreit, 'Imagination and Transformations to Sustainable and Just Futures', *Elementa: Science of the Anthropocene* 8:1 (2020), 3. https://doi.org/10.1525/elementa.2020.081.

107   John Urry, 'Consuming the Planet to Excess', *Theory, Culture and Society* 27:2/3 (2010), 198. https://doi.org/10.1177/0263276409355999.

108   'Science Fiction', *Historical Dictionary of Science Fiction* (2022). Available at https://sfdictionary.com/view/209 [accessed 6 February 2023].

109   Brian Attebery, *Strategies of Fantasy* (Bloomington: Indiana University Press, 1992), 107.

110   Gary K. Wolfe, *Evaporating Genres: Essays on Fantastic Literature* (Middletown, CT: Wesleyan University Press, 2011), 18–20.

111   Ezio Manzini, D*esign, When Everybody Designs: An Introduction to Design for Social Innovation* (Cambridge, MA: MIT Press, 2015).

112   Attebury, *Strategies of Fantasy,* 107.

113   Farah Mendelsohn, *Diana Wynne Jones: Children's Literature and the Fantastic Tradition* (Abingdon: Routledge, 2005), xv.

114   Contributed by Judith Sharkey: https://fashionfictions.org/2021/03/25/world-70/.

115   Wolfe, *Evaporating Genres*, 21.

116   Contributed by Annalisa Espino Lim, Nicholas See Wen Bin, Denise Yeo, Brian Loh Keng Chee and Caitlyn Rose Baird: https://fashionfictions.org/2022/03/18/world-152/.

117   Jones was well aware of the potential for her books to become lodged in her readers' psyches: 'Books, especially fantasy, are remembered from childhood. It has entered this person's consciousness at a time when ideas were still forming, waking their sense of wonder and forcing their ideas in a new direction – enlarging their imagination, in fact – and by the mere fact of always being in their mind from then on, has influenced that

reader's entire personality. Permanently.' Diana Wynne Jones, *Reflections: On the Magic of Writing* (New York: Greenwillow Books, 2012), 73.

118 Charlie Butler, 'Reflecting on *Reflections*', in *Reflections: On the Magic of Writing* by Diana Wynne Jones (New York: Greenwillow Books, 2012), xxi.

119 Diana Wynne Jones, *The Lives of Christopher Chant* (London: HarperCollins, 2008 [1988]), 158.

120 Dunne and Raby, *Speculative Everything*, 84–5.

121 James Auger, 'Speculative Design: Crafting the Speculation', *Digital Creativity* 24:1 (2013), 13. https://doi.org/10.1080/14626268.2013.767276

122 Wright, Nyberg, De Cock and Whiteman, 'Future Imaginings', 652.

123 Glasser, 'Toward Robust Foundations for Sustainable Well-Being Societies', 64.

124 Tim Dant, *Material Culture in the Social World: Values, Activities, Lifestyles* (Buckingham: Open University Press, 1999), 93.

125 Brian Attebery, *The Fantasy Tradition in American Literature: From Irving to Le Guin* (Bloomington: Indiana University Press, 1980) 2.

126 Ibid., 2.

127 Attebery, *Strategies of Fantasy*, 54.

128 Kathryn Hume, *Fantasy and Mimesis: Responses to Reality in Western Literature* (Abingdon: Routledge, 2014 [1984]), 8.

129 Zittoun, Hawlina and Gillespie, 'Imagination', 4.

130 Attebery, *Strategies of Fantasy*, 141.

131 Garforth, *Green Utopias*, 10.

132 Attebery, *Strategies of Fantasy*, 129.

133 Richard Sandford, 'Ideas of the Future and their Place in Young People's Internal Conversation', PhD thesis, University of Bristol (2021), 130.

134 Contributed anonymously: https://fashionfictions.org/2021/04/25/world-97/.

135 Seymour, *Bad Environmentalism*, 234.

136 Jones, *Reflections*, 171.

137 Richard Schechner, *Performance Studies: An Introduction*, 3rd edition (Abingdon: Routledge, 2013), 89.

138 Jones, *Reflections*, 225.

139 Cassie Robinson (@cassierobinson), 'Lots people think the work of "collective imagination" is a nice-to-have or only about visioning a potential future', Twitter, 23 March 2022: https://twitter.com/CassieRobinson/status/1506526786577960960.

140 Mendelsohn, *Diana Wynne Jones*, xxi.

Chapter 2

1   A concise version of this guide is included in Activity 2.1.

2   Fashion Fictions interactive generator, https://fashionfictions.github.io/generator/.

3   Pedro J. S. Vieira de Oliveira and Luiza Prado de O. Martins, 'Designer/Shapeshifter: A De-colonial Redirection for Speculative and Critical Design', in *Tricky Design: The Ethics of Things*, edited by Tom Fisher and Lorraine Gamman (London: Bloomsbury, 2018), 106.

4   Tania Zittoun, Hana Hawlina and Alex Gillespie, 'Imagination', in *The Palgrave Encyclopedia of the Possible*, edited by Vlad P. Glăveanu (Cham: Palgrave Macmillan, 2021), 2. https://doi.org/10.1007/978-3-319-98390-5_68-1.

5   Donella Meadows, 'Envisioning a Sustainable World', in *Creating a Sustainable and Desirable Future: Insights from 45 Global Thought Leaders*, edited by Robert Costanza and Ida Kubiszewski (Singapore: World Scientific, 2014), 9.

6   'The Language of Sci-Fi', *Word of Mouth*, BBC Radio 4 [radio broadcast], 11 April 2022. Available at https://www.bbc.co.uk/programmes/m00162v4 [accessed 6 February 2023].

7   The former approach is described as 'recasting' and the latter as 'pastcasting' in Roy Bendor, Elina Eriksson and Daniel Pargman, 'Looking Backward to the Future: On Past-Facing Approaches to Futuring', *Futures* 125 (2021). https://doi.org/10.1016/j.futures.2020.102666.

8   Lisa Garforth, *Green Utopias: Environmental Hope Before and After Nature* (Cambridge: Polity, 2017), 14.

9   Arturo Escobar, 'Welcome to Possibility Studies', *Possibility Studies and Society* 1:1–2 (2023), 57. https://doi.org/10.1177/27538699231171450.

10   Mario Blaser, 'Life Projects', in *Pluriverse: A Post-Development Dictionary*, edited by Ashish Kothari, Ariel Salleh, Arturo Escobar, Federico Demaria and Alberto Acosta (New Delhi: Tulika Books, 2019), 236.

11   Ann Light, 'Collaborative Speculation: Anticipation, Inclusion and Designing Counterfactual Futures for Appropriation', *Futures* 134 (2021), 5. https://doi.org/10.1016/j.futures.2021.102855.

12   Brian Attebery, *Strategies of Fantasy* (Bloomington: Indiana University Press, 1992), 141.

13   Gary K. Wolfe, *Evaporating Genres: Essays on Fantastic Literature* (Middletown, CT: Wesleyan University Press, 2011), 23.

14   Rob Hopkins, 'Why Is Now the Moment for Social Imagination?', Joseph Rowntree Foundation, 16 May 2022. Available at https://www.jrf.org.uk/blog/why-now-moment-social-imagination [accessed 6 February 2023].

15   Attebery, *Strategies of Fantasy*, 3.

16   Ibid., 3–4.

17   Zittoun, Hawlina and Gillespie, 'Imagination', 3.

18   Attebery, *Strategies of Fantasy*, 126.

19   Ibid., 127.

20   Ibid.

21   James Auger, 'Speculative Design: Crafting the Speculation', *Digital Creativity* 24:1 (2013), 2. https://doi.org/10.1080/14626268.2013.767276.

22   Garforth, *Green Utopias*, 11.

23   Joachim Halse, 'Ethnographies of the Possible', in *Design Anthropology: Theory and Practice*, edited by Wendy Gunn, Ton Otto and Rachel Charlotte Smith (London: Berg, 2013), 182.

24   World 2, Enactment i (see Figure 3.17); World 91, Enactment i (see page 78).

25   World 62, Enactment i (see page 68).

26   World 27, Enactment i (see page 62) and World 54, Enactment i (see page 81).

27   World 45, Enactment i (see Figure 7.11) and World 91, Enactment ii: https://fashionfictions.org/2023/04/08/world-91-enactment-ii-meet-the-mushrooms-report/.

28   Contributed by Amandine Maillard Bourgeois: https://fashionfictions.org/2021/09/21/world-127/.

29   Further details and case study video: https://fashionfictions.org/2023/11/27/world-127-enactment-i-report/.

30   Mette Gislev Kjærsgaard and Laurens Boer, 'The Speculative and the Mundane in Practices of Future-Making: Exploring Relations between Design Anthropology and Critical Design', paper for seminar *Collaborative Formation of Issues* (22–23 January 2015), Aarhus, Denmark.

31   Garforth, *Green Utopias*, 14.

32   Attebery, *Strategies of Fantasy*, 107.

33   Vlad P. Glăveanu, *Wonder: The Extraordinary Power of an Ordinary Experience* (London: Bloomsbury, 2020), 15.

34   Vlad P. Glăveanu, 'Creativity and Wonder', *Journal of Creative Behaviour* 53:2 (2019), 172.

35   Glăveanu, *Wonder*, 42.

36   Attebery, *Strategies of Fantasy*, 67.

37   Thomas Princen, *Treading Softly: Paths to Ecological Order* (Cambridge, MA: MIT Press, 2010), 188.

38   Martin Parker, George Cheney, Valerie Fournier and Chris Land, 'Introduction', in *The Routledge Companion to Alternative Organisation*, edited by Martin Parker, George Cheney, Valérie Fournier and Chris Land (Abingdon: Routledge, 2018), 19.

39   Cameron Tonkinwise, 'I Prefer Not To: Anti-Progressive Designing', in *UnDesign: Critical Practices at the Intersection of Art and Design*, edited by Gretchen Coombs, Andrew McNamara and Gavin Sade (Abingdon: Routledge, 2019), 82–3.

40   Cally Gatehouse, 'A Hauntology of Participatory Speculation', in *Proceedings of the 16th Participatory Design Conference 2020 – Participation(s) Otherwise – Volume 1 (PDC '20)* (New York: Association for Computing Machinery, 2020), 138. https://doi.org/10.1145/3385010.3385024.

41   Vlad P. Glăveanu, 'Wonder', in *The Palgrave Encyclopedia of the Possible*, edited by Vlad P. Glăveanu (Cham: Palgrave Macmillan, 2021), 1773.

42   Fashion Fictions, Wonder-Capture Activity, https://fashionfictions.org/wonder-capture/

43   The dataset can be accessed at http://doi.org/10.5281/zenodo.13369853.

44 Virginia Braun and Victoria Clarke, *Thematic Analysis: A Practical Guide* (London: SAGE, 2022).

45 If you take any of these ideas forward, please let me know! I'd love to hear from you: amy@amytwiggerholroyd.com.

46 Fashion Fictions: https://fashionfictions.org.

Chapter 3

1 Narrative Initiative, *Toward New Gravity: Charting a Course for the Narrative Initiative* (2017), 12. Available at https://narrativeinitiative.org/resource/toward-new-gravity/ [accessed 5 February 2024].

2 Marie-Laure Ryan, 'Narrative', in *Routledge Encyclopedia of Narrative Theory*, edited by David Herman, Manfred Jahn and Marie-Laure Ryan (Abingdon: Routledge, 2005), 347.

3 Contributed by Vicki Harris: https://fashionfictions.org/2022/11/15/world-178/.

4 Joseph T. Shipley, *The Origins of English Words: A Discursive Dictionary of Indo-European Roots* (Baltimore: Johns Hopkins University Press, 1984), 427.

5 Rob Pope, *Studying English Literature and Language: An Introduction and Companion*, 3rd edition (Abingdon: Routledge, 2012), 242.

6 Ibid., 251.

7 Barbara Benjamin, 'The Case Study: Storytelling in the Industrial Age and Beyond', in *Storytelling in a Liminal Time*, edited by Boria Sax (Leeds: Emerald Publishing Limited, 2006), 160.

8 Ruth Finnegan, 'Storying the Self: Personal Narratives and Identity', in *Consumption and Everyday Life*, edited by Hugh Mackay (London: SAGE, 1997), 65–112.

9 Richard Kearney, *On Stories* (London: Routledge, 2002), 4.

10 Benjamin, 'The Case Study', 161.

11 Kearney, *On Stories,* 13.

12 Narrative Initiative, *Toward New Gravity,* 12.

13 Alice Sachrajda, 'From Narrative Theory to Narrative Practice: Cultivating the Pop Culture for Social Change …', Inter-Narratives, 5 August 2022. Available at https://inter-narratives.org/community-insight/from-narrative-theory-to-narrative-practice-cultivating-the-pop-culture-for-social-change/ [accessed 5 February 2024].

14 Mathilda Tham, 'Languaging Fashion and Sustainability: Towards Synergistic Modes of Thinking, Wording, Visualising and Doing Fashion and Sustainability', *Nordic Textile Journal* 3:1 (2010), 16.

15 Ibid.

16 Sacha Kagan, 'Proving the World More Imaginary? Four Approaches to Imagining Sustainability in Sustainability Research', *Österreich Z Soziol* 44: Suppl. 2 (2019), 163. https://doi.org/10.1007/s11614-019-00378-9.

17 Ibid., 161, original emphasis.

18   Sheila Jasanoff, 'Future Imperfect: Science, Technology, and the Imaginations of Modernity', in *Dreamscapes of Modernity: Sociotechnical Imaginaries and the Fabrication of Power*, edited by Sheila Jasanoff and Sang-Hyun Kim (Chicago: University of Chicago Press, 2015), 4.

19   Imagine, Oslo Metropolitan University: https://imagine.oslomet.no.

20   Jon Alexander, *Citizens: Why the Key to Fixing Everything Is All of Us* (Kingston upon Thames: Canbury Press, 2022), 96.

21   Martin Parker, George Cheney, Valerie Fournier and Chris Land, 'Introduction', in *The Routledge Companion to Alternative Organisation*, edited by Martin Parker, George Cheney, Valérie Fournier and Chris Land (Abingdon: Routledge, 2018), 10.

22   Alexander, *Citizens*, 94.

23   Harold Glasser, 'Toward Robust Foundations for Sustainable Well-Being Societies: Learning to Change by Changing How We Learn', in *Sustainability, Human Well-Being, and the Future of Education*, edited by Justin W. Cook (Cham: Palgrave Macmillan, 2019), 40.

24   Cameron Tonkinwise, '"I Prefer Not To": Anti-Progressive Designing', in *Undesign: Critical Practices at the Intersection of Art and Design*, edited by Gretchen Coombs, Andrew McNamara and Gavin Sade (Abingdon: Routledge, 2019), 81.

25   Dan Lockton and Stuart Candy, 'A Vocabulary for Visions in Designing for Transitions', in *Proceedings of DRS2018 International Conference*, vol. 3 (2018), Design Research Society, Limerick, Ireland, 918.

26   Glasser, 'Toward Robust Foundations for Sustainable Well-Being Societies', 50.

27   Manjana Milkoreit, 'Imaginary Politics: Climate Change and Making the Future', *Elementa: Science of the Anthropocene* 5:62 (2017). https://doi.org/10.1525/elementa.249

28   Alexander, *Citizens*, 15.

29   Narrative Initiative, *Toward New Gravity*, 23.

30   A detailed account of this analysis can be found in Amy Twigger Holroyd, 'Writing Sustainable Fashion Worlds', in *Sustainability and the Fashion Industry: Can Fashion Save the World?*, edited by Annick Schramme and Nathalie Verboven (Abingdon: Routledge, 2024), 19–35.

31   James Drisko and Tina Maschi, *Content Analysis* [ebook] (New York: Oxford University Press, 2015). Accessed via Oxford Scholarship Online.

32   This is a subjective process; I may have inferred different meanings to those that the author intended, especially considering that many contributors will have different cultural references to me and that some have written in English as a second language.

33   The analysis spreadsheet is available from Fashion Fictions Worlds 1–120 analysis, zenodo,http://doi.org/10.5281/zenodo.6991840.

34   Tham, 'Languaging Fashion and Sustainability', 16.

35   Of the first 250 fictions published on the website, 105 were created by UK-based contributors.

36   Cripping Masculinity: https://crippingmasculinity.com.

37   Rosie Findlay and Johannes Reponen, 'Introduction', in *Insights on Fashion Journalism*, edited by Rosie Findlay and Johannes Reponen (Abingdon: Routledge, 2023), 5.

38 Kate Nelson Best *The History of Fashion Journalism* (London: Bloomsbury Academic, 2018), 15–44.

39 Katie Baker Jones, 'American *Vogue* and Sustainable Fashion (1990–2015): A Multimodal Critical Discourse Analysis', *Clothing and Textiles Research Journal* 38:2 (2020), 105. https://doi.org/10.1177/0887302X19881508.

40 Ibid., 115.

41 Ibid., 116.

42 Ibid., 115.

43 Michael Mann, *Macmillan Student Encyclopedia of Sociology* (London: Macmillan, 1983), 154.

44 Thomas Wanner, 'The New "Passive Revolution" of the Green Economy and Growth Discourse: Maintaining the "Sustainable Development" of Neoliberal Capitalism', *New Political Economy* 20:1 (2015), 23. https://doi.org/10.1080/13563467.2013.866081.

45 Jones, 'American *Vogue* and Sustainable Fashion (1990–2015)', 115.

46 *Display Copy*: https://displaycopy.com.

47 Contributed by Victoria Coutts: https://fashionfictions.org/2020/11/16/world-24/.

48 Rosie Findlay, 'Fashion as Mood, Style as Atmosphere: Literary Non-Fiction Fashion Writing on SSENSE and in London Review of Looks', in *Insights on Fashion Journalism*, edited by Rosie Findlay and Johannes Reponen (Abingdon: Routledge, 2023), 147.

49 Femke de Vries and Ruby Hoette, 'Introduction', *A Magazine Reader* 02 (November 2018), 5. Available at https://www.femkedevries.com/wordpress/wp-content/uploads/2020/09/The-Readers-Of-A-Newspaper-Magazine-Or-Book-Are-The-People-Who-Read-It.-A-Magazine-Reader-02.pdf [accessed 27 February 2024].

50 Morna Laing, 'Sustainability and the Fashion Media: Micro-Utopia, Social Dreaming and Hope in the Margins', *Fashion Theory* (2024). https://doi.org/10.1080/1362704X.2024.2339937.

51 Femke de Vries, *A Magazine Reader*. Available at https://www.femkedevries.com/a-magazine-reader/ [accessed 27 February 2024].

52 FutureFashionMedia, *Welcome to the FutureFashionMedia exhibition*.

53 Emily Spivack, *Worn Stories* (New York: Princeton Architectural Press, 2014), 6.

54 Contributed by Nikita S.B.: https://fashionfictions.org/2021/07/14/world-120/.

55 Contributed by Amy Twigger Holroyd.

56 Contributed by Salome Egger.

57 Contributed by Johanna Zanon.

58 Contributed anonymously: https://fashionfictions.org/2021/09/27/world-131/.

59 Contributed by Matthew Crowley.

60 Stage 2 group: Tamar Millen, Ruhee Das Chowdhury and Leah Das.

61 Contributed by Jeannine Diego.

62 Stage 2 group: Sally Cooke, Charlotte Tupper and an anonymized contributor.

63 *Oxford English Dictionary*, 'Deed (noun)' (2023). Available at https://www.oed.com/dictionary/deed_n?tab=meaning_and_use [accessed 25 February 2024].

64 For links to FigShare 'deeds', see World 27, Enactment i report: https://fashionfictions.org/2023/01/08/world-27-enactment-i-report/,

65 Contributed by Karly Grant: https://fashionfictions.org/2021/04/23/world-80/

66 Tham, 'Languaging Fashion and Sustainability', 17.

67 Brian Attebery, *Strategies of Fantasy* (Bloomington: Indiana University Press, 1992), 6.

68 Ibid.

69 Kjersti Fløttum, 'Language and Climate Change', in *The Role of Language in the Climate Change Debate*, edited by Kjersti Fløttum (Abingdon: Routledge, 2017), 1.

70 Tham, 'Languaging Fashion and Sustainability', 14.

71 Kate Fletcher and Mathilda Tham, *Earth Logic Fashion Action Research Plan* (London: The J J Charitable Trust, 2019), 61.

72 Ibid., 63.

73 Robin Wall Kimmerer, *Braiding Sweetgrass: Indigenous Wisdom, Scientific Knowledge, and the Teachings of Plants* (Minneapolis: Milkweed Editions, 2013), 50.

74 Matthew Schneider-Mayerson and Brent Ryan Bellamy, 'Introduction', in *An Ecotopian Lexicon*, edited by Matthew Schneider-Mayerson and Brent Ryan Bellamy (Minneapolis: University of Minnesota Press, 2019), 7.

75 Allison Ford and Kari Marie Norgaard, 'Ghurba', in *An Ecotopian Lexicon*, edited by Matthew Schneider-Mayerson and Brent Ryan Bellamy (Minneapolis: University of Minnesota Press, 2019), 72–81.

76 Refuvescence, The Werríng, To Wormdazzle: https://bureauoflinguisticalreality.com/portfolio/werring/.

77 Sandra Niessen, 'Defashion', *Climate Words* (2022). Available at https://climatewords.org [accessed 2 October 2023].

78 Stage 2 group: Elly Platt, Talia Hussain and Martin Benes.

79 Contributed by Amy Twigger Holroyd: https://fashionfictions.org/2020/05/22/world-4/.

80 Stage 2 contributor: Benjamin-Rose Ingall.

81 Fletcher and Tham, *Earth Logic Fashion Action Research Plan*, 61.

82 Contributed by Talia Hussain.

83 Stage 2 group: Wendy Ward and Jana Melkumova-Reynolds.

84 Watch the videos: World 62, Enactment i: recipe: https://fashionfictions.org/2023/02/08/world-62-enactment-i-recipe/.

85 Roland Barthes, *The Fashion System*, translated by Matthew Ward and Richard Howard (Berkeley and Los Angeles: University of California Press, 1983 [1967]), 3.

86 Ibid., 4.

87 Collaborative description written by Vanessa Brown, Sally Cooke, Benjamin-Rose Ingall and Annebella Pollen.

88 Collaborative description written by Veronica Isaac, Alison Peck and two anonymized Fashion Fictions contributors.

89   De Vries and Hoette, 'Introduction', 3.

90   De Vries and Hoette, 'Introduction', 3.

91   Enactment devised by Amy Twigger Holroyd, based on prototype created by Wendy Ward and Jana Melkumova-Reynolds and fiction by Talia Hussain.

92   Access the template: World 62 planner: https://bit.ly/World62template.

93   Find the videos embedded in the step-by-step enactment recipe: World 62, Enactment i: recipe: https://fashionfictions.org/2023/02/08/world-62-enactment-i-recipe/.

94   Natalia Eernstman and Arjen E. J. Wals, 'Locative Meaning-making: An Arts-based Approach to Learning for Sustainable Development', *Sustainability* 5 (2013), 1654. https://doi.org/10.3390/su5041645.

95   Torkild Thanem and David Knights, *Embodied Research Methods* (London: SAGE, 2019), 3. https://doi.org/10.4135/9781529716672.

96   Maurice Merleau-Ponty, *The Phenomenology of Perception*, translated by Colin Smith (London: Routledge & Kegan Paul, 1962 [1945]), 94.

97   Ibid., 169.

98   Rebecca Schneider, *Performing Remains: Art and War in Times of Theatrical Reenactment* (Abingdon: Routledge, 2011).

99   Jeremy Deller, The Battle of Orgreave, 15–17 June 2001, https://www.artangel.org.uk/project/the-battle-of-orgreave/.

100   Charlotte Canning, 'Feminist Performance as Feminist Historiography', *Theatre Survey* 45:2 (November 2004), 230. https://doi.org/10.1017/S0040557404000183.

101   Scott Magelssen, 'Introduction', in *Enacting History*, edited by Scott Magelssen and Rhona Justice-Malloy (Tuscaloosa: University of Alabama Press, 2011), 6.

102   *Queen Elizabeth I: A Timewatch Guide*, BBC4 (13 November 2019). I was delighted to encounter some Totnes Elizabethans for myself (still on a Tuesday) while finishing this book.

103   Stuart Candy and Kelly Kornet, 'Turning Foresight Inside Out: An Introduction to Ethnographic Experiential Futures', *Journal of Futures Studies* 23:3 (2019), 5. DOI:10.6531/JFS.201903_23(3).0002

104   Tobias Revell, Justin Pickard and Georgina Voss, 'Valuing Utopia in Speculative and Critical Design', in *Economic Science Fictions*, edited by William Davies (London: Goldsmiths Press, 2018), 290.

105   Ibid., 288.

106   Joachim Halse, 'Ethnographies of the Possible', in *Design Anthropology: Theory and Practice*, edited by Wendy Gunn, Ton Otto and Rachel Charlotte Smith (London: Berg, 2013), 180–96; Thomas Binder, 'The Things We Do: Encountering the Possible', in *Design Anthropological Futures*, edited by Rachel Charlotte Smith, Kasper Tang Vangkilde, Mette Gislev Kjærsgaard, Ton Otto, Joachim Halse and Thomas Binder (London: Bloomsbury, 2016), 267–81.

107   Contributed by Maria Fernanda León, Candelaria Baptiste, Nathalia Huertas, Laura M. Restrepo and Gabriela Cruz, https://fashionfictions.org/2024/02/23/world-221/.

108   Kimberly Tony Korol-Evans, 'Dinner: Impossible, "Medieval Mayhem" at the Maryland Renaissance Festival', in *Enacting History*, edited by Scott Magelssen and Rhona Justice-Malloy (Tuscaloosa: University of Alabama Press, 2011), 158.

109 Richard Schechner, *Performance Studies: An Introduction*, 3rd edition (Abingdon: Routledge, 2013), 34.

110 Ibid., 35.

111 Richard Schechner, *Between Theater and Anthropology* (Philadelphia: University of Pennsylvania Press, 1985), 114.

112 Ibid., 113.

113 Contributed by Amy Twigger Holroyd: https://fashionfictions.org/2020/05/22/world-2/.

114 Schechner, *Between Theater and Anthropology*, 99.

115 Ibid., 39.

116 Linda Hutcheon, *A Theory of Adaptation*, 2nd edition (Abingdon: Routledge, 2013), 2.

117 Frances Babbage, *Augusto Boal* (London: Routledge, 2004), 45.

118 Chris Seeley and Peter Reason, 'Expressions of Energy: An Epistemology of Presentational Knowing', in *Knowing Differently: Arts-Based and Collaborative Research*, edited by Pranee Liamputtong and Jean Rumbold (New York: Nova Science Publishers, Inc., 2008), 12.

119 Contributed by Wendy Ward, https://fashionfictions.org/2021/03/09/world-54/.

120 https://www.moma.org/collection/works/136307.

121 Halse, 'Ethnographies of the Possible', 192.

122 Babbage, *Augusto Boal*, 42.

Chapter 4

1 Mary Schoeser, *World Textiles: A Concise History* (London: Thames & Hudson, 2003), 50–3, 71–2.

2 Edwina Ehrman, *Fashioned from Nature* (London: V&A Publishing, 2018), 55, 58, 65.

3 Ibid., 55.

4 Jenny Evans, 'Animal Print', in *Fashion Photography Archive* (London: Bloomsbury, 2015). http://dx.doi.org/10.5040/9781350934429-FPA198.

5 Amy Twigger Holroyd, Jennifer Farley Gordon and Colleen Hill, *Historical Perspectives on Sustainable Fashion: Inspiration for Change* (London: Bloomsbury, 2023), 123–4.

6 Changing Markets Foundation, *Fossil Fashion: The Hidden Reliance of Fast Fashion on Fossil Fuels* (Changing Markets Foundation, 2021), 12.

7 Twigger Holroyd, Gordon and Hill, *Historical Perspectives on Sustainable Fashion*, 22–3.

8 Lucy Siegle, 'Burning Issue: How Fashion's Love of Leather is Fuelling the Fires in the Amazon', *The Guardian*, 29 August 2019. Available at https://www.theguardian.com/fashion/2019/aug/29/burning-issue-how-fashions-love-of-leather-is-fuelling-the-fires-in-the-amazon [accessed 6 June 2021].

9 *A Snapshot of Change: One Year of Fashion Loved by Forests*, Canopy (2014): https://web.archive.org/web/20160425004723/https://canopyplanet.org/wp-content/uploads/2015/03/Canopy_Snapshot_Nov2014.pdf.

10   Tansy Hoskins, 'Cotton Production Linked to Images of the Dried Up Aral Sea Basin', *The Guardian*, 1 October 2014. Available at https://www.theguardian.com/sustainable-business/sustainable-fashion-blog/2014/oct/01/cotton-production-linked-to-images-of-the-dried-up-aral-sea-basin [accessed 6 February 2023].

11   Madeleine Cobbing and Yannick Vicaire, *Destination Zero: Seven Years of Detoxing the Fashion Industry* (Hamburg: Greenpeace, 2018).

12   Changing Markets Foundation, *Fossil Fashion*, 27.

13   Damian Carrington, 'Microplastics Found in Human Blood for First Time', *The Guardian*, 24 March 2022. Available at https://www.theguardian.com/environment/2022/mar/24/microplastics-found-in-human-blood-for-first-time [accessed 5 February 2023].

14   House of Commons Environmental Audit Committee, *Fixing Fashion: Clothing Consumption and Sustainability* (London, 2019), 40. Available at https://publications.parliament.uk/pa/cm201719/cmselect/cmenvaud/1952/full-report.html [accessed 5 February 2024].

15   Robin Sooklall, 'Fashion Industry and the Realities of Waste Colonialism', *Centric*, 25 July 2023. Available at https://centric.org.uk/blog/fashion-industry-and-the-realities-of-waste-colonialism/ [accessed 5 February 2024].

16   Sarah Johnson, '"It's Like a Death Pit": How Ghana Became Fast Fashion's Dumping Ground', *The Guardian*, 5 June 2023. Available at https://www.theguardian.com/global-development/2023/jun/05/yvette-yaa-konadu-tetteh-how-ghana-became-fast-fashions-dumping-ground [accessed 5 February 2024].

17   Transformers Foundation, *Cotton: A Case Study in Misinformation* (New York, 2021), 7. Available at https://www.transformersfoundation.org/cotton-report-2021 [accessed January 30, 2022].

18   Contributed anonymously: https://fashionfictions.org/2021/06/22/world-118/.

19   'Meet Microsilk™', Bolt Threads. Available at https://boltthreads.com/technology/microsilk/ [accessed 5 February 2023].

20   Contributed by Michael Garand: https://fashionfictions.org/2021/10/22/world-142/.

21   Paul Wapner, *Living Through the End of Nature: The Future of American Environmentalism* (Cambridge, MA: MIT Press, 2010), 81.

22   Ibid., 104.

23   Ibid., 80.

24   Anna Lehtonen, Arto Salonen, Hannele Cantell and Laura Riuttanen, 'A Pedagogy of Interconnectedness for Encountering Climate Change as a Wicked Sustainability Problem', *Journal of Cleaner Production* 199 (2018), 861. https://doi.org/10.1016/j.jclepro.2018.07.186.

25   Contributed by Anne Reimers: https://fashionfictions.org/2021/04/25/world-96/.

26   Contributed by Zuza Sebekova: https://fashionfictions.org/2021/09/22/world-130/.

27   HereWear, 'Man-Made Cellulosic (MMC) Fibres'. Available at https://herewear.tcbl.eu/man-made-cellulosic-mmc-fibres [accessed September 7, 2024].

28   Ananas Anam, 'About Us'. Available at https://www.ananas-anam.com/about-us/ [accessed July 18, 2021].

29   Ehrman, *Fashioned from Nature*, 71.

30 Vanessa Brown, 'Is Coolness Still Cool?', *Journal for Cultural Research* 25:4 (2021), 429–45. https://doi.org/10.10 80/14797585.2021.2000837.

31 UNESCO, *Education for Sustainable Development Goals: Learning Objectives* (Paris: UNESCO, 2017), 10.

32 Contributed by Yeo Tian Poh, Amanda Teoh, Vrinda Maheshwari, Chloe Ysabel Tan and Pang Chong Jia Wyona: https://fashionfictions.org/2021/05/12/world-112/.

33 Contributed by Kate Fletcher: https://fashionfictions.org/2020/07/21/world-16/.

34 Wapner, *Living Through the End of Nature*, 55.

35 Ibid., 54.

36 Marius de Geus, *Ecological Utopias: Envisioning the Sustainable Society* (Utrecht: International Books, 1999).

37 Arne Naess, *There Is No Point of No Return* (London: Penguin Books, 2021 [1986]), 1–20.

38 Contributed by Jade Lord: https://fashionfictions.org/2020/07/17/world-13/.

39 Contributed anonymously: https://fashionfictions.org/2021/05/12/world-111/.

40 Contributed anonymously: https://fashionfictions.org/2021/04/05/world-75/.

41 Contributed by Elaine Igoe: https://fashionfictions.org/2020/12/17/world-40/.

42 Contributed by Katherine Pogson.

43 Stage 2 contributor: Jade Lord.

44 Ehrman, *Fashioned from Nature*, 67.

45 Malcolm Barnard, *Fashion Theory: An Introduction* (Abingdon: Routledge, 2014), 70.

46 Sara Idacavage, 'The Development of Fast Fashion', in *Berg Encyclopedia of World Dress and Fashion: Global Perspectives*, edited by Joanne B. Eicher and Phyllis G. Tortora (Oxford: Berg, 2010). http://dx.doi. org/10.2752/9781847888594.EDch101421.

47 Contributed by Alice-Marie Archer.

48 Alice-Marie Archer Studio: https://alicemariearcher.com

49 Rebecca Burgess, *Fibershed: Growing a Movement of Farmers, Fashion Activists, and Makers for a New Textile Economy* (White River Junction: Chelsea Green Publishing, 2019), 14.

50 'Mission & Vision', Fibershed. Available at https://fibershed.org/mission-vision [accessed 5 February 2023].

51 Wapner, *Living Through the End of Nature*, 6.

52 Ibid.

53 Lisa Garforth, *Green Utopias: Environmental Hope Before and After Nature* (Cambridge: Polity, 2017), 139.

54 Ibid., 138.

55 Ibid., 33.

56 Vanessa Machado de Oliveira, *Hospicing Modernity: Facing Humanity's Wrongs and the Implications for Social Activism* (Berkeley, CA: North Atlantic Books, 2021), 27.

57 Contributed by Beth Pagett.

58   Stage 2 group: Victoria Frausin and Rachel Ward.

59   Contributed by Sarah Kilkenny.

60   Stage 2 group: Katherine Pogson and an anonymized contributor.

61   Donna Haraway, *Staying with the Trouble: Making Kin in the Chthulucene* (Durham, NC: Duke University Press, 2016), 10.

62   Ibid., 29.

63   Ibid., 4.

64   Contributed by Daphne Mohajer va Pesaran: https://fashionfictions.org/2021/03/13/world-63/.

65   Contributed by Elie Seksig: https://fashionfictions.org/2021/11/19/world-146/.

66   Haraway, *Staying with the Trouble*, 13.

67   Contributed by Jane Norris.

68   Haraway, *Staying with the Trouble*, 55.

69   Femke de Vries, 'Which Animal Is Present in your Garment?' Available at https://www.femkedevries.com/which-animal-is-present-in-your-garment [accessed 5 February 2024].

70   Ibid.

71   Katie David, 'What is the Anthropocene and Why Does it Matter?', *Natural History Museum* (undated). Available at https://www.nhm.ac.uk/discover/what-is-the-anthropocene.html [accessed April 27, 2024].

72   Evan Berry, *Devoted to Nature: The Religious Roots of American Environmentalism* (Oakland: University of California Press, 2015), 182.

73   Merlin Sheldrake, *Entangled Life: How Fungi Make Our Worlds, Change Our Minds, and Shape Our Futures* (London: Penguin Random House, 2020), 5.

74   Emily Farra, 'You Aren't Tripping: Fungi Are Taking Over Fashion', *Vogue*, 2 April 2021. Available at https://www.vogue.com/article/fungi-mushrooms-fashion-inspiration-mycelium [accessed 5 February 2023].

75   Natasha Bird, 'Va Va Shroom', *Elle*, 27 July 2022. Available at https://www.elle.com/uk/fashion/trends/a40655873/mushroom-trends-fashion/ [accessed 5 February 2023].

76   Sheldrake, *Entangled Life*, 10, 201.

77   Ibid., 214–5.

78   Ibid., 9.

79   Ibid., 6.

80   Ibid., 120.

81   Philip Sheldrake, *Spirituality: A Brief History* (Chichester: John Wiley & Sons, 2013), Chapter 1. ProQuest Ebook Central. http://ebookcentral.proquest.com/lib/ntuuk/detail.action?docID=7103704.

82   Ibid., ch. 1.

83   Sheldrake, *Entangled Life*, 129.

84   Ibid., 228.

85   Ibid., 4–6.

86   Ibid., 11.

87   Ibid.

88   Ibid., 16.

89   Bron Taylor, *Dark Green Religion: Nature Spirituality and the Planetary Future* (Berkeley: University of California Press, 2010), 15.

90   Robin Wall Kimmerer, *Braiding Sweetgrass: Indigenous Wisdom, Scientific Knowledge, and the Teachings of Plants* (Minneapolis: Milkweed Editions, 2013), 56.

91   Ibid., 57.

92   'humble, adj.', *OED Online*, December 2022 (Oxford: Oxford University Press). Available at https://www.oed.com/view/Entry/89298 [accessed 5 February 2023].

93   Sheldrake, *Entangled Life*, 3.

94   Anna Lowenhaupt Tsing, *The Mushroom at the End of the World: On the Possibility of Life in Capitalist Ruins* (Princeton: Princeton University Press, 2015), vii.

95   Hannah Marriott, 'Nature Looms Large at Alexander McQueen's Autumn/Winter Show in New York', *The Guardian*, 16 March 2022. Available at https://www.theguardian.com/fashion/2022/mar/16/nature-looms-large-at-alexander-mcqueens-autumnwinter-show-in-new-york [accessed February 6, 2023].

96   Ibid.

97   Sheldrake, *Entangled Life*, 237.

98   Ibid., 234.

99   Ibid., 193.

100   Enactment devised by Amy Twigger Holroyd, based on prototype created by Elly Platt, Talia Hussain and Martin Benes and fiction by Suzanne Rowland.

101   Further details and case study video: World 91, Enactment iii report: https://fashionfictions.org/2023/11/27/world-91-enactment-iii-report/.

102   Lynne Hume, *The Religious Life of Dress: Global Fashion and Faith* (London: Bloomsbury Academic, 2013), 37–43.

103   Ibid., 53.

104   Ibid., 105–8.

105   Ibid., 2.

106   Ibid., 1.

107   Linda B. Arthur, 'Introduction: Dress and the Social Control of the Body', in *Religion, Dress and the Body*, edited by Linda B. Arthur (Oxford: Berg, 1999), 5.

108   Ibid., 2.

109   Contributed by Alexandra Jones: https://fashionfictions.org/2024/07/15/world-248/.

110 Contributed anonymously: https://fashionfictions.org/2021/09/21/world-128/.

111 Hume, *The Religious Life of Dress*, 130.

112 Britannica, *Encyclopedia of World Religions* (2006), 988–9.

113 Ibid.

114 Hume, *The Religious Life of Dress*, 131.

115 Dan Whisker, 'The Possibility of Shamanism: A Genealogy of Anthropological Appropriations', *History and Anthropology*, 24:3 (2013), 344–62. https://doi.org/10.1080/02757206.2013.761982.

116 Bron Taylor, 'Earthen Spirituality or Cultural Genocide?: Radical Environmentalism's Appropriation of Native American Spirituality', *Religion*, 27:2 (1997), 183–215. https://doi.org/10.1006/reli.1996.0042.

117 Ehrman, *Fashioned from Nature*, 27.

118 Contributed by Sally Cooke: https://fashionfictions.org/2020/07/13/world-10/.

119 Hume, *The Religious Life of Dress*, 107.

120 Contributed by East London Textile Arts: https://fashionfictions.org/2021/09/27/world-132/.

121 https://fashionfictions.org/2021/01/05/world-45/.

122 Stage 2 group: Gautham Krishna, Rachael Matthews and an anonymized contributor.

123 Otto von Busch and Jeanine Viau, 'Introduction', in *Silhouettes of the Soul: Meditations on Fashion, Religion, and Subjectivity*, edited by Otto von Busch and Jeanine Viau (London: Bloomsbury, 2022), 3.

124 William McDonough and Michael Braungart, *Cradle to Cradle: Remaking the Way We Make Things* (London: Vintage, 2009), 26.

Chapter 5

1 Textile Tales, 'An Industry in Decline' (undated). Available at https://www.textiletales.co.uk/history/an-industry-in-decline [accessed 25 February 2024].

2 Amy Twigger Holroyd, Jennifer Farley Gordon and Colleen Hill, *Historical Perspectives on Sustainable Fashion: Inspiration for Change* (London: Bloomsbury, 2023), 84–91.

3 Benjamin Selekman, *The Clothing and Textile Industries in New York and Its Environs, Present Trends and Probable Future Developments* (New York: Regional Plan of New York and its Environs, 1925), 23.

4 Peter Dicken, *Global Shift: Mapping the Changing Contours of the Global Economy*, 7th edition (London: SAGE, 2015), 453.

5 Marianne McCune, '"Our Industry Follows Poverty": Success Threatens a T-Shirt Business', *NPR*, 2 December 2013. Available at https://www.npr.org/sections/money/2013/12/04/247360787/our-industry-follows-poverty-success-threatens-a-t-shirt-business [accessed 6 February 2024].

6 Dicken, *Global Shift*, 461.

7 Ibid., 463.

8   Marc Levinson, *The Box: How the Shipping Container Made the World Smaller and the World Economy Bigger*, 2nd edition (Princeton: Princeton University Press, 2016), 4.

9   Ibid., 4.

10   McCune, 'Our Industry Follows Poverty'.

11   Levinson, *The Box*, 2.

12   Christopher Breward, 'Fashion Cities', in *Berg Encyclopedia of World Dress and Fashion: Global Perspectives* edited by Joanne B. Eicher and Phyllis G. Tortora (Oxford: Berg, 2010), 226.

13   Ibid., 229.

14   Ibid., 226.

15   Elizabeth Wilson, *Adorned in Dreams: Fashion and Modernity*, revised and updated edition (London: I.B.Tauris, 2003), 138.

16   World 83. Contributed by Emily Jego-Rolfe: https://fashionfictions.org/2021/04/23/world-83/.

17   World 149. Contributed by Anna Howard: https://fashionfictions.org/2021/11/23/world-149/.

18   World 144. Contributed by Maha Abdalla, Neha Chauhan and Shahzaadee Valli: https://fashionfictions.org/2021/10/28/world-144/.

19   Contributed by Molly O'Neil: https://fashionfictions.org/2021/04/23/world-92/.

20   Contributed by Sara E. Bernat: https://fashionfictions.org/2020/12/12/world-36/.

21   World 36, Exploration F: https://fashionfictions.org/2022/08/25/world-36-exploration-f/.

22   Kate Fletcher, 'Haberdashemergency', *Fashion Ecologies*. Available at http://fashionecologies.org/haberdashemergency/ [accessed 26 February 2024].

23   Tara Donaldson, 'Automation in Apparel could make a Strong Cost-Savings Case for Nearshoring by 2025, McKinsey Says', *Sourcing Journal* (Online), 11 October 2018. Available at https://sourcingjournal.com/topics/sourcing/automation-nearshoring-mckinsey-survey-123086/ [accessed 8 February 2024].

24   Fibershed: https://fibershed.org.

25   Contributed by Amelia Twine: https://fashionfictions.org/2022/11/15/world-175/.

26   Contributed by Ileana Jalil Kentros: https://fashionfictions.org/2021/04/16/world-76/.

27   Contributed by Holly McQuillan: https://fashionfictions.org/2021/03/09/world-53/.

28   Tim Cresswell, *Place: An Introduction*, 2nd edition (Chichester: Wiley Blackwell, 2015), 76.

29   Kyle Chayka, 'The Tyranny of the Algorithm: Why Every Coffee Shop Looks the Same', *The Guardian*, 16 January 2024. Available at https://www.theguardian.com/news/2024/jan/16/the-tyranny-of-the-algorithm-why-every-coffee-shop-looks-the-same [accessed 6 February 2024].

30   Cresswell, *Place*, 75.

31   Sue Clifford and Angela King, *England In Particular* (London: Hodder & Stoughton, 2006), ix.

32   Ibid., xiii.

33   Contributed by Nick Gant: https://fashionfictions.org/2020/12/17/world-42/.

34   Contributed anonymously: https://fashionfictions.org/2024/07/31/world-250/.

35   Donna Dee Hardy, 'The Scottish Waulking Song: "The Boat Will Come"', *ERIC* (undated). Available at https://eric.ed.gov/?id=ED294805 [accessed 25 February 2024].

36   Margaret Maynard, *Dress and Globalisation* (Manchester: Manchester University Press, 2004).

37   Carla Jones and Ann Marie Leshkowich, 'The Globalization of Asian Dress: Re-Orienting Fashion or Re-Orientalizing Asia', in *The Anthropology of Dress and Fashion: A Reader*, edited by Brent Luvaas and Joanne B. Eicher (London: Bloomsbury, 2019), 296.

38   Alison Goodrum, *The National Fabric: Fashion, Britishness, Globalization* (Oxford: Berg Publishers, 2005) 37.

39   Ibid.

40   Contributed by Sally Cooke.

41   Saaniya Sharma, 'Climate Change & Fashion Waste Colonialism', *Carbon Literacy Project* (2023). Available at https://carbonliteracy.com/climate-change-fashion-waste-colonialism/ [accessed 6 February 2024].

42   Rwanda was the only country to implement this policy via high import taxes; pushback from both local vendors and from major exporters, including the USA, dissuaded the other states from taking action. Franck Kuwonu, 'Protectionist Ban on Imported Used Clothing', *Africa Renewal* (December 2017–March 2018). Available at https://www.un.org/africarenewal/magazine/december-2017-march-2018/protectionist-ban-imported-used-clothing [accessed 26 February 2024].

43   Amy Twigger Holroyd, 'Finding Distinctiveness in the Dustbin: Engendering a Sense of Place through Waste', *The Journal of Resourcefulness* 1 (2018), 70–9. Available at https://www.rekindle.org.nz/collections/the-journal-of-resourcefulness [accessed 6 February 2024].

44   Contributed by Sally Cooke: https://fashionfictions.org/2023/02/24/world-183/.

45   Rachael Matthews, *Rag Manifesto: Making, Folklore and Community* (Stroud: Quickthorn, 2024).

46   Contributed by Amy Twigger Holroyd: https://fashionfictions.org/2020/05/22/world-5/.

47   Contributed by Vanessa Brown.

48   Jillian Kestler-D'Amours, 'Nunavut Woman accuses U.K. Fashion Label of Appropriating Inuit Design', *Toronto Star*, 26 November 2015. Available at: https://www.thestar.com/news/canada/2015/11/26/nunavut-woman-accuses-uk-fashion-label-of-appropriating-inuit-design.html [accessed 7 February 2024].

49   Ibid.

50   Jones and Leshkowich, 'The Globalization of Asian Dress', 295.

51   Nirmal Puwar, 'Multicultural Fashion … Stirrings of Another Sense of Aesthetics and Memory', *Feminist Review* 72 (2002), 64. https://www.jstor.org/stable/1396022.

52   Ibid., 63.

53   Jarune Uwujaren, 'The Difference Between Cultural Exchange and Cultural Appropriation', *Everyday Feminism*, 30 September 2013. Available at http://everydayfeminism.com/2013/09/cultural-exchange-and-cultural-appropriation [accessed 7 February 2024].

54   Tony Blackshaw, *Key Concepts in Community Studies* (London: SAGE, 2010), 12.

55   Gerard Delanty, *Community*, 3rd edition (Abingdon: Routledge, 2018), 2.

56 Wilson, *Adorned in Dreams*, 144.

57 Ibid., 150.

58 Bonnie English and Nazanin Hedayat Munroe, *A Cultural History of Western Fashion: From Haute Couture to Virtual Couture* (London: Bloomsbury, 2022), 113.

59 Ray Oldenburg, *The Great Good Place: Cafés, Coffee Shops, Bookstores, Bars, Hair Salons, and Other Hangouts at the Heart of a Community*, 2nd edition (Cambridge, MA: Da Capo Press, 1997), 119.

60 Bethan Alexander and Marta Blazquez Cano, 'Futurising the Physical Store in the Omnichannel Retail Environment', in *Exploring Omnichannel Retailing*, edited by Wojciech Piotrowicz and Richard Cuthbertson (Cham: Springer Nature Switzerland, 2019), 197–223.

61 Leeds Community Clothes Exchange, established in 2008 and now with over 3,000 members, is a notable example: https://leedscommunityclothesexchange.com/about/.

62 Contributed by Becca Warner.

63 Contributed by Jay McCauley Bowstead: https://fashionfictions.org/2020/09/11/world-17/.

64 Contributed by Sally Cooke.

65 Stage 2 group: Mor Schwartz Foulser, Alis Le May and Nadine Mellor.

66 Stitched Up, *About*. Available at https://stitchedup.coop/about/ [accessed 7 February 2024].

67 Matti Kurzeja, Katja Thiele and Britta Klagge, 'Makerspaces: Third Places for a Sustainable (Post-Growth) Society?', in *Post-Growth Geographies: Spatial Relations of Diverse and Alternative Economies*, edited by Bastian Lange, Martina Hülz, Benedikt Schmid and Christian Schulz (Bielefeld: transcript Verlag, 2022), 162.

68 Le Textile Lab. https://letextilelab.com/.

69 Contributed by Natalia Bernal, Luisa Bula, Sofía Montagut, Joel Manevich and David Duarte: https://fashionfictions.org/2024/02/23/world-225/.

70 Oldenburg, *The Great Good Place*.

71 Kurzeja, Thiele and Klagge, 'Makerspaces', 159.

72 Oldenburg, *The Great Good Place*.

73 Kurzeja, Thiele and Klagge, 'Makerspaces', 166.

74 Ibid., 160, 165.

75 Martin Langlinderer, '"Hobbyhimmel" – An Open Workshop in the Context of Post-Growth', in *Post-Growth Geographies: Spatial Relations of Diverse and Alternative Economies*, edited by Bastian Lange, Martina Hülz, Benedikt Schmid and Christian Schulz (Bielefeld: transcript Verlag, 2022), 213.

76 Kurzeja, Thiele and Klagge, 'Makerspaces', 165.

77 Collective Mending Sessions: https://www.collectivemendingsessions.com.

78 Peter Ward, *The Clean Body: A Modern History* (Montreal: McGill-Queen's University Press, 2019), 89.

79 Ibid., 90.

80 Stage 2 group: Kaavya Virmani, Tom Chin and Lorraine Warde.

81   Langlinderer, 'Hobbyhimmel', 215.

82   Clare Jane Daněk, 'Working Alone, Working Together: Exploring Craft Learning in Open Access Community Making Spaces', PhD thesis, University of Leeds (2024), 28.

83   Kurzeja, Thiele and Klagge, 'Makerspaces', 169.

84   Ibid., 168.

85   Ann Shivers-McNair, *Beyond the Makerspace: Making and Relational Rhetorics* (Ann Arbor: University of Michigan Press, 2021), 5.

86   Kurzeja, Thiele and Klagge, 'Makerspaces', 168.

87   Ibid., 169.

88   Ibid., 159.

89   Shivers-McNair, *Beyond the Makerspace*, 99.

90   Ibid., 102.

91   John Field, *Social Capital*, 3rd edition (Abingdon: Routledge, 2017), 2.

92   Contributed by Annebella Pollen.

93   Contributed by Sally Cooke.

94   Catherine Bell, *Ritual: Perspectives and Dimensions*, revised edition (Oxford: Oxford University Press, 1997), 138.

95   Richard Schechner, *Performance Studies: An Introduction*, 3rd edition (Abingdon: Routledge, 2013), 87.

96   Byung-Chul Han, *The Disappearance of Rituals: A Topology of the Present*, translated by Daniel Steuer (Cambridge: Polity, 2020), 2.

97   Bell, *Ritual*, 138–69.

98   Ibid., 108.

99   Ibid., 109.

100   Contributed by Karly Grant: https://fashionfictions.org/2021/04/23/world-80/.

101   Ward, *The Clean Body*, 188.

102   Stage 2 group: Flavia Loscialpo, Anja Connor-Crabb, Wendy Chan and an anonymized contributor.

103   Bell, *Ritual*, 103.

104   Ibid., 169.

105   Ibid.

106   Han, *The Disappearance of Rituals*, 7.

107   Ibid., 8.

108   Bell, *Ritual*, 94.

109   Contributed by Sindhu, Dawama, Keran and Jerome: https://fashionfictions.org/2021/05/12/world-106/.

110   Bell, *Ritual*, 95.

111 Ibid.

112 Schechner, *Performance Studies*, 67.

113 Ibid., 72.

114 Arvind Venkataramani and Adam Menter, 'Integrating Self and Systems Through Ritual: Toward Deeper Systems Practice', *Proceedings of Relating Systems Thinking and Design* (Ahmedabad, 2020).

115 Joanna Macy and Molly Brown, *Coming Back to Life: The Updated Guide to The Work That Reconnects* (Gabriola Island: New Society Publishers, 2014), 152.

116 World 27, Enactment i film: https://fashionfictions.org/2023/05/08/world-27-enactment-i-film/.

117 Han, *The Disappearance of Rituals*, 4.

118 Bell, *Ritual*, 137.

119 Enactment devised by Amy Twigger Holroyd, based on prototype created by Sally Cooke, Charlotte Tupper and anonymized Fashion Fictions contributor and fiction by Jeannine Diego. Watch a film of the first enactment: https://fashionfictions.org/2023/05/08/world-27-enactment-i-film/.

120 World 27, Enactment ii report: https://fashionfictions.org/2023/05/08/world-27-enactment-ii-report/.

121 Linda Welters and Abby Lillethun, 'Introduction', in *The Fashion Reader*, 2nd edition, edited by Linda Welters and Abby Lillethun (Oxford: Berg, 2011), 3.

122 Joanne Entwistle, *The Fashioned Body*, 3rd edition (Cambridge: Polity, 2023), 3, original emphasis.

123 Wilson, *Adorned in Dreams*, 3.

124 Ibid., 64.

125 Sandra Niessen, 'Afterword: Fashion's Fallacy', in *Modern Fashion Traditions: Negotiating Tradition and Modernity through Fashion*, edited by M. Angela Jansen and Jennifer Craig (London: Bloomsbury, 2016), 209.

126 Joanne B. Eicher, 'Introduction', in *National Geographic: Fashion* by Cathy Newman (Washington, DC: National Geographic, 2001), 17.

127 Jennifer Craik, *Fashion: The Key Concepts* (Oxford: Berg, 2009), 19, original emphasis.

128 Linda Welters and Abby Lillethun, *Fashion History: A Global View* (London: Bloomsbury, 2018), 72.

129 Ibid., 15.

130 Aubrey Cannon, 'Cultural and Historical Contexts of Fashion', in *Consuming Fashion: Adorning the Transnational Body* edited by Anne Brydon and Sandra Niessen (Oxford: Berg, 1998), 31.

131 Ibid., 23.

132 Welters and Lillethun, *Fashion History*, 72.

133 Sandra Niessen, 'Fashion, its Sacrifice Zone, and Sustainability', *Fashion Theory* 24:6 (2020), 864. https://doi.org/10.1080/1362704X.2020.1800984.

134 Contributed by Amanda Saunders: https://fashionfictions.org/2020/11/17/world-25/.

135 World 54, Enactment i film: https://fashionfictions.org/2022/09/03/world-54-enactment-i-film/.

136 Tiziana Ferrero-Regis, 'Re-Framing Fashion: From Original and Copy to Adaptation', in *Fashion-Wise*, edited by Maria Vaccarella and Jacquelyn Foltyn (Leiden: Brill, 2019), 350.

137 Susan B. Kaiser, *The Social Psychology of Clothing: Symbolic Appearances in Context*, revised 2nd edition (New York: Fairchild, 1997).

138 Ward, *The Clean Body*, 85.

139 Contributed by Julie Ripley: https://fashionfictions.org/2021/04/23/world-89/.

140 Contributed by Maz Hedgehog: https://fashionfictions.org/2020/07/06/world-8/.

141 Arto Laitinen and Anne Birgitta Pessi, 'Solidarity: Theory and Practice, An Introduction', in *Solidarity: Theory and Practice*, edited by Arto Laitinen and Anne Birgitta Pessi (Lanham: Lexington Books, 2014), 2.

142 Delanty, *Community*, 53.

143 Laitinen and Pessi, 'Solidarity', 8.

144 Ibid., 9.

145 Fred Dallmayr, *Freedom and Solidarity: Toward New Beginnings* (Lexington: University Press of Kentucky, 2015), 196.

146 Laitinen and Pessi, 'Solidarity', 5.

147 Clean Clothes Campaign, 'Direct Solidarity' (undated). Available at https://cleanclothes.org/direct-solidarity [accessed 25 February 2024].

148 Enactment devised by Amy Twigger Holroyd, based on prototype created by Johnny O'Flynn, Gillian Allsopp, Kate Harper and anonymized Fashion Fictions contributor and fiction by Wendy Ward. Watch a film of the first enactment: https://fashionfictions.org/2022/09/03/world-54-enactment-i-film/.

149 Access the cards: https://bit.ly/World54cards.

150 Access the scenarios: https://bit.ly/World54scenarios.

Chapter 6

1 Contributed by Jade Lord: https://fashionfictions.org/2021/03/26/world-71/.

2 Martin Parker, *Shut Down the Business School: What's Wrong with Management Education* (London: Pluto Press, 2018), 111.

3 Elena Karpova, Grace I. Kunz and Myrna B. Garner, *Going Global: The Textile and Apparel Industry*, 4th edition (London: Bloomsbury, 2021), 26.

4 Victor K. Fung, William K. Fung and Jerry (Yoram) Wind, *Competing in a Flat World: Building Enterprises for a Borderless World* (Upper Saddle River: Wharton School Publishing/Pearson Education, 2008), 15.

5 Parker, *Shut Down the Business School*, x.

6 Edwina Ehrman, *Fashioned from Nature* (London: V&A Publishing, 2018), 21.

7 Alice Payne, *Designing Fashion's Future: Present Practice and Tactics for Sustainable Change* (London: Bloomsbury, 2021), 82.

8   Ibid., 86.

9   Alison Toplis, *The Hidden History of the Smock Frock* (London: Bloomsbury, 2021).

10 Contributed by Sasha de Koninck: https://fashionfictions.org/2021/03/13/world-57/.

11 Contributed by Rev. Dr Ali Leach, Esq.: https://fashionfictions.org/2021/03/06/world-52/.

12 Contributed by Christina Suntovski: https://fashionfictions.org/2021/04/23/world-81/.

13 Sheila Rowbotham, 'A New Vision of Society: Women Clothing Workers and the Revolution of 1848 in France', in *Chic Thrills: A Fashion Reader*, edited by Juliet Ash and Elizabeth Wilson (London: Pandora Press, 1992), 189.

14 Ibid., 195.

15 Ibid., 196.

16 Lorezno Fe, 'The GKN workers' fight continues', *Red Pepper*, 13 March 2024. Available at https://www.redpepper.org.uk/economics-unions-work/work-trade-unions/the-gkn-workers-fight-continues/ [accessed 13 April 2024].

17 Contributed by Sally Cooke: https://fashionfictions.org/2022/08/27/world-173/.

18 Sparks Bristol: https://sparksbristol.co.uk/departments/fashion/.

19 Contributed by William Sullivan: https://fashionfictions.org/2021/03/16/world-65/.

20 Contributed anonymously: https://fashionfictions.org/2021/04/23/world-82/.

21 Contributed by Louize Harries.

22 Stage 2 group: Mats Siffels, Sally Cooke and Amy Twigger Holroyd.

23 Contributed by Pavwan Ahmad, Tamara Naoura and Tania Dubayssi: https://fashionfictions.org/2021/10/28/world-145/.

24 Contributed by Emily Jego-Rolfe: https://fashionfictions.org/2021/04/23/world-83/.

25 Contributed by Tamsin Johnson: https://fashionfictions.org/2020/11/16/world-23/.

26 Contributed by Lizzie Harrison: https://fashionfictions.org/2020/07/13/world-12/.

27 Ekaterina Gerasimova and Sof'ia Chuikina (2009) 'The Repair Society', *Russian Studies in History* 48:1, 64. https://doi.org/10.2753/RSH1061-1983480104.

28 Claudia Elisabeth Henninger, Nina Bürklin and Kirsi Niinimäki, 'The Clothes Swapping Phenomenon – When Consumers Become Suppliers', *Journal of Fashion Marketing and Management* 23:3 (2019), 327–44.

29 Nuw: https://www.thenuwardrobe.com.

30 Contributed by Modise Tsiu and an anonymous collaborator: https://fashionfictions.org/2021/10/22/world-143/.

31 Contributed by Katie Hill: https://fashionfictions.org/2020/11/17/world-26/.

32 Contributed by Stephanie Wooster: https://fashionfictions.org/2022/11/15/world-176/.

33 Contributed by Lindy Boerman: https://fashionfictions.org/2021/03/09/world-55/.

34 Mary Dellenbaugh-Losse, Nils-Eyk Zimmermann and Nicole de Vries, *The Urban Commons Cookbook: Strategies and Insights for Creating and Maintaining Urban Commons* (2020), 65–72. http://urbancommonscookbook.com.

35 Ted Rau, 'Sociocracy – Basic Concepts and Principles', Sociocracy for All (2020). Available at https://www.sociocracyforall.org/sociocracy/ [accessed 9 March 2024].

36 Catherine Alexander, 'The Third Sector', in *The Human Economy*, edited by Keith Hart, Jean-Louis Laville and Antonio David Cattani (Cambridge: Polity, 2010), 213.

37 Contributed by Spenninger Melissa, Belina Lim Fang Ci, Chin Meei, Alcina, Indira Varma, Hyesoo Im and Mannat Nurpuri: https://fashionfictions.org/2022/03/18/world-159/.

38 Peter Dicken, *Global Shift: Mapping the Changing Contours of the Global Economy*, 7th edition (London: SAGE, 2015), 461.

39 Remake, 'FAQ: The Garment Worker Protection Act (SB62)' (undated). Available at https://remake.world/stories/faq-the-garment-worker-protection-act-sb62/ [accessed 12 April 2024].

40 Tiffanie Darke, 'Fast fashion: the French are bringing Shein and Temu to heel. Can Britain follow suit?', *The Guardian*, 16 March 2024. Available at https://www.theguardian.com/commentisfree/2024/mar/16/fast-fashion-french-bringing-shein-and-temu-to-heel-can-britain-follow-suit [accessed 12 April 2024].

41 Ulrich Brand, Barbara Muraca, Éric Pineault, Marlyne Sahakian, Anke Schaffartzik, Andreas Novy, Christoph Streissler, Helmut Haberl, Viviana Asara, Kristina Dietz, Miriam Lang, Ashish Kothari, Tone Smith, Clive Spash, Alina Brad, Melanie Pichler, Christina Plank, Giorgos Velegrakis, Thomas Jahn, Angela Carter, Qingzhi Huan, Giorgos Kallis, Joan Martínez Alier, Gabriel Riva, Vishwas Satgar, Emiliano Teran Mantovani, Michelle Williams, Markus Wissen and Christoph Görg, 'From Planetary to Societal Boundaries: An Argument for Collectively Defined Self-Limitation', *Sustainability: Science, Practice and Policy*, 17:1 (2021), 279. https://doi.org/10.1080/15487733.2021.1940754.

42 Contributed by Iris Do Tho Uyen, Cheryl Chueh Xin Yi, Woo Miko, Lee Jimin and Tasya Aurellia: https://fashionfictions.org/2021/05/12/world-109/.

43 Contributed by Victoria Frausin: https://fashionfictions.org/2021/03/13/world-59/.

44 Angela McRobbie, Daniel Strutt and Carolina Bandinelli, *Fashion as Creative Economy: Micro-Enterprises in London, Berlin and Milan* (Cambridge: Polity Press, 2023), 72.

45 Amsterdam Donut Coalition: https://doughnuteconomics.org/groups-and-networks/1.

46 Kiri Langmead, Chris Land and Daniel King, 'Can Management Ever Be Responsible? Alternative Organizing and the Three Irresponsibilities of Management', in *Research Handbook of Responsible Management*, edited by Oliver Laasch, Roy Suddaby, R. Edward Freeman and Dima Jamali (Cheltenham: Edward Elgar Publishing, 2020), 52.

47 Parker, *Shut Down the Business School*, 114.

48 J. K. Gibson-Graham, Jenny Cameron and Stephen Healey, *Take Back the Economy* (Minneapolis: University of Minnesota Press, 2013), 11–13.

49 Brand et al., 'From Planetary to Societal Boundaries', 281.

50 workers.coop, *The Worker Co-operative Code* (2023), 3. Available at https://www.workers.coop/wp-content/uploads/2023/04/WorkerCoopCode_2023.pdf [accessed 1 April 2024].

51 Langmead, Land and King, 'Can Management Ever be Responsible?', 50.

52 Massimo De Angelis and David Harvie, 'the Commons', in *The Routledge Companion to Alternative Organisation*, edited by Martin Parker, George Cheney, Valérie Fournier and Chris Land (Abingdon: Routledge, 2018), 280.

53 David Bollier, 'The Commons, Short and Sweet', 15 July 2011. Available at https://www.bollier.org/commons-short-and-sweet [accessed 12 April 2024].

54 Leila Dawney, 'Introduction', in *We Are Commoners: Creative Acts of Commoning* (Birmingham: Craftspace, 2022), 4.

55 J. M. Neeson, *Commoners: Common Right, Enclosure and Social Change in England, 1700–1820* (Cambridge: Cambridge University Press, 1993).

56 Dellenbaugh-Losse, Zimmermann and de Vries, *The Urban Commons Cookbook*.

57 *The Commoner's Catalog for Changemaking*: https://www.commonerscatalog.org.

58 Zoe Gilbertson, *Learning to be We: Exploring Democratic Enterprise for the UK Fibreshed Movement and Beyond* (South West England Fibreshed/Liflad, 2023). Available at https://www.southwestenglandfibreshed.co.uk/wp-content/uploads/2023/10/Learning-to-be-We-Report-SWEF-2023-updated.pdf [accessed 12 April 2024].

59 The Linen Project, 'Shared Stewardship' (undated). Available at https://thelinenproject.online/the-linen-economy/shared-stewardship/ [accessed 12 April 2024].

60 Our Common Market: https://www.ourcommon.market.

61 Amy Twigger Holroyd, *Folk Fashion: Understanding Homemade Clothes* (London: I.B. Tauris, 2017), 11–12.

62 https://fashionfictions.org/2021/01/05/world-43/.

63 Curated by Craftspace. Virtual tour: https://craftspace.co.uk/wac-exhibition/.

64 Bastien Kerspern, 'Economic Design Fictions: Finding the Human Scale', in *Economic Science Fictions*, edited by William Davies (London: Goldsmiths Press, 2018), 261.

65 Brand et al., 'From Planetary to Societal Boundaries', 280.

66 Contributed by Matthew Crowley: https://fashionfictions.org/2021/02/04/world-49/.

67 Contributed by Ann-Sophie Maria Mueller, Natasha Tjandradinata, Payal Vinod Harilela, Reyhan Faustino and Vivian Darlene Utomo: https://fashionfictions.org/2021/05/12/world-107/.

68 Parker, *Shut Down the Business School*, 115.

69 Fredric Jameson, *Archaeologies of the Future: The Desire Called Utopia and Other Science Fictions* (London: Verso, 2005), xiii.

70 Contributed by Xi Fang: https://fashionfictions.org/2022/04/19/world-166/.

71 Contributed anonymously: https://fashionfictions.org/2021/04/23/world-88/.

72 Edwina Ehrman, *Fashioned from Nature* (London: V&A Publishing, 2018), 36.

73 Ibid., 71.

74 Amy Twigger Holroyd, Jennifer Farley Gordon and Colleen Hill, *Historical Perspectives on Sustainable Fashion: Inspiration for Change* (London: Bloomsbury, 2023), 108.

75 WRAP, *Textiles 2030 Annual Progress Report 2022–23* (2023). Available at https://wrap.org.uk/sites/default/files/2023-11/textiles-2030-annual-progress-report-2022-23.pdf [accessed 29 January 2024].

76 Changing Markets Foundation, *Licence to Greenwash: How Certification Schemes and Voluntary Initiatives are Fuelling Fossil Fashion* (2022). Available at https://changingmarkets.org/report/licence-to-greenwash-how-certification-schemes-and-voluntary-initiatives-are-fuelling-fossil-fashion/ [accessed 12 April 2024].

77   Contributed by Emily Rickard and Amy Twigger Holroyd: https://fashionfictions.org/2021/01/05/world-47/.

78   William E. Thompson and Jennifer C. Gibbs, *Deviance & Deviants: A Sociological Approach* (Chichester: John Wiley & Sons, 2016), 7.

79   Contributed anonymously: https://fashionfictions.org/2021/10/22/world-140/.

80   Contributed by Despina-Nafsika Haidemenos: https://fashionfictions.org/2021/04/23/world-84/.

81   Contributed by Doris Domoszlai-Lantner: https://fashionfictions.org/2020/12/12/world-37/.

82   Contributed by Gisèle Legionnet-Klees: https://fashionfictions.org/2021/03/13/world-58/.

83   Contributed anonymously: https://fashionfictions.org/2024/07/15/world-241/.

84   Contributed by Joselin Marvina Wongso, Ong Hui Yin Cheryl, Amrit Kaur and Muhammad Sadiq bin Mohamed Shah: https://fashionfictions.org/2023/03/17/world-200/.

85   Contributed by Ceren Unler Sen, Irmak Tas and Sedef Kilinc: https://fashionfictions.org/2023/01/13/world-180/.

86   Twigger Holroyd, Gordon and Hill, *Historical Perspectives on Sustainable Fashion*, 144.

87   Contributed by Laetitia Forst: https://fashionfictions.org/2021/03/13/world-64/.

88   Contributed by Shyann Rosario: https://fashionfictions.org/2021/10/22/world-139/.

89   Thompson and Gibbs, *Deviance & Deviants*, 10.

90   Frederike Ambagtsheer, 'The Black Market in Human Organs', in *Deviant Globalization: Black Market Economy in the 21st Century*, edited by Nils Gilman, Jesse Goldhammer and Steven Weber (London: Bloomsbury Academic, 2011), 74.

91   https://fashionfictions.org/2020/05/22/world-1/.

92   Larissa Zakharova, 'How and What to Consume: Patterns of Soviet Clothing Consumption in the 1950s and 1960s', in *Communism and Consumerism: The Soviet Alternative to the Affluent Society*, edited by Timo Vihavainen and Elena Bogdanova (Leiden: Brill, 2015), 90.

93   Ibid., 107.

94   Contributed by Caroline Raybould.

95   Stage 2 group: Maz Hedgehog, Annebella Pollen and Kara Adey.

96   A. Braverman, *Nekotorye voprosy razvitiia sovremennoi odezhdy. Novaia tekhnika i tekhnologiia shveinogo proizvodstva* (Kiev: Obshchestvo 'Znanie', 1964), 31–2, quoted in Zakharova, 'How and What to Consume', 88.

97   Kimberley Brownlee, *Conscience and Conviction: The Case for Civil Disobedience* (Oxford: Oxford University Press, 2012), 18.

98   Oscar Berglund and Daniel Schmidt, *Extinction Rebellion and Climate Change Activism: Breaking the Law to Change the World* (Cham: Palgrave Macmillan, 2020), 27–8.

99   Extinction Rebellion, *This Is Not a Drill: An Extinction Rebellion Handbook* (London: Penguin, 2019), 2.

100   Harold Glasser, 'Toward Robust Foundations for Sustainable Well-Being Societies: Learning to Change by Changing How We Learn', in *Sustainability, Human Well-Being, and the Future of Education*, edited by Justin W. Cook (Cham: Palgrave Macmillan, 2019), 40.

101 Christopher Wright, Daniel Nyberg, Christian De Cock and Gail Whiteman, 'Future Imaginings: Organizing in Response to Climate Change', *Organisation* 20:5 (2013), 648. https://doi.org/10.1177/1350508413489821.

102 Stockholm Resilience Centre, 'Planetary Boundaries' (undated). Available at https://www.stockholmresilience.org/research/planetary-boundaries.html [accessed 20 April 2024].

103 Global Footprint Network: https://www.footprintnetwork.org.

104 Giorgos Kallis, *Limits: Why Malthus was Wrong and Why Environmentalists Should Care* (Stanford: Stanford University Press, 2019), 61.

105 Ibid., 58.

106 Ibid., 5.

107 Brand et al., 'From Planetary to Societal Boundaries', 265.

108 Ibid., 275.

109 Ibid., 275.

110 Ibid., 281.

111 Kate Fletcher, *Craft of Use: Post-Growth Fashion* (Abingdon: Routledge, 2016), 242.

112 Lisa Garforth, *Green Utopias: Environmental Hope Before and After Nature* (Cambridge: Polity, 2017), 16.

113 Kallis, *Limits*, 128.

114 Ibid., 128.

115 Ibid.

116 Brand et al., 'From Planetary to Societal Boundaries', 275.

117 Martin Parker, 'Alternatives to Management Ideas', in *The Oxford Handbook of Management Ideas*, edited by Andrew Sturdy, Stefan Heusinkveld, Trish Reay and David Strang (Oxford: Oxford Academic), 502.

118 Brand et al., 'From Planetary to Societal Boundaries', 275, original emphasis.

119 Contributed by Souporni Nath: https://fashionfictions.org/2023/04/19/world-207/.

120 Contributed by #sameclotheseveryday: https://fashionfictions.org/2020/07/21/world-15/.

121 Amy Twigger Holroyd, 'Writing Sustainable Fashion Worlds', in *Sustainability and the Fashion Industry: Can Fashion Save the World?*, edited by Annick Schramme and Nathalie Verboven (Abingdon: Routledge, 2024), 29.

122 Contributed by Sally Cooke.

123 Stage 2 group: Alison Peck, Cathy Rudman, Julie Ripley and an anonymized contributor.

124 Thomas Princen, *Treading Softly: Paths to Ecological Order* (Cambridge, MA: MIT Press, 2010), 69–70.

125 Kate Fletcher and Mathilda Tham, *Earth Logic Fashion Action Research Plan* (London: The J J Charitable Trust, 2019), 45.

126 Deborah Campbell and Aaron Kool, 'Mitigation and Adaptation', *MIT Climate Portal* (undated). Available at https://climate.mit.edu/explainers/mitigation-and-adaptation [accessed 20 April 2024].

127 Ibid.

128 Kyle P. Whyte, 'Indigenous Science (Fiction) for the Anthropocene: Ancestral Dystopias and Fantasies of Climate Change Crises', *Environment and Planning E: Nature and Space* 1:1–2 (2018), 226. https://doi.org/10.1177/2514848618777621.

129 Daniel Nyberg, Christopher Wright and Vanessa Bowden, *Organising Responses to Climate Change: The Politics of Mitigation, Adaptation and Suffering* (Cambridge: Cambridge University Press, 2022), 115.

130 Campbell and Kool, 'Mitigation and Adaptation'.

131 Nyberg, Wright and Bowden, *Organising Responses to Climate Change*, 124.

132 Douglas Rushkoff, *Survival of the Richest: Escape Fantasies of the Tech Billionaires* (London: Scribe, 2022).

133 Timothy W. Luke, 'Earth Breaking Bad: The Politics of Deep Adaptation', in *The Palgrave Handbook of Environmental Politics and Theory*, edited by Joel Jay Kassiola and Timothy W. Luke (Cham: Palgrave Macmillan, 2023), 89–103.

134 Dougald Hine, *At Work in the Ruins: Finding Our Place in the Time of Science, Climate Change, Pandemics and All the Other Emergencies* (White River Junction: Chelsea Green, 2023), 179.

135 Paul Kingsnorth and Dougald Hine, *Uncivilisation: The Dark Mountain Manifesto* (Oxford: The Dark Mountain Manifesto, 2019 [2009]), 30.

136 Cameron Tonkinwise, 'I Prefer Not To: Anti-Progressive Designing', in *UnDesign: Critical Practices at the Intersection of Art and Design*, edited by Gretchen Coombs, Andrew McNamara and Gavin Sade (Abingdon: Routledge, 2019), 80.

137 Patrick O'Hare and Dagna Rams, 'Introduction – Circular Economies', in *Circular Economies in an Unequal World*, edited by Patrick O'Hare and Dagna Rams (London: Bloomsbury, 2024), 4–5.

Chapter 7

1 Diana Wynne Jones, *Conrad's Fate* (London: HarperCollins, 2005).

2 Max Haiven and Alex Khasnabish, 'What Is the Radical Imagination? A Special Issue', *Affinities* 4:2 (2010), ii–iii.

3 Julia Bentz, Letícia do Carmo, Nicole Schafenacker, Jörn Schirok and Sara Dal Corso, 'Creative, Embodied Practices, and the Potentialities for Sustainability Transformations', *Sustainability Science* 17 (2022), 690. https://doi.org/10.1007/s11625-021-01000-2.

4 Brian Eno, 'Foreword', in Jon Alexander, *Citizens: Why the Key to Fixing Everything Is All of Us* (Kingston upon Thames: Canbury Press, 2022), 8.

5 Vlad P. Glăveanu, 'Wonder', in *The Palgrave Encyclopedia of the Possible*, edited by Vlad P. Glăveanu (Cham: Palgrave Macmillan, 2021), 1778.

6 Alexander, *Citizens: Why the Key to Fixing Everything Is All of Us*, 98.

7 https://fashionfictions.org/wonder/.

8 Martin Parker, George Cheney, Valérie Fournier and Chris Land, 'Introduction', in *The Routledge Companion to Alternative Organisation*, edited by Martin Parker, George Cheney, Valérie Fournier and Chris Land (Abingdon: Routledge, 2018), 18.

9 Vanessa Machado de Oliveira, *Hospicing Modernity: Facing Humanity's Wrongs and the Implications for Social Activism* (Berkeley, CA: North Atlantic Books, 2021), 93.

10 Lewis Akenji, Magnus Bengtsson, Viivi Toivio and Michael Lettenmeier, *1.5-Degree Lifestyles: Towards A Fair Consumption Space for All: Summary for Policy Makers* (Berlin: Hot or Cool Institute, 2021), 5.

11 Frank W. Geels and Johan Schot, 'The Dynamics of Transitions: A Socio-Technical Perspective', in *Transitions to Sustainable Development: New Directions in the Study of Long Term Transformative Change*, edited by John Grin, Jan Rotmans and Johan Schot (Abingdon: Routledge, 2010), 58.

12 Frank W. Geels, 'Analysing the Breakthrough of Rock 'n' Roll (1930–1970): Multi-regime Interaction and Reconfiguration in the Multi-level Perspective, *Technological Forecasting and Social Change* 74:8 (2007), 1411–31. https://doi.org/10.1016/j.techfore.2006.07.008.

13 Elizabeth Shove and Nicola Spurling, 'Sustainable Practices: Social Theory and Climate Change', in *Sustainable Practices: Social Theory and Climate Change*, edited by Elizabeth Shove and Nicola Spurling (Abingdon: Routledge, 2014), 2.

14 Alice Payne, *Designing Fashion's Future: Present Practice and Tactics for Sustainable Change* (London: Bloomsbury, 2021), 85.

15 Ursula K. Le Guin, *Words are My Matter: Writings on Life and Books* (New York: Mariner, 2019), 114.

16 Martin Parker, George Cheney, Valérie Fournier and Chris Land, 'The Question of Organization: A Manifesto for Alternatives', *Ephemera* 14:4 (2014), 628.

17 Andrew Sayer, 'Power, Sustainability and Well Being: An Outsider's View', in *Sustainable Practices: Social Theory and Climate Change*, edited by Elizabeth Shove and Nicola Spurling (Abingdon: Routledge, 2014), 168.

18 Elizabeth Shove, Mika Pantzar and Matt Watson, *The Dynamics of Social Practice: Everyday Life and How It Changes* (London: SAGE, 2012), 12.

19 Ibid., 12.

20 Anthony Giddens, *The Constitution of Society* (Cambridge: Polity Press, 1984), 2.

21 Sayer, 'Power, Sustainability and Well Being', 168.

22 John Grin, Jan Rotmans and Johan Schot, *Transitions to Sustainable Development: New Directions in the Study of Long Term Transformative Change* (Abingdon: Routledge, 2010).

23 Michele-Lee Moore and Manjana Milkoreit, 'Imagination and Transformations to Sustainable and Just Futures', *Elementa: Science of the Anthropocene* 8:1 (2020), 4. https://doi.org/10.1525/elementa.2020.081.

24 Erik Olin Wright, *Envisioning Real Utopias* (London: Verso, 2010), 298.

25 Giuseppe Feola, 'Degrowth and the Unmaking of Capitalism', *ACME: An International Journal for Critical Geographies* 18:4 (2019), 979. https://doi.org/10.14288/acme.v18i4.1790.

26 Ibid., 978.

27 Harold Glasser, 'Toward Robust Foundations for Sustainable Well-Being Societies: Learning to Change by Changing How We Learn', in *Sustainability, Human Well-Being, and the Future of Education*, edited by Justin W. Cook (Cham: Palgrave Macmillan, 2019), 50.

28 Stephen Sterling, 'Transformative Learning and Sustainability: Sketching the Conceptual Ground', *Learning and Teaching in Higher Education* 5 (2010–11), 25.

29 Amish Morrell and Mary Ann O'Connor, 'Introduction', in *Expanding the Boundaries of Transformative Learning: Essays on Theory and Praxis*, edited by Edmund O'Sullivan, Amish Morrell and Mary Ann O'Connor (New York: Palgrave Macmillan, 2002), xvii.

30 Walidah Imarisha, 'Intro', in *Octavia's Brood: Science Fiction Stories from Social Justice Movements*, edited by Walidah Imarisha and adrienne maree brown (Oakland: AK Press, 2015), 4.

31 Nicole Seymour, *Bad Environmentalism: Irony and Irreverence in the Ecological Age* (Minneapolis: University of Minnesota Press, 2018), 21.

32 Debbie Gascoyne, '"Why Don't You Be a Tiger?": The Performative, Transformative, and Creative Power of the Word in the Universes of Diana Wynne Jones', *Journal of the Fantastic in the Arts* 21:2 (2010), 217. https://www.jstor.org/stable/i24352197.

33 Tania Zittoun, Hana Hawlina and Alex Gillespie, 'Imagination', in *The Palgrave Encyclopedia of the Possible*, edited by Vlad P. Glăveanu (Cham: Palgrave Macmillan, 2021), 3. https://doi.org/10.1007/978-3-319-98390-5_68-1.

34 Ibid., 5, original emphasis.

35 Ibid., 2.

36 Vlad P. Glăveanu, *Wonder: The Extraordinary Power of an Ordinary Experience* (London: Bloomsbury, 2020), 4.

37 Vlad P. Glăveanu, *The Possible: A Sociocultural Theory* (Oxford: Oxford University Press, 2021), 5.

38 Vlad P. Glăveanu, 'The Possible as a Field of Inquiry', *Europe's Journal of Psychology*, 14:3 (2018), 527. https://doi.org/10.5964/ejop.v14i3.1725.

39 Frances Babbage, *Augusto Boal* (London: Routledge, 2004), 40.

40 Augusto Boal, *Theater of the Oppressed* (London: Pluto Press, 1979), 141.

41 Babbage, *Augusto Boal*, 62.

42 Scott Magelssen, 'Tourist Performance in the Twenty-first Century', in *Enacting History*, edited by Scott Magelssen and Rhona Justice-Malloy (Tuscaloosa: University of Alabama Press, 2011), 193.

43 Byung-Chul Han, *The Disappearance of Rituals: A Topology of the Present*, translated by Daniel Steuer (Cambridge: Polity, 2020), 11.

44 Contributed by Manuela Cadena, Santiago Colmenares, Mariana León, Estefania Mariño and Mariana Rojas: https://fashionfictions.org/2024/02/23/world-224/.

45 Chris Riedy, 'Storying the Future: Storytelling Practice in Transformative Systems', in *Storytelling for Sustainability in Higher Education*, edited by Petra Molthan-Hill, Heather Luna, Tony Wall, Helen Puntha and Denise Baden (Abingdon: Routledge, 2020), 71.

46 Ella Saltmarshe, 'Using Story to Change Systems', *Stanford Social Innovation Review*, 20 February 2018. Available at https://ssir.org/articles/entry/using_story_to_change_systems [accessed 10 March 2024].

47 Ibid.

48 Matthew Schneider-Mayerson and Brent Ryan Bellamy, 'Introduction', in *An Ecotopian Lexicon*, edited by Matthew Schneider-Mayerson and Brent Ryan Bellamy (Minneapolis: University of Minnesota Press, 2019), 3.

49 Quoted in Meir Rinde, 'Imagining a Postcarbon Future', *Distillations Magazine*, 11 October 2016. Available at https://www.sciencehistory.org/stories/magazine/imagining-a-postcarbon-future/ [accessed 10 March 2024].

50   Brian Eno, 'Foreword', 8.

51   Abena P. A. Busia, 'Teaching Toni Cade Bambara Teaching: Learning with the Children in Toni Cade Bambara's "The Lesson"', in *Savoring the Salt: The Legacy of Toni Cade Bambara*, edited by Linda Janet Holmes and Cheryl A. Wall (Philadelphia: Temple University Press, 2008), 183.

52   Moore and Milkoreit, 'Imagination and Transformations to Sustainable and Just Futures', 3.

53   Rolf A. Zwaan, 'Situation Model', in *Routledge Encyclopedia of Narrative Theory*, edited by David Herman, Manfred Jahn & Marie-Laure Ryan (Abingdon: Routledge, 2005), 535.

54   Ursula K. Le Guin, *The Lathe of Heaven* (New York: Scribner, 1971), 14.

55   John Wood, *Design for Micro-Utopias: Making the Unthinkable Possible* (Abingdon: Routledge, 2017), 133–4.

56   adrienne maree brown, 'Outro', in *Octavia's Brood: Science Fiction Stories from Social Justice Movements*, edited by Imarisha and brown (Oakland: AK Press, 2015), 279.

57   Moore and Milkoreit, 'Imagination and Transformations to Sustainable and Just Futures', 2.

58   Saltmarshe, 'Using Story to Change Systems'.

59   Ibid.

60   Riedy, 'Storying the Future', 71.

61   Glasser, 'Toward Robust Foundations for Sustainable Well-Being Societies', 50.

62   Alexander, *Citizens*, 134.

63   Manjana Milkoreit, 'Imaginary Politics: Climate Change and Making the Future', *Elementa. Science of the Anthropocene* 5:62 (2017), 7. https://doi.org/10.1525/elementa.249.

64   Ibid., 2.

65   Ibid., 11.

66   Rachel Weidinger, 'Four Baskets: Necessary Capacities for Narrative Change', *Narrative Initiative*, 30 July 2020. Available at https://narrativeinitiative.org/blog/four-baskets-necessary-capacities-for-narrative-change/ [accessed 10 March 2024]. Another useful framework for getting stories out into the world can be found in Riedy, 'Storying the Future', 85–6.

67   Imarisha, 'Intro', 5.

68   Alastair Fuad-Luke, Anja-Lisa Hirscher and Katharina Moebus, 'Introduction', in *Agents of Alternatives: Re-designing Our Realities* (Berlin: Agents of Alternatives, 2015), 12.

69   Lara Monticelli, 'Prefigurative Politics Within, Despite and Beyond Contemporary Capitalism', in *The Future Is Now: An Introduction to Prefigurative Politics*, edited by Lara Monticelli (Bristol: Bristol University Press, 2022), 32.

70   Ibid., 36.

71   Jilly Traganou, 'The Paradox of the Commons: The Spatial Politics of Prefiguration in the Case of Christiania Freetown', in *The Future Is Now: An Introduction to Prefigurative Politics*, edited by Lara Monticelli (Bristol: Bristol University Press, 2022), 105.

72   Tobias Revell, Justin Pickard and Georgina Voss, 'Valuing Utopia in Speculative and Critical Design', in *Economic Science Fictions*, edited by William Davies (London: Goldsmiths Press, 2018), 287.

73   Monticelli, 'Prefigurative Politics Within, Despite and Beyond Contemporary Capitalism', 32.

74   Ibid., 25.

75   Kiri Langmead, Chris Land and Daniel King, 'Can Management Ever Be Responsible? Alternative Organizing and the Three Irresponsibilities of Management', in *Research Handbook of Responsible Management*, edited by Oliver Laasch, Roy Suddaby, R. Edward Freeman and Dima Jamali (Cheltenham: Edward Elgar Publishing, 2020), 52.

76   Ibid., 47.

77   Erik Olin Wright, *How to Be an Anticapitalist in the 21st Century* (London: Verso, 2019), 120.

78   Our Common Market: https://www.ourcommon.market.

79   Growing A.R.C./A.R.C. en croissance, LinkedIn: https://www.linkedin.com/company/a-r-c-en-croissance-growing-a-r-c/.

80   David Graeber, *The Utopia of Rules: On Technology, Stupidity, and the Secret Joys of Bureaucracy* (London: Melville House, 2015), 96.

81   Carol A. Jones, *A History of Nottingham School of Design* (Nottingham: Nottingham Trent University, 1993).

82   Christopher Richardson, *A City of Light: Socialism, Chartism and Co-operation – Nottingham 1844*, 2nd edition (Nottingham: Loaf on a Stick Press, 2015).

83   Ibid., 115.

84   I would love someone to take this idea forward. Could it be you?

85   Arvind Venkataramani and Adam Menter, 'Integrating Self and Systems Through Ritual: Toward Deeper Systems Practice', *Proceedings of Relating Systems Thinking and Design* (Ahmedabad, 2020), 14, 1.

86   Enactment i recipe: https://fashionfictions.org/2023/03/07/world-45-enactment-i-material-mindfulness-recipe/.

87   Lucy Wright, 'What Is Dusking?', Tradfolk, 9 October 2023. Available at https://tradfolk.co/art/writing/what-is-dusking/ [Accessed 1 April 2024].

88   Lucy Wright, 'Dusking' (2023). Available at https://www.lucywright.art/works/dusking [accessed 1 April 2024].

89   Tradfolk, 'Dusking 2023: A round-up', 1 November 2023. Available at https://tradfolk.co/performance/morris-dancing/dusking-round-up/ [accessed 1 April 2024].

90   Heila Lotz-Sisitka, Arjen Wals, David Kronlid and Dylan McGarry, 'Transformative, Transgressive Social Learning: Rethinking Higher Education Pedagogy in Times of Systemic Global Dysfunction', *Current Opinion in Environmental Sustainability* 16 (2015), 77. https://doi.org/10.1016/j.cosust.2015.07.018.

91   Alexander, *Citizens*, 182–5.

92   https://fashionfictions.org/wonder/.

93   Parker, Cheney, Fournier and Land, 'The Question of Organization', 623.

94   Glăveanu, 'Wonder', 1776.

95   Victor Turner, *From Ritual to Theatre* (New York: PAJ Publications, 1982), 28.

96   Wood, *Design for Micro-Utopias*, 133.

97   Loes Damhof and Jitske Gulmans, 'Imagining the Impossible: An Act of Radical Hope', *Possibility Studies & Society* 1:1–2 (2023), 52, original emphasis. https://doi.org/10.1177/27538699231174821.

Select Bibliography

Alexander, J. (2022), *Citizens: Why the Key to Fixing Everything Is All of Us*, Kingston upon Thames: Canbury Press.

Attebery, B. (1992), *Strategies of Fantasy*, Bloomington: Indiana University Press.

Bell, C. (1997), *Ritual: Perspectives and Dimensions*, revised edition, Oxford: Oxford University Press.

Bentz, J., Do Carmo, L, Schafenacker, N., Schirok, J. and Dal Corso, S. (2022), 'Creative, Embodied Practices, and the Potentialities for Sustainability Transformations', *Sustainability Science* 17, 687–99.

Boal, A. (1979), *Theater of the Oppressed*, London: Pluto Press.

Candy, S. and Kornet, K. (2019), 'Turning Foresight Inside Out: An Introduction to Ethnographic Experiential Futures', *Journal of Futures Studies* 23:3, 3–22.

Damhof, L. and Gulmans, J. (2023), 'Imagining the Impossible: An Act of Radical Hope', *Possibility Studies & Society* 1:1–2. https://doi.org/10.1177/27538699231174821.

Davies, W. (ed.) (2018), *Economic Science Fictions*, London: Goldsmiths Press.

Dellenbaugh-Losse, M., Zimmermann, N-E. and de Vries, N. (2020), *The Urban Commons Cookbook: Strategies and Insights for Creating and Maintaining Urban Commons*. http://urbancommonscookbook.com.

Duggan, J., Lindley, J. and McNicol, S. (2017), 'Near Future School: World Building Beyond a Neoliberal Present with Participatory Design Fictions', *Futures* 94. https://doi.org/10.1016/j.futures.2017.04.001.

Dunne, A. and Raby, F. (2013), *Speculative Everything: Design, Fiction, and Social Dreaming*, Cambridge, MA: The MIT Press.

Ehrman, E. (2018), *Fashioned from Nature*, London: V&A Publishing.

Escobar, A. (2023), 'Welcome to Possibility Studies', *Possibility Studies and Society* 1:1–2, 56–9.

Farias P. G., Bendor, R. and van Eekelen, B. F. (2022), 'Social Dreaming Together: A Critical Exploration of Participatory Speculative Design', in *Participatory Design Conference 2022: Volume 2*, 19 August–1 September 2022, Newcastle upon Tyne. https://doi.org/10.1145/3537797.3537826.

Feola, G. (2019), 'Degrowth and the Unmaking of Capitalism', *ACME: An International Journal for Critical Geographies* 18:4, 977–97.

Fletcher, K. and Tham, M. (2019), *Earth Logic Fashion Action Research Plan*, London: The J J Charitable Trust.

Fry, T. (2023), *Writing Design Fiction: Relocating a City in Crisis*, London: Bloomsbury.

Garforth, L. (2017), *Green Utopias: Environmental Hope Before and After Nature*, Cambridge: Polity.

Gibson-Graham, J. K., Cameron, J. and Healey, S. (2013), *Take Back the Economy*, Minneapolis: University of Minnesota Press.

Glasser, H. (2019), 'Toward Robust Foundations for Sustainable Well-Being Societies: Learning to Change by Changing How We Learn', in J. W. Cook (ed.), *Sustainability, Human Well-Being, and the Future of Education*, Cham: Palgrave Macmillan, 31–90.

Glăveanu, V. P. (2020), *Wonder: The Extraordinary Power of an Ordinary Experience*, London: Bloomsbury.

Glăveanu, V. P. (2021), *The Possible: A Sociocultural Theory*, Oxford: Oxford University Press.

Halse, J. (2013), 'Ethnographies of the Possible', in W. Gunn, T. Otto and R. C. Smith (eds), *Design Anthropology: Theory and Practice*, London: Berg, 180–96.

Haraway, D. (2016), *Staying with the Trouble: Making Kin in the Chthulucene*, Durham, NC: Duke University Press.

Hickel, J. (2020), *Less is More: How Degrowth will Save the World*, London: Windmill Books.

Hine, D. (2023), *At Work in the Ruins: Finding Our Place in the Time of Science, Climate Change, Pandemics and All the Other Emergencies*, White River Junction: Chelsea Green.

Jansen, M. A. and Craik, J. (2016), *Modern Fashion Traditions: Negotiating Tradition and Modernity through Fashion*, London: Bloomsbury.

Jones, D. W. (2012), *Reflections: On the Magic of Writing*, New York: Greenwillow Books.

Kallis, G. (2019), *Limits: Why Malthus was Wrong and Why Environmentalists Should Care*, Stanford: Stanford University Press.

Kuzmanovic, M. and Gaffney, N. (2017), 'Enacting Futures in Postnormal Times', *Futures* 86, 107–17. https://doi.org/10.1016/j.futures.2016.05.007.

Lange, B., Hülz, M., Schmid, B. and Schulz, C. (eds), *Post-Growth Geographies: Spatial Relations of Diverse and Alternative Economies*, Bielefeld: transcript Verlag.

Light, A. (2021), 'Collaborative Speculation: Anticipation, Inclusion and Designing Counterfactual Futures for Appropriation', *Futures* 134. https://doi.org/10.1016/j.futures.2021.102855.

Machado de Oliveira, V. (2021), *Hospicing Modernity: Facing Humanity's Wrongs and the Implications for Social Activism*, Berkeley, CA: North Atlantic Books.

Magelssen, S. and Justice-Malloy, R. (eds) (2011), *Enacting History*, Tuscaloosa: University of Alabama Press.

Markussen, T., Knutz, E. and Lenskjold, T. (2020), 'Design Fiction as a Research Practice in the Social Field', *Temes de Disseny* 36: 16–39. https://doi.org/10.46467/TdD36.2020.16-39.

Milkoreit, M. (2017), 'Imaginary Politics: Climate Change and Making the Future', *Elementa: Science of the Anthropocene* 5:62. https://doi.org/10.1525/elementa.249.

Mitrović, I., Auger, J., Hanna, J. and Helgason, I. (eds) (2021), *Beyond Speculative Design: Past – Present – Future*, Split: SpeculativeEdu/Arts Academy, University of Split, 2021. https://speculativeedu.eu/beyond-speculative-design-past-present-future/.

Monticelli, L. (ed.) (2022), *The Future Is Now: An Introduction to Prefigurative Politics*, Bristol: Bristol University Press.

Moore, M-L. and Milkoreit, M. (2020), 'Imagination and Transformations to Sustainable and Just Futures', *Elementa: Science of the Anthropocene* 8:1. https://doi.org/10.1525/elementa.2020.081.

Mulgan, G. (2020), *The Imaginary Crisis (and How We Might Quicken Social and Public Imagination)*. https://demoshelsinki.fi/wp-content/uploads/2020/04/the-imaginary-crisis-web.pdf.

Parker, M. (2018), *Shut Down the Business School: What's Wrong with Management Education*, London: Pluto Press.

Parker, M., Cheney, G., Fournier, V. and Land, C. (eds) (2018), *The Routledge Companion to Alternative Organisation*, Abingdon: Routledge.

Payne, A. (2021), *Designing Fashion's Future: Present Practice and Tactics for Sustainable Change*, London: Bloomsbury.

Riedy, C. (2020), 'Storying the Future: Storytelling Practice in Transformative Systems', in P. Molthan-Hill, H. Luna, T. Wall, H. Puntha and D. Baden (eds), *Storytelling for Sustainability in Higher Education* (Abingdon: Routledge), 71–87.

Schechner, R. (1985), *Between Theater and Anthropology*, Philadelphia: University of Pennsylvania Press.

Schechner, R. (2013), *Performance Studies: An Introduction*, 3rd edition, Abingdon: Routledge.

Scott, K., Bakker, C. and Quist, J. (2012), 'Designing Change by Living Change', *Design Studies* 33:3, 279–97. https://doi.org/10.1016/j.destud.2011.08.002.

Sheldrake, M. (2020), *Entangled Life: How Fungi Make Our Worlds, Change Our Minds, and Shape Our Futures*, London: Penguin Random House.

Schmelzer, M., Vetter, A. and Vansintjan, A. (2022), *The Future is Degrowth: A Guide to a World Beyond Capitalism*, London: Verso.

Schneider-Mayerson, M. and Bellamy, B. R. (eds) (2019), *An Ecotopian Lexicon*, Minneapolis: University of Minnesota Press.

Seymour, N. (2018), *Bad Environmentalism: Irony and Irreverence in the Ecological Age*, Minneapolis: University of Minnesota Press.

Shove, E. and Spurling, N. (eds) (2014), *Sustainable Practices: Social Theory and Climate Change*, Abingdon: Routledge.

Smith, R. C., Vangkilde, K. T., Kjærsgaard, M. G., Otto, T., Halse, J. and Binder, T. (eds) (2016), *Design Anthropological Futures*, London: Bloomsbury.

Thanem, T. and Knights, D. (2019), *Embodied Research Methods*, London: SAGE.

Tonkinwise, C. (2019), '"I Prefer Not To": Anti-Progressive Designing', in G. Coombs, A. McNamara and G. Sade (eds), *Undesign: Critical Practices at the Intersection of Art and Design*, Abingdon: Routledge, 74–84.

Tyszczuk, R. (2021), 'Collective Scenarios: Speculative Improvisations for the Anthropocene', *Futures* 134. https://doi.org/10.1016/j.futures.2021.102854.

Wanner, T. (2015), 'The New "Passive Revolution" of the Green Economy and Growth Discourse: Maintaining the "Sustainable Development" of Neoliberal Capitalism', *New Political Economy* 20:1, 21–41. https://doi.org/10.1080/13563467.2013.866081.

Wapner, P. (2010), *Living Through the End of Nature: The Future of American Environmentalism*, Cambridge, MA: MIT Press.

Welters, L. and Lillethun, A. (2018), *Fashion History: A Global View*, London: Bloomsbury.

Wilson, E. (2003), *Adorned in Dreams: Fashion and Modernity*, revised and updated edition, London: I.B.Tauris.

Wood, J. (2017), *Design for Micro-Utopias: Making the Unthinkable Possible*, Abingdon: Routledge.

Wright, C., Nyberg, D., De Cock, C. and Whiteman, G. (2013), 'Future Imaginings: Organizing in Response to Climate Change', *Organization* 20:5, 647–58. https://doi.org/10.1177/1350508413489821.

Wright, E. O. (2010), *Envisioning Real Utopias*, London: Verso.

Zittoun, T., Hawlina, H. and Gillespie, A. (2021), 'Imagination', in V. P. Glăveanu (ed.), *The Palgrave Encyclopedia of the Possible*, Cham: Palgrave Macmillan. https://doi.org/10.1007/978-3-319-98390-5_68-1.

Index